ALFRED
NOBEL

ALFRED NOBEL

·

A Biography

KENNE FANT

Translated from the Swedish
by Marianne Ruuth

ARCADE PUBLISHING • NEW YORK

First English-language Edition

First published in Sweden by Norstedts Förlag, Stockholm

Designed by GDS / Jeffrey L. Ward

Library of Congress Cataloging-in-Publication Data

Fant, Kenne, 1923–
    [Alfred Bernhard Nobel.   English]
    Alfred Nobel : a biography / Kenne Fant ; translated from the
Swedish by Marianne Ruuth.
        p.   cm.
    Includes index.
    ISBN 1-55970-222-2
    1. Nobel, Alfred Bernhardt, 1833–1896.   2. Chemical engineers —
Sweden — Biography.   I. Title.
TP268.5.N7F3613   1993
660'.092 — dc20
    [B]   93-28235

Published in the United States by Arcade Publishing, Inc., New York
Distributed by Little, Brown and Company

10 9 8 7 6 5 4 3 2 1

BP

Printed in the United States of America

PREFATORY NOTE

Were it not for his extensive correspondence, Alfred Nobel (1833–1896) would have remained an enigma to this day — a shadow behind a name known the world over. We are fortunate that Nobel always made copies of his letters, even when they were very private. They form a veritable autobiography, and give flesh and blood to the bronze figure minted in profile on each Nobel prize. Of special interest are those papers the Nobel Foundation has placed in the Swedish National Archives, for they include 218 letters, handwritten in German, each carefully numbered, that Nobel sent to his Austrian mistress, Sofie Hess, during the years 1878–1895. Selections are reproduced here. Readers interested in looking at the complete letters are directed to the Nobel Collection, located in the Swedish National Archives, Dossier No. 301, shelf XXVI, volumes A, B, C, and D.

To this collection can now be added twenty additional letters written by Nobel to his older brother, Robert, during the years 1878–1895, which have been kept by his family for many years. Through the efforts of the late Kristina Winberg — the driving force behind the creation of Sweden's Nobel Museum — those letters were made available to me.

I make extensive use of them all in this biography, for they permit Alfred Nobel to tell his own story.

For the continuing assistance I have received during my writing from the chairman of the Nobel Foundation, Dr. Stig Ramel, I am deeply grateful. Further, I wish to thank the following individuals who, in different ways, have been especially helpful: Kjell Espmark, Sven Fagerberg, and Per Anders Fogelström; the late director of the Technical Museum, Sigvard Strandh, as well as its present director, Erik Lundblad; Dr. Sven Ingemar Olofsson; professors David H. Ingvar and Fredrik Lund; museum director Gertie Ågren; and the person responsible for the Nobel documents in the National Archives, Carin Tisell. A special thank you to this book's creative Swedish publisher — Lasse Bergström.

For the American edition, I am pleased to thank everyone at Arcade Publishing and in particular, for his invaluable assistance, my editor, Timothy Bent.

Kenne Fant

ALFRED NOBEL'S LIFE AND WORK
A Summary

1833   Alfred Nobel is born in the family home at 9 Norrlands-gatan in Stockholm on October 21.

1842   At age nine, he is reunited with his father, who emigrated to St. Petersburg, Russia, in 1838.

1850   When Alfred turns seventeen, his father finances a study trip to America, partly to give Alfred an opportunity to work for and learn from the inventor John Ericsson, partly to make him give up once and for all his dreams of becoming a writer.

1860   For the first time, Alfred succeeds in making nitroglycerine explode.

1863   Alfred leaves St. Petersburg for good, and settles with his parents at Heleneborg in Stockholm. Under primitive conditions, he continues his nitroglycerine experiments. On October 14, he is given his first patent for his "method of preparing gunpowder for both blasting and shooting."

1864   On September 3, the shed in which the experiments have been taking place explodes. Alfred receives only minor injuries, but five people are killed, among them his youngest brother, Emil.

1865   On November 8, Alfred obtains permission from the German authorities to build a nitroglycerine factory in Krümmel, outside Hamburg.

1866   At age thirty-three, Alfred makes his second journey to America, this time to assert his patent rights and establish a continuous production of dynamite. On May 7, he gets his British patent for dynamite.

1867   Alfred is granted a patent for his epoch-making invention, the Nobel igniter.

1868   On May 26, the United States grants him a patent for dynamite.

1870   Alfred establishes a dynamite factory in Paulilles, in the south of France.

1871   According to Alfred, dynamite is now "beginning to enter into world industry." He lays the cornerstone for a factory in Ardeer, Scotland.

1873   At forty, Alfred settles in Paris at Avenue Malakoff.

1875   Alfred invents a blasting gelatin that is free of explosion
        risk from impact or friction.

1876   During the spring, Alfred, 43, meets Bertha Kinsky, 33, in
        Paris. He falls in love with her almost immediately and asks
        if her "heart is free." It is not — on June 12, she marries
        the young baron Arthur von Suttner. That fall, Alfred be-
        gins an eighteen-year, tumultuous relationship with an Aus-
        trian flower salesgirl, Sofie Hess.

1879   "The Naphtha Production Company Brothers Nobel," or
        Branobel, is formed in Russia, with Ludvig joining Robert
        and Alfred as the driving force.

1883   In March, Alfred returns to St. Petersburg for a visit to
        help his brother Ludvig out of a temporary fiscal crisis.
        Ludvig has become known as Russia's uncrowned oil king.

1884   Alfred invents smokeless gunpowder, ballistite.

1886   In collaboration with his French partner, Paul Barbe, Alfred
        unites all his dynamite companies into a trust, a process
        that he jokingly refers to as "the trustification."

1887   France grants Alfred a patent for his smokeless gunpowder.

1890   Although he has offered the French government manufac-
        turing rights, an offer it refused, the chauvinistic French
        press accuses Alfred of being a traitor when he signs an
        agreement with the Italian government to manufacture bal-
        listite. Feeling wronged, Alfred leaves Paris for San Remo,
        Italy. Contributing to his low spirits is Paul Barbe's suicide,
        and the discovery that he had been speculating wildly in
        nitroglycerine behind Alfred's back.

1893   Alfred's decision to leave the arena of business notwith-
        standing, he buys the Swedish armament works at Bofors.
        He hires a young engineer named Ragnar Sohlman, who
        becomes one of the two executors of his will. Alfred re-
        ceives an honorary doctor's degree in Uppsala (Sweden),
        one of the few worldly honors he values.

1895   In Paris, Alfred signs his third and final last will and tes-
        tament. He is mortified to learn he has lost the British patent
        for his smokeless gunpowder. Evident patent intrusion has
        taken place, but English courts — in the so-called cordite
        case — deny his claim for damages. Alfred is bitter, not
        because of the money, but because his honor as an inventor
        has been questioned.

1896   Alfred dies on December 10 in San Remo.

ALFRED
NOBEL

Chapter 1

I am sometimes forced to delay onerous business and contractual duties for weeks, yes, sometimes months, due to lack of time. To think of writing an autobiographical sketch, under such circumstances, is absolutely impossible, unless it were as brief as a police blotter description, which is, I think, the most eloquent of all.

> Alfred Nobel — pitiful creature, ought to have been suffocated by a humane physician when he made his howling entrance into this life. Greatest virtues: keeping his nails clean and never being a burden to anyone. Greatest weaknesses: having neither wife and kids nor sunny disposition nor hearty appetite. Greatest single request: to not be buried alive. Greatest sin: not worshiping Mammon. Important events in his life: none.

Is that not enough and more than enough? And what, in our time, would fit under the headline "Important Events"? The ten billion suns moving in the astral bubble we call the Milky Way would be ashamed of their smallness were they conscious of the whole scope of the universe. Who has time to read biographies, and who can be so naive or fatuous as to take an interest in them — that's what I find myself asking myself.

Alfred Nobel wrote these lines in 1887 in response to a request from his brother Ludvig, the eldest of the Nobel brothers, who had begun to research the family genealogy. Ludvig had long been pleading with Alfred both to write his own autobiography and to write down all he knew about their ancestors. Ludvig was not satisfied with Alfred's brief document, however, and urged his brother again for a more complete account.

Again Alfred declined. "Why tire yourself with biographical essays?" he wrote back. "Nobody reads essays about people other than actors and murderers, preferably the latter, who have accomplished their grisly feats on the battlefield or indoors. Our family already knows just about everything about our father, for example, and whether or not the general public gets to see his biography seems of meager interest."

Very possibly, Alfred Nobel honestly felt that his life was so commonplace as not to deserve profound reflection, much less publication. He showed almost total disinterest in uncovering family history.

Three years before his death, Alfred Nobel was urged yet once more to write about himself. In 1893, an honorary Doctor of Philosophy degree was to be conferred upon him. Accepting this high honor meant agreeing to compose an autobiographical sketch, and he did. Again, however, it was of the "police-blotter variety," to borrow his own expression:

> The undersigned was born on October 21, 1833, and acquired his education through private tutoring, without ever attending an institution of higher learning; has been active especially in the field of applied chemistry, through the development of explosives known as dynamite and blasting gelatin, as well as smokeless gunpowder, also known by the names of ballistite and C-89. Member of the Royal Swedish Academy of Science since 1884, of the Royal Institute in London, and of Société des Ingénieurs Civils in Paris. Since 1880 he has been a Knight of the Order of the North Star. Holds rank of officer in the French Legion of Honor. Publications: only a lecture in the English language, which was awarded a silver medal.

Alfred Nobel often maintained he cared little for honorary titles and official distinctions, but he did value both his honorary doctor's degree and his membership in the Academy of Science. The bantering tone of a letter to his friend and colleague Alarik Liedbeck strengthens the impression that he was pleased to be elected: "It would almost be a pity if I should kick the bucket now since exceedingly interesting things are going on for me. Since the monsters have made me into a doctor of philosophy, I have become even more of a philosopher than before and now believe that the word *utility* is a relative term."

Trying to sum up his life in one terse sentence, he offered the following: "I am a misanthrope and yet utterly benevolent, have more than one screw loose yet am a super-idealist who digests philosophy more efficiently than food."

Given Nobel's strong distaste for blowing his own horn, when he was confronted with spontaneous expressions of admiration, he actually experienced a sense of shame, as if a feeling of unworthiness had taken possession of him. His reflections might then take on a tone of sarcasm: "How pitiful to strive to be someone or something in the motley crowd of 1.4 billion two-legged, tailless apes running around on our revolving earth projectile."

But Nobel did strive to be someone. In the letter to Ludvig quoted above, he speaks of being "forced to delay onerous business and contractual duties for weeks," when the reality was that his workdays were absurdly long. He would frequently work for fifteen, even twenty hours without rest. It was as if he wanted to exhaust himself in order to ward off melancholy. Since he detested meetings, he often put his orders in writing. He could write twenty to thirty letters a day, and he seldom went to bed before midnight.

The brief self-portrait he wrote in connection with his honorary doctor's degree notes, somewhat surprisingly, that he is a Knight of the Order of the North Star and had reached rank of officer in the French Legion of Honor. In his letters, on the other hand, he continually pokes fun at "all the world's grand stars and honor badges, carried either on chest, stomach, or back" and asks to be "spared metal trinkets and iron plater's snippery." In one letter he mocks, "My honor badges have no explosive foundation. For the Swedish Order of the North Star I have to thank my cook, since her art appealed to a high-born stomach. I received my French order because of my close acquaintance with a cabinet member, my Brazilian Rose Order because I was accidentally introduced to Dom Pedro, and, finally, the famous Bolivia Order, because Max Philipp had seen Niniche[1] and wanted to illustrate the happenstance way in which honors and decorations are given out."

Still, Alfred did not refuse the "metal trinkets," as he called them. Perhaps he recalled Goethe's observation that "decorations and titles protect one against many a jostling shove in the crowd." But the founder of the Nobel prizes was by no means an exhibitionist. When it was suggested that he should pose for the Russian painter Makoffsky, he reacted with acidic humor: "I have met Makoffsky," he wrote, "and promise that as soon as God our Father in His benevolence makes my snout thirty years younger — so that it will be

[1] Farce popular at the time.

worthy of oil and color — I will, like a patient child, pose for him and present to posterity a simulation of my interesting, handsome, and resplendent hog-bristle beard."

He had an equal aversion to publicity. When the publisher of an illustrated book listing famous and outstanding Swedes wrote him, Nobel replied courteously but firmly: "I will with pleasure subscribe to this interesting and worthwhile project. But I request that my portrait be omitted from this collection. So far as I know, I have not earned any renown nor have I any taste for its buzz." Nobel found it impossible to maintain his self-esteem if he had to seek the esteem of others. Not even in the beginning of his career did he exhibit any active need to be in the public eye. In that respect, he seems today to be a transition figure between the eras of self-effacement and self-promotion.

On one occasion Nobel did vent displeasure at not having received an honor. For some unknown reason he was not invited to attend the inauguration of the St. Gotthard Railway (in the Swiss Alps) in the spring of 1882, despite the fact that this epic achievement had been facilitated by his new gelatin dynamite. Deeply hurt, he wrote, in a letter to Sofie Hess: "It is said that the dynamite and the explosive gelatin have, by accelerating the completion of the railway, saved millions in interest alone. But that has to be wrong. Had that been the case, not even the most ill-mannered churl would have neglected to send me an invitation to the occasion." His irritation does suggest a powerful need for some recognition hidden behind his seeming indifference.

Given the uncommonly vehement disparity between his public and private personas, Alfred Nobel's letters are particularly invaluable to our understanding and appreciation of him. The private correspondence allows readers to locate the undercurrents in his life: his self-absorption, his loneliness, and his belief in the absurdity of existence. Many of the private letters seem to have been written during those moments when the demons of melancholy — the "spirits of Niflheim [the land of the dead in Norse mythology]," as he frequently called them — were on the offensive. When they attacked, work was his only escape. Its soothing effect was immediate: chest pains, difficulties in breathing, and the headaches that haunted him his whole life would all disappear as if by magic. Work even diminished his feelings of loneliness, although he could not make them disappear altogether. In a letter to his sister-in-law, Edla, Ludvig's wife, Nobel writes:

What a contrast between us. You, surrounded by love, joy, noise, pulsating life, caring and being cared for, caressing and being caressed, anchored by contentment; I, roving, without compass or rudder, like a useless and desolate wreck, without happy memories from the past, without the false but beautiful visions of the future that illusions create, without vanity, which is a blunt but ready and willing self-beautifier, without family, which is the only afterlife to expect, without friends for my heart or enemies for my bile, but with a self-criticism that shows every blemish in its unembellished ugliness and every inability in a merciless light. A self-portrait with such contours is not suitable reading for a home of joy and contentment and befits only the wastepaper basket to which it is headed.

When his brother Robert tried to tempt Alfred into visiting him and Ludvig in Baku, Russia, where their oil business was located, he received the following reply: "The one and only thing that would entice me to come there would be the company — yours and perhaps Ludvig's — but the waterless, dusty, oil-stained desert itself offers me nothing in the way of temptation. I want to live among trees and bushes — silent friends who respect my nervousness — and flee whenever I can both metropolises and deserts."

It is true that Nobel would "flee" now and then. In fact, he would frequently disappear without telling anyone where he'd gone. In his solitude, he would sometimes adopt a bitter voice, as in this letter to Robert: "You allude to my many friends. Where are they? At the cloudy bottom of a fleeting illusion or attached to the clinking sound of coins. Believe me — most of one's friends in life are dogs you've fed with someone else's meat, or worms who have fed on you. Grateful stomachs and grateful hearts are twins."

Passages such as these remind us that in his youth Nobel seriously considered a career as a writer. All his life he derived nearly as much pleasure experimenting with language as he did experimenting with acids and powders in his laboratory. In both instances his design was to blast through convention. Like many reserved, inhibited people, Nobel felt liberated by the written word. Like many writers, he also felt its weight. A dark shadow often falls over his private letters, such as the one in which he portrays himself as "a worthless brooding instrument, alone in the world and with thoughts heavier than anyone can imagine." The image is that of the writer buried beneath the responsibility of being the conscience of his race. Other examples abound. After a brief stay at a health resort, he writes: "The earth is a vale of tears through which walk worm-eaten corpses, and those in this anatomical museum of a spa who can move more than one step a minute are relatively healthy. But it is probably inexpensive to stay here, since one quickly loses one's appetite by watching one's fellow creatures." Such a misanthropic vision is similar to that of the German philosopher Arthur Schopenhauer, who once wrote, "This world is the worst of all possible worlds, a fact that is confirmed even by experience." Both quotes express the feeling of doom and demise that reigned in many European intellectual circles during the latter part of the nineteenth century. Even as a young man, Nobel believed he had arrived at an immutable opinion regarding human nature "by studying and drawing knowledge from the pages in Nature's own large book."

He frequently played the doomsayer with an impish glint in his eye, however. Nobel's great friend and later executor of his will, Ragnar Sohlman, deserves credit for puncturing the myth of Nobel as a man who suffered without reprieve in an earthly torture chamber. "Dr. Nobel could talk and philosophize in such an entertaining manner that it was pure pleasure and delight to his rapt audience. To spend an hour chatting with him was both a remarkable joy and a challenging exercise, because you had to stay on your toes to follow the wild sallies of his unexpected turns of thought and startling paradoxes. He would soar like a wind-driven swallow from one subject to another and, as seen against the rapid flight of his thought, our globe would shrink and its distances melt, becoming trivial."

Sohlman describes Nobel's voice as somewhat raspy and his tone of voice tinged with melancholy, at times with sarcasm. Nobel could converse with ease in five languages: Swedish, German, English, French, and Russian. He did not mind being challenged during an animated discussion, and when he in turn presented his counter-arguments, he always did so in an even-tempered and intellectually convincing manner. Sohlman's portrait of Nobel is often surprising: "Nobel's outward behavior created the impression that he was rather high-strung. His movements and gestures were lively, his walk slightly mincing, his facial expressions volatile, as was his conversational manner, spiced as it was with sudden sallies of wit and outbursts of ideas. At times his whims bordered on the absurd and seemed purely intended to épater les bourgeois [scandalize the middle class]. To Nobel's Swedish countrymen, unused to his somewhat cosmopolitan conversational manner, he seemed perplexing, to put it mildly."[2]

Ragnar Sohlman also touches upon the paradox of Nobel's interest in the peace movement, given his lifelong involvement with munitions and armaments: "Alfred Nobel himself was conscious of such inconsistency and tried, in his correspondence with Bertha von Suttner[3] — and doubtless within himself — to defend it. He believed that the act of perfecting the means of destruction would have a greater chance of doing away with wars than all the peace conferences."

Sohlman continues: "In reality, that hardly explains his interest in weapon inventions, which was, rather, a result of his vigorous inventive instincts. Once, when we were discussing experiments with explosive armor-breaking hand grenades that would succeed in penetrating armor-plate and exploding behind it, he said, 'Well, you know, we are actually dealing with rather demonic devices. But as problems, they are so interesting, purely as technical problems — financial or commercial considerations aside — and because of that alone so fascinating.'"

Actions are a yardstick by which values can be measured, and in addition to his "demonic devices," Alfred Nobel left a legacy of lasting importance. Through his prizes, this restless, eternal wanderer — whom Victor Hugo termed "Europe's richest vagabond" — has forever etched his name in human memory.

[2] Ragnar Sohlman, *Ett Testamente,* originally published by Norstedt & Söners Förlag, Stockholm, 1950; revised edition published by Bokförlaget Atlantis AB, Stockholm, 1983. English version entitled *The Legacy of Alfred Nobel* published by The Bodley Head, London, 1983.
[3] Bertha von Suttner, peace activist, author of the popular and pacifistic novel *Die Waffen nieder* (1889), translated as *Lay Down Arms!* and winner of the Nobel Peace Prize in 1905.

Chapter 2

On both of his parents' sides, we can trace Alfred Nobel's roots back to the seventeenth century. The credit for uncovering his genealogical background lies partly with Ludvig Nobel (1831–1888), who meticulously researched the lives of their ancestors, but mostly with the late Professor Henrik Schück, who completed the work. Schück and Ragnar Sohlman provided an account of their research in the Nobel Foundation's memorial publication on the occasion of its twenty-fifth anniversary in 1926.

The first person known to carry the name Nobel was Petrus Olai Nobelius (1655–1707) from Skåne, a southern Swedish province. Petrus matriculated at Uppsala University's law faculty in 1682. His name was actually Peder Olufsson but, as was the custom, he latinized the name of his native region, Östra Nöbbelöv, located in the southeastern part of Skåne, not far from the city of Simrishamn. The young Petrus Olai, hungry for knowledge and musically gifted, was Alfred Nobel's great-great grandfather. A notation in the university's *Album Studiosorum* for February 21, 1682, reads: *"Petrus Olai Nobelius e Scania."* He never took any degree, but that was not an uncommon occurrence at Uppsala University in the seventeenth century; in fact, it would have been rare to do so, at least from the law faculty.

The album also denotes Petrus Olai as *"musicus,"* meaning that he belonged to the academic orchestra and thereby enjoyed the benefit of a royal scholarship. For a full ten years, he was the object of this kingly favor, but since he had to make the modest scholarship sum go further, he became a tutor to two young noblemen, Samuel and Frans Appelbom. In spite of his humble origins, Petrus Olai's musical talent brought him into the leading academic circles around Olof Rudbeck (1630–1702), who, at age thirty-two, had become rector of the university and was for years its spiritual leader.

As a musical scholarship student, Petrus Olai, without needing to pursue his law studies with any energy, could count on a position whenever there was an opening. One did not need a law degree even to become a judge, but in 1694 Petrus did acquire some practical experience as an apprentice to a magistrate named Gyllencreutz, as well as at Stockholm's magistrates' court. On March first of the following year, with the support of a "Doctoris Olai Rudbeckii recommendation," he sought *venia auscultandi* ("favorable hearing") at the Svea Circuit Court of Appeals, which was granted. Not long thereafter the court considered him "for a District Judge Office Capable and Able."

As a newly appointed district judge over Oland's and Frosaker's jurisdictional districts in Uppland, Petrus Olai was ready to enter into marriage. The bride-to-be, Wendela Rudbeck (1667–1710), was none other than the daughter of the same Olof Rudbeck who had recommended him to his office.

Petrus Olai and Wendela married in March of 1696, and their first child was born in December of the same year. They participated with obvious pleasure in the gay social scene of the university city, and throughout his life Petrus moved with total ease at the highest strata of society. A private letter tells of the great gala that was arranged in connection with King Karl XII's coronation on May 3, 1698: ". . . with short speeches by four voices which were the learned old Rudbeckus as well as his daughters and son-in-law, the district judge Mr. Nobelius."

Wendela Catharina's father was the multitalented intellectual giant often called the "Leonardo da Vinci of the North." In addition to his literary and scientific interests, Rudbeck was an animated singer, composer, and draftsman, who etched illustrations for his scientific works. Perhaps Alfred Nobel's father inherited that artistic talent, since, much later, in St. Petersburg, he painted watercolors of his inventions. Olof Rudbeck's mental range seems almost incomprehensibly vast, and it is hard to find his match in Swedish intellectual history. He is probably best known today (in Sweden, principally) as the author of the remarkable work, *Atlantica*, the first part of which was published in 1679.[1]

The marriage between Petrus Olai and Wendela produced eight children, of which only two sons survived. Petrus Olai himself did not reach old age. He was often unwell and made lengthy visits to health resorts to undergo various treatments. For instance, in 1706 he requested His Royal Majesty to grant him a leave of absence from his position as district judge to be able to "take the waters."

---

[1] A long, heavily annotated humanist treatise, *Atlantica* set out to prove that Plato's fictional island of Atlantis (discussed in his dialogue, *Timaeus*) was in actuality Sweden, and that therefore Sweden was the cradle from which culture spread to the rest of the world.

The youngest of the two surviving sons was Olof Pärsson Nobelius (1706–1760), Alfred Nobel's great grandfather. As Uppsala
University's drawing master, Olof's scientific drawings were praised
by Carl von Linné. Olof was also a skillful miniaturist. Only two
examples of his art survive: portraits of him and his wife, which are
still owned by the Nobel family.

As with several of Alfred Nobel's ancestors, Olof Pärsson Nobelius's life was darkened by difficult financial circumstances. In 1756
his income was so small that he had to borrow 1,200 Swedish dollars[2]
from the university against security and interest. Two years later, he
petitioned the consistory — the highest administrative organ at the
university — in order to "better my rather weak provisions," and
asked that "some addition to my small salary may favorably be
granted." In consideration of his frail health, he was granted "One
Hundred Fifty Dollar copper coins from the purse Rectoris and also
six Barrels of Grain, half rye and half malt, from the Mill here
located." His condition worsened, however, and he died on February
18, 1760. Three days later, "the Drawing Master Nobelius was buried
in the cemetery." The simple burial cost only thirty-nine dollars. A
little over 125 years later, when he believed himself to be ruined by
the so-called Panama Scandal, Alfred may have devoted a thought
or two to Olof Nobelius's bitter fate. He would have had cause to,
for he was born into a bankrupt estate.

Olof Nobelius had seven children by his wife Anna Walling
(1718–1787). After her husband's death, she had barely enough
money to buy food each day, yet she still managed to give her children
a decent upbringing and a few of them a good education. Her oldest
son, Petrus, joined the army and in 1788 advanced to the rank of
ensign in Österbotten's regiment.

Her youngest son, Immanuel, was born in 1757 and enrolled at
age fifteen in the Cathedral School in Uppsala. He wanted to become
a physician, but because the preparation time was too long and expensive, he chose instead to become a military barber-surgeon. Unable to accept the conditions in the Karlskrona naval squadron, he
asked to be transferred to the Uppsala regiment. Immanuel was the
first Nobelius to change his Latin name to Nobell, which he short-
ened to Nobel in 1785.

---

[2] First minted in 1534, the *riksdaler* (here, "Swedish dollar") became the main cur-
rency in 1766. In 1855, it was replaced by the *krona,* or crown, which is worth
1/4 riksdaler, or 100 öre, and is still in use in Sweden today.

Immanuel Nobel was sent as barber-surgeon to Svartholmen's fortress. Shortly after, he returned to Uppsala, where "the father of Swedish surgery," Olof af Acrel, on July 21, 1789, awarded him a journeyman's license. Although already thirty-two years old, Immanuel was still formally a *studiosus Chirurgiae* [a student of surgery]. That he was successful in his studies is evident from the medical faculty minutes of June 15, 1791: ". . . the Scholarship list was examined and it was found that the decease of student Hjerpe in Finland has freed a room, to which occupation the Faculty designated Emanuel [*sic*] Nobel, Uplandus."

Immanuel received no degree other than the designation *studiosus Chirurgiae* and had actually no legal right to practice even the profession of barber-surgeon. Despite his lack of diplomas, he applied to become "Hospital-Physician in Wenersberg," a position he was granted in 1794 and kept until 1796. Thereafter, he became "*vice provincialmedicus*," "city barber-surgeon in Gefle," and "hospital physician." He was noted and rewarded for his contributions in connection with the introduction of vaccination. Like his son and grandson, Immanuel never obtained an academic degree, yet he practiced various professions with success.

Immanuel Nobel married twice. His first marriage produced three children, of whom two died at an early age. After his first wife, Anna Kristina Rosell (1760–1795), a mayor's daughter from Karlstad, died, he remarried in 1800. His new wife was Brita Katarina Ahlberg, the daughter of a shipper in Gävle. She gave birth to three children. The oldest was Immanuel, the father of Alfred Nobel, born March 24, 1801, and christened two days later.

Chapter 3

About the childhood of Immanuel Nobel (1801–1872), we know little except that he was born into poverty. Immanuel would never recover from the humiliations that he was exposed to in his childhood; these haunted him his entire life, creating an inferiority complex that was not alleviated by his occasional success. A contributing factor was his lack of basic schooling. Immanuel's father had taught him to read, write, and count, but took his son out of school at age fourteen. Consequently, this robust, natural genius would have difficulty writing a grammatically faultless letter, and his handwriting was unpracticed, to put it mildly, as evidenced in his handwritten, 112–page autobiography, which was found hidden away in the home of a descendant.

Immanuel began to earn his living as soon as he left school. Like so many other destitute youths of his time, he chose the sea, although a contributing factor could have been that his maternal grandfather was a shipper. In a notation in the Gävle shipping office's yearbook for 1815, one reads that "the youth Emanuel [*sic*] Nobel has been permitted to enlist to serve at the shipping office."

Full of initiative but with little interest in book learning, the lad signed on as cabin boy on a ship named the *Thetis*. Three years as a sailor gave the young Immanuel a chance to see the world. He became familiar with life in the ports of the Mediterranean countries and the Near East. His salary was five Swedish dollars per month.

According to the church register, he returned to his homeland in 1819. His talent for drawing and mechanics soon became evident, and with great enthusiasm he began studying with a master builder in his hometown of Gävle. He may have been the draftsman who drew the triumphal arch for King Karl XIV Johan's visit to the city. Though it seems unlikely that an eighteen-year-old youth, whose only qualification was that he had just begun to study construction, would have been given this task, the following was printed in the Christmas 1819 issue of Gävle's newspaper: "This glorious triumphal arch was drawn by the eighteen-year-old Emanuel [*sic*] Nobel, thereby laying the foundation for his career. He returned last year after a few years as a sailor and is studying architecture."

Whether true or not, it is clear that as early as 1818 Immanuel

had gone to Stockholm to learn more about drawing. His name can
be found on the roster of architecture students at the Academy of
Liberal Arts for the year 1818–1819. After a few years of study,
which he financed by working for a master builder, Immanuel received the academy's fourth medal on January 25, 1824, and was
awarded the Tessin Medal[1] a year later. In 1825, he was accepted at
the Royal Academy's mechanical school, where he attended lectures
and submitted drawings. The drawings received some attention, because he received a larger scholarship of sixty dollars "for a well-
executed model of a portable house" and another "for a model of a
spiral staircase."

That same year, Immanuel Nobel requested no fewer than three
patents: the first for his "planing machine"; the second for "a mangle
machine with ten rollers" and "a mechanical movement"; the third
for an invention to transform rotation movement to a back and forth
movement "by means of the use of ropes and without cogs." The
applications were submitted to the Technical Institute's teacher col-
legium for comments. "This invention is . . . a completely new and
as yet unachieved improvement," begins one of the reports.

Inventing was an important step forward for Immanuel. In spite
of his meager theoretical training, he began submitting more patent
applications; most were approved. As a result, he became increasingly
sought after as a building contractor. As Nobel biographer Sigvard
Strandh writes, "Within the building and construction technology,
it was mostly stalwart men with practical knowledge — not the
theorists — who were making the greatest contributions. That holds
true for almost the entire nineteenth century."[2]

Immanuel's practical way of doing things — reminiscent of his
ancestor, Olof Rudbeck, for whom no problem was unsolvable —
brought him one assignment after another. One of his more famous
works was a building in the Stockholm City Garden. The so-called
Ronska house was erected on a cliff shelf at the edge of a steep
mountainside. The house needed to be propped up, and Immanuel
found a way to do it. He blasted (with gunpowder, since this was
long before his son invented dynamite) recesses in the mountain and
stabilized the building with heavy plinths. This was deemed a heroic

[1] Named for Nicodemus Tessin (1654–1728), Sweden's foremost architect of the
time, who won international fame as the designer of Stockholm's royal castle.
[2] Sigvard Strandh, *Alfred Nobel — mannen, verket, samtiden* [Alfred Nobel — The
Man, His Work, His Times], published by Natur & Kultur, Stockholm, 1983. No
English translation available.

feat in professional circles, and it was acknowledged he had saved the house from almost certain doom.

The esteem of his colleagues led to new assignments, and Immanuel did all work to satisfaction. On his own, he built a "moveable wooden house," indicating again how far ahead of his time he was. He constructed tool machines that are considered revolutionary by experts. Probably because his father had been a barber-surgeon, he developed a system for the manufacture of surgical equipment. He invented floating mattresses and pontoon sections, using an inflatable elastic rubber.

In 1827, Immanuel married the daughter of an accountant, Andriette Ahlsell (1805–1889), and theirs was a uniquely happy marriage.

By 1831, the couple's finances were strong enough for them to buy a small house on Langholmen in Stockholm. Their firstborn, Robert, was then two, and his brother Ludvig was born that year. Everything seemed to be turning out well for the young family, when suddenly Immanuel was hit by one setback after another. Three of his barges, loaded with expensive building material, sank, and a finished stone chest went down while being towed. He was forced to rebuild a building wing he had already restored at heavy cost. Worst of all, the family's house burned down on December 31, 1832.

The following month, Immanuel had no choice but to declare bankruptcy. Official documents paint a disheartening picture of the family's living conditions. Immanuel had rented a simple apartment on the outskirts of Stockholm, in the Tobaksspinnaren block in Maria parish. Although the yearly rent was low, he had trouble paying it. The bankruptcy papers reveal that the furnishings were the simplest imaginable: a few tables and beds, a few beat-up chairs, six sets of sheets, three pillow cases, "copper and iron" valued at about twenty Swedish dollars, and glasses and china worth ten. Immanuel had to move his family again, this time to even simpler lodgings in a house across the yard at number 11 Norrlandsgatan.

An objective study of the bankruptcy case might conclude that Immanuel had acted in a highly irresponsible manner, and that he ought not to have involved himself in as many risky undertakings as he did. On the other hand, there is overwhelming proof of his powers of initiative and ingenuity. Immanuel's various contracts included ventures as diverse as a suspension bridge over Skurusund, repair of the Anjou house at the Grand Plaza, the Petersen house at the Monk Bridge, and a laundry at Jakobsberg.

In his petition to Stockholm's magistrates' court, he attributed his losses to a "series of misfortunes" and estimated them at 15,471 Swedish dollars 32 schillings. In a later paper, dated January 11, 1833, he acknowledges resignedly that "such losses have exceeded me, and, in spite of my good will it is impossible for me to compensate in full the debts and obligations in which I presently stand toward all my Creditors. Therefore I see myself forced to apply for official summons and proceedings on behalf of all Creditors in order to surrender to them all of my personal belongings salvaged from the flames. . . ."

The bankruptcy proceedings went on for more than a year, but Immanuel was not free of debts even when they were over. On the contrary, in 1837, his creditors turned high-handed, threatening him with debtor's prison. Not until the beginning of the 1850s was he totally free of debt and all his creditors paid in full. Even if Immanuel sometimes gave the impression of being a dreamer and an eccentric, his sense of honor was well developed.

Chapter 4

Alfred Bernhard Nobel was born on October 21, 1833, in a room on the second floor at the back of a three-story apartment building on Stockholm's northern periphery. Today, the address is 9 Norrlandsgatan, and the block is now located in the center of the city. The original house was torn down in 1934. A small limestone slab commemorates Nobel as an "inventor, supporter of culture, friend to peace."

Whether Alfred was a wanted child or not, we don't know. We do know that in the tax assessment statement for 1833, after the bankruptcy, his father Immanuel was described as "poor" and as an "artist." His wife had already given birth to three children and lost her firstborn. When their home burned down during her husband's absence, a fire that destroyed all the furniture, she had risked her own life to save her children.

It was thus into a ravaged home that Alfred first saw the light of day. He was so weak that he nearly died at birth. He would remain sickly and frail all his life.

Despite Alfred's unwillingness to write down his life history in any systematic fashion, we do know something about his childhood and the circumstances under which he grew up. The humiliations caused by the bankruptcy figure prominently in *Nemesis,*[1] a play he began to write late in life and finished not long before his death. A tragedy involving incest and betrayal, *Nemesis* feeds upon the intensity of childhood trauma. Beatrice, the main character, reflects upon what has driven her to an act of revenge against her father:

---

[1] Nobel's *Nemesis* was inspired by the English poet Percy Bysshe Shelley's tragic drama *The Cenci* (1819), the story of Count Francesco Cenci, a sixteenth-century Roman nobleman who becomes incestuously passionate about his daughter, Beatrice. Beatrice, her brother Bernard, and their stepmother Lucretia plot to kill Francesco. Their plot is discovered and they are tortured before being condemned to death by the pope. After Alfred's death in 1896, his family considered the play a discredit to him and had the entire edition destroyed. The only remaining copy of the play is kept at the Nobel Foundation in Stockholm.

I admit that I have often failed, that feelings of hate and bitterness have deep roots in my heart; but you know, since nothing escapes you, that it is compassion for my brothers and my poor mother, that it is their being unfairly and terribly tortured that has fostered my hate.

[Act II, scene xi]

Later in the play, another character echoes the sense of entrapment and futility that informs the work:

My whole being is a source of hate; my first childhood memory is of trying to bite the tyrant. My whole thread of life is spun by Nemesis.

[Act IV, scene i]

Alfred's early memories may have had to do with freezing, for he feared and hated the cold his whole life. Icy drafts surely swept the simple house, heated only by an iron stove and a Dutch oven. Smoky oil lamps provided the light (half a century would pass before the great transformation brought about by the introduction of electricity). The children were probably always coughing from the sulfuric smoke burning in their throats. Garbage was thrown into a corner of the backyard beside the privies, where fat rats ran riot.

Food had to be rationed and, rather than meat, dried codfish was served almost every day. Another passage from *Nemesis* seems appropriate, if also (like the entire play) melodramatic:

You who read in my heart the misery of my whole life, you know that ever since my childhood days I have been the victim of abuse of every imaginable kind. Hunger, lashings, insults — nothing has been spared me.

[Act II, scene xi]

Life for poor people in Stockholm during the 1830s was barely tolerable. Since nobody had been able to solve basic sanitary problems, one epidemic followed another. More people were dying than being born. Thousands of infants perished from diphtheria and whooping cough. In addition, the country was hit by a depression, resulting in political unrest. Tailwinds from the July revolution in Paris in 1830 reached Sweden and encouraged activist groups who were militating in opposition to the established order.

According to records from the time, thousands of tradesmen declared bankruptcy, but the knowledge that they had brothers in misfortune did not make Immanuel's family feel any less grim about life. Under the circumstances, some might feel that Immanuel ought to have learned a lesson from his free-enterprise experiences and gone out looking for employment, but he did not. Encouraged by his patient wife, he continued his activities as an entrepreneur and inventor, although on an increasingly limited scale. Sigvard Strandh says that at this point Immanuel looked "with great enthusiasm into the possibilities of using the elastic qualities of rubberized material in a land mine. But nobody wanted to listen to him. Sweden now had its first rubber industry — the only problem was that it had no customers."

Andriette's father was a relatively well-to-do accountant and controller at the governmental barracks in Stockholm. Having been raised with a strong sense of responsibility, she was thrifty and hard-working — qualities that came in handy when it came to managing their meager finances. Alfred's brother Robert said in his old age that "One of my most painful childhood memories is when my mother sent me out to buy dinner food for the whole family for twelve shillings and I lost the little coin." About a year before his death, Ludvig recounted how he and Robert had been entrusted with selling matches on street corners in order to "contribute a few extra coins to our livelihood."

Andriette's workday began before dawn. She made clothes for her children from cheap remnants, always seeing to it that they were patched and clean. Taking on the major part of the everyday burdens seemed natural to her — just as it did to most of her female contemporaries. During the 1830s, Andriette's greatest sorrow was that her husband did not have his own workroom. She might also have regretted that he was unable to accept any invitations from business acquaintances, since the Nobels' small living quarters prevented any return invitations. The harsh pressure from the outside did create a remarkable unity within the family, however, and the marriage survived until Immanuel's death in 1872.

There were some moments of happiness. In middle age, Alfred

wrote to his mistress Sofie Hess[2] from Paris: "If Stockholm were not situated three steps from the North Pole, I would leap over there for Christmas and extend my plate toward the porridge bowl." He missed the Swedish Christmas rituals: *dopp i grytan* (bread dipped into a special broth), the Christmas Eve fish, the dancing around the Christmas tree, the singing of "Silent Night." Christmas Eve was the one evening of the year when even poor children had enough to eat.

[2] Sofie Hess (1850–1912), later Sofie von Kapivar, became Alfred's mistress in 1878. Their correspondence is reproduced later in this biography.

Chapter 5

Often I see myself again, in my imagination, enclosed in my real mother's embrace, being caressed and kissed with tenderness, as if a mother could be an angel or an angel could be a mother. I can still see her sorrowful, melancholy, tear-filled expression.

Nemesis, Act III, scene xi

August Strindberg (1849–1912), who two decades later would attend the same school as Alfred Nobel, Jacob Parish Apologist School, suggests in his autobiography[1] that mother worship is a substitute for a lost belief in God. There is a remarkable agreement between Nobel and Strindberg in this (as well as in other coincidences: both died at age sixty-three, and at both burials Sweden's future archbishop, Nathan Söderblom, officiated).

After he had started school, his mother was Alfred's universe. She would sit up nights with him and keep him company. He describes her vigilance in a poem that he wrote in 1851, in English, when he was eighteen:

> My cradle looked a deathbed, and for years
> a mother watched with ever anxious care,
> so little chance, to save the flickering light,
> I scarce could muster strength to drain the breast,
> and the convulsions followed, till I gasped
> upon the brink of nothingness — my frame
> a school for agony with death for goal.

These seven lines are part of a 419-line poem written under the influence of Shelley, whose idealism had made an indelible impression on Alfred. According to Henrik Schück, the poem takes the "form of a poetic epistle and reveals without a doubt a literary talent, which under other circumstances could possibly have developed into something. Its main interest to us lies in its autobiographical details. . . ."[2]

---

[1] August Strindberg, *Tjänstekvinnans son* [The Servant Woman's Son], published in 1887. Strindberg's father was a wealthy man, and his mother was a servant working in his house. An English translation was published in 1913.

[2] Henrik Schück and Ragnar Sohlman were asked by the Nobel Foundation's board of directors to write a memorial piece about the family for the twenty-fifth anniversary of the foundation.

Alfred's constant ill health kept him from taking part in his siblings' and other children's games:

> We find him now a boy. His weakness still
> makes him a stranger in the little world,
> wherein he moves. When fellow boys are playing
> he joins them not, a pensive looker-on,
> and thus debarred the pleasures of his age
> his mind keeps brooding over those to come.

In a way Alfred remained a "pensive looker-on" his whole life. His parents' social disgrace was the foundation for his bitterest childhood memories. Tensions enveloped his father and mother; after the evening meal they would sit by the lamp, silent and bent over their work, he with his accountings and drawings, she with her sewing. Neither was able to break the troubled silence, and as an adolescent Alfred would write that "reality so brutally spoiled my young heart's idealistic world." The deepest lines of his character had been etched.

Alfred's maternal grandmother's maiden name was Carolina Roospigg, and she came from the barren and god-fearing province of Småland. From her, Andriette had inherited a clear sense of right and wrong, and she was constantly impressing upon her sons the importance of remaining unreservedly honest. The impression stuck: Robert, Ludvig, and not least, Alfred embraced commendable (and, for their time, highly exceptional) business ethics. Alfred's growing bitterness derived in part from his sense that people around him did not measure up to his standards. That they were driven by greed exacerbated his suspiciousness and his disgust. His way of honoring his mother's memory was by remaining scrupulously honest. Anton Chekhov (1860–1904) once wrote that "from our father we received our talent, from our mother our soul." The Nobel brothers would have agreed.

Although Immanuel Nobel's difficulties were partly self-inflicted, one cannot deny that he had considerable intelligence and a talent for invention. He was also a man of indomitable courage, and he had an energy that could move mountains. His imagination was unlimited, even if many of its products had no commercial value.

Alfred would later criticize both his father and his brother Ludvig for thinking the financing of a project secondary. To Alfred, solving the matter of financing was primary.

As a father, Immanuel was fair, if demanding. He sometimes had trouble controlling his temper, but even Alfred could flare up quickly. His letters refer to that "Nobel blood that easily starts to boil."

When Alfred was four, a decisive event took place in the family's life. During a party, Immanuel made the acquaintance of a Finnish-Russian civil servant named Lars Gabriel von Haartmann, who was the governor of Turku, Finland, and the man presiding over the Czar's commission for promoting industry and trade. Immanuel led the conversation around to his favorite subject: land mines. Von Haartmann's interest was aroused. He urged Immanuel to come to Turku, where he could introduce him to the right people.

Surrounded by impatient creditors and threatened by debtor's prison, Immanuel felt he had little to lose by going. He told his family they would follow as soon as circumstances allowed. Immanuel's decision to go was based on his hope to be able "to realize my plans and win encouragement for my industrious exertions, which I clearly realize will never succeed in my own country where I have experienced so many undeserved misfortunes."

On December 4, 1837, Immanuel waved farewell to his family on the pier from the railing of a sailing ship, his destination Turku. For Andriette and her three boys, the next few years would mean endless deprivations that began the minute the ship was out of sight. Andriette had no idea how she would support herself and her children.

Her father came to the rescue, supplying her with enough cash to keep the wolf from the door. With the help of her relatives and a few friends, Andriette managed to open a store for dairy products and vegetables, not far from their home. By doing everything herself and working from early morning to late at night she managed to turn a small profit. Once the threat of starvation had passed, she could begin to plan her children's education.

The year Immanuel left for Turku, Andriette had already enrolled her eldest son Robert in Jacob Parish Apologist School's first grade. Two years later, it was Ludvig's turn, and when Alfred turned seven in 1840, he started at the same school.

Jacob was known as the school for ragamuffins, because the children of the poor went there, while children of middle-class or upper-class families went to Klara School. According to August

Blanche's tales of early nineteenth-century Stockholm,[3] the students were in a constant state of war with each other. They fought battles among barrels, carts, and parcels of goods, among hawkers, tradesmen, and peddlers and on a schoolyard that was overshadowed by commercial buildings.

It was a setting straight out of a Dickens novel. The oil lamps in the classrooms gave off fumes; not until the end of the 1870s were they exchanged for gas burners. Since no ventilation system existed and the windows were equipped with inner glass panes that were nearly impossible to open, the rooms were seldom if ever aired out. Each room had a selection of carpet beaters: long, medium, and short — since thrashing was considered an effective cure for intellectual shortcomings. A student who had made six spelling mistakes could be called forward to the teacher's desk. "Put your fingers on the edge!" Then the teacher raised the carpet beater and dealt six stinging lashes across the fingers.

Beating was widely practiced, as Claes Lundin's and August Strindberg's Old Stockholm clearly shows: "Every schoolboy at Jacob counted that day when he had escaped beating as most unusual. After morning prayers came the moment of punishment for those whose beating had been postponed from the preceding day, and then the lashes rained during every hour of lessons."[4]

In 1860, Strindberg's father took him out of Klara School and put him into Jacob, where Strindberg compared his new peers to his former schoolmates. Jacob pupils, he wrote, were "less well-dressed with ulcerous noses, had ugly facial features and stank." Yet, he felt more "intimate" with them than he had with pupils at Klara, who had a habit of turning up their noses at most things and most people.

Alfred spent two long semesters at Jacob. Before his industriousness and talent were noted, he must have felt that pupils had no civil rights. They were supposed to be grateful just for being allowed to go to school.

The school was financed partly through so-called term fees, "voluntary" fees collected in humiliating ways at the end of each semester. Groups of teachers and pupils went from door to door

[3] August Blanche (1811–1868), *Hyrkuskens berättelser* [Stories of a Coachman], published in Sweden in 1857. No English translation available.
[4] Claes Lundin and August Strindberg, *Gamla Stockholm* [Old Stockholm], published in Sweden in 1882. No English translation available.

playing music. Every family was supposed to contribute what they felt they could afford. Some parents were unable to pay anything; others refused out of stinginess. Despite the fact that Jacob Parish was home to government workers and royal court attendants, the sums collected were frequently pitifully small. Whether Andriette contributed anything is not known.

Naturally, her own and her boys' thoughts revolved around Immanuel, hoping that he would manage to create a secure future for them with his inventions. In addition to the mines, he was working on a number of other projects, dealing mainly with military equipment. As a true patriot, it pained him doubly that the Swedish defense apparatus had been indifferent to his proposals. When, more than a half-century later, Alfred Nobel bought the Bofors works, he turned it into one of the world's largest weapons manufacturers with the idea of making the Swedish defense system less dependent on foreign industry. The year before his death, he wrote to Ragnar Sohlman: "There will be a lively time at Bofors as soon as we achieve some tangible results with any one of our current new projects. It would be fun to see old Sweden rival Germany and England when it comes to weapons." The circle seems to close: Alfred completed what his father had begun.

As if wanting to compensate his mother for all her sacrifices, young Alfred plowed through his homework with tenacious stamina. He was quickly proving himself a model student and received the highest grade, A, for what was called "Power of Comprehension." He received the same grade for "Industriousness" and "Manners." As a comparison, Ludvig received a B in "Power of Comprehension," B/C in "Industriousness," and A/B in "Manners."

His teachers' praise made Alfred feel special. The frail boy who had such difficulty asserting himself among his older brothers and their friends was now suddenly distinguishing himself. Diligence and talent had already, at age eight, set him apart.

Immanuel Nobel was delighted to hear that Alfred, somewhat to his surprise, had turned out to have such academic talent. Normally stingy with praise, Immanuel made an exception for Alfred, as we find in a letter to his brother-in-law, Ludvig Ahlsell: ". . . my good and industrious Alfred is highly valued both by his parents and his brothers for his knowledge as well as for his untiring work ability, which nothing can replace." Five years later, he tried to characterize his sons: "What fate has given less of to one, another seems to have received in richer measure. According to my evaluation, Ludvig has the most brains, Alfred the greatest discipline, and Robert the greatest sense of enterprise but also a perseverance that amazed me several times last winter." Ludvig went on to become a highly successful entrepreneur in St. Petersburg, and Robert would reap success as an oil exporter in Baku, but it was Alfred's combination of all three qualities that took him the furthest.

During his two semesters at Jacob, Alfred came in contact with children from other social classes. At the physical drill exhibitions, in which both Klara and Jacob students participated, as well as at the ceremonies on the last day of each semester, class differences were striking. Some children wore sailor's suits and velvet jackets with white vests. Others wore leather short pants, oiled leather boots, and homemade clothes. Photographs show straight-backed bourgeois parents wearing stiff collars and tall hats that looked like chimneys. The mothers of poor children look like charwomen, and the fathers are bent and warped from hard manual labor.

In all probability, the social injustices Alfred observed early in life contributed to his later declaring himself a social democrat. At the time he was one of Europe's richest men and controlled more than ninety companies spread out around the globe. We might understand why the world greeted his alleged political conviction with some distrust, for though a social democrat, he was opposed to granting voting rights to everyone. However, Alfred, like his brother Ludvig, had a pronounced social conscience. Both felt compassion for the weak and the powerless and translated this feeling into action.

Finally, Alfred's father, who had been constructing mines both for land and sea defense, first in Turku and later in St. Petersburg, became successful enough to send for his family. On October 21, 1842, a passport was issued for "Mrs. Nobel with children, all minors."

By the time they were ready to leave, Andriette had already found time to teach the boys a few Russian words. Alfred, who had an excellent ear for languages, would very soon teach himself Russian so well that after only a year in his new country he could speak it fluently.

Chapter 6

After five long years of separation, the family boarded a ship in Stockholm's harbor to be reunited with Immanuel Nobel.

During his year-long stay in Turku, Immanuel had lived in the house of a well-to-do family named Scharlin. Governor von Haartmann kept his promise and brought him into contact with influential individuals within the Russian defense ministry. They hinted he would get quite a few assignments were he to establish himself in St. Petersburg.

Nineteenth-century St. Petersburg was a cosmopolitan city. Nicholas I (1796–1855) was czar, and ruled with such ruthlessness that he earned the nickname "the crowned policeman." (He was not unopposed, however. Twelve hours before he wanted to pass through the center of the city the main streets had to be closed because of bomb threats). From the moment of Immanuel's arrival in St. Petersburg in December of 1838, he found success as a manufacturer, inventor, and industrial designer. The Russian government had long adopted a benevolent attitude toward foreigners who wished to establish themselves in the capital. In 1702, to attract talented and energetic entrepreneurs who might create work for the local residents, Peter the Great opened Russian doors to outsiders. And in 1817 the Swedish king Karl XIV Johan and Czar Alexander I concluded a treaty that exempted all Swedes living in Russia from taxation and military service. The presence of men like Immanuel Nobel in Russia was very welcome.

That he was a born inventor is evident from an illuminating episode mentioned in an obituary published in a weekly family magazine on September 20, 1872:

> Immanuel Nobel made his first invention at the tender age of six. It was a sun glass — a prism — consisting of a piece of ice. From the frozen surface of a bucket of water, he had cut out a suitable piece, shaping it with a knife to make it fit into a wooden ring after which it was smoothed and polished between the little boy's hands. When the piece of ice had frozen inside the wooden ring, his first experiment

was begun. Oh miracle! With shining eyes the little boy watched as a piece of paper, folded several times and placed under the ice, ignited and burned through. After that he tried and succeeded in lighting his father's tobacco pipe using the same method. How proud the little fellow was when his invention won him praise from his father, not a man known to waste words of praise.

Immanuel's theoretical foundation might have been imperfect, and there were indeed gaps in his general knowledge, but his intuition compensated. Alfred inherited the quality in rich measure. Alfred's relationship to his optimistic and outgoing father was complicated, however. With the years, father and son would grow apart even though they worked together. To Alfred, his father's way of thinking and business philosophy were more and more out of step with the times. But the eight-year-old Alfred who came to St. Petersburg swelled with pride at his father's accomplishments in a foreign country.

Andriette and children arrived in a mail coach loaded to over-flowing with suitcases, books, and household goods. Immanuel was waiting for them with horse and carriage and his own coachman. Alfred's eyes must have grown as large as saucers when he discovered that in this strange new country you could even own human beings. Serfdom was not abolished in Russia until 1863.

In the 1840s there were few railroads in Russia, and Andriette and her young sons had been forced to travel the many miles from Turku over rough roads in an uncomfortable vehicle. By the time of their arrival in the Russian capital, the autumn air was damp and misty, and days were short.

The large, open streets around St. Peter's Cathedral were home to thousands of starving orphans who lived entirely on charity. Some well-to-do families felt it their duty to give them extra food, and Alfred undoubtedly took notice, since he was always generous once he became financially independent. Following the Russian tradition, he would put aside considerable resources for the destitute and ignore only the most outrageous donation requests.

In all of Alfred Nobel's vast correspondence, there is no mention of his first impressions of St. Petersburg. Fortunately, another eye-witness, the Swedish nurse Maja Huss, wrote down her experiences in the city, where she was later employed to care for Edla Nobel's sister. (Among the Swedish upper class, it was common practice during prolonged stays abroad to employ a nurse, most often from the Red Cross in Stockholm.) The letters Huss has passed on are, in her daughter's words, "living images and impressions from a forgotten epoch." For instance, we are told that "my [salary of] 95 öre a day is 95 öre, whether I am with the Nobels or with X, Y, or Z. Perhaps even less, since I have to pay one crown [100 öre] here for what I get for 75 öre at home. It's also sad to drink champagne when one's only dress is splitting at the seams."

Continues Maja Huss, "The Neva is a splendid, beautiful wide river, with kilometer-long bridges crossing it. There is palace after palace — among them the Winter Palace. You must not think that the Neva's water goes through any kind of filter — no, sewage from the cholera barracks goes into it and from there it continues directly into our pipes."

We learn that on the Thirteenth Day of Christmas the Neva's water is blessed with great ceremony. "People are running over and filling their water pitchers with the cholera soup blessed by the bishops. I have a sensitive stomach and get diarrhea immediately after drinking a cup of tea."

Like Alfred, Maja Huss drove through the city shortly after she arrived: "We have to stop in front of the Kassan Cathedral, situated in Petersburg's heart, the Nevsky, and force our way through the crowds to the church. Inside, the brilliance of gold and silver is almost blinding. Only black-robed bishops are allowed into the inner, most holy sanctum." The Swedish nurse then remarks on the overwhelming smell of incense and wax candles. The monotonous drone of the priests going through twelve gospels makes her dizzy. The great feast day of the year is Easter: "Hams and veal steaks find their way into the homes. They are also eating blini — a kind of round pancake served directly from the griddle and eaten with sour cream, caviar, and smoked fish."

On a trip to the Alexander Nevsky priory, the most distinguished in Petersburg, located on an island in the Neva, she notes that it "can look brilliant in the midday sun [viewed] from one of the bridges." She cites the legend, which has it that Alexander Nevsky's priory is situated on the very spot where "Grand Duke Alexander in the year 1241 won a great victory over the Swedes and their allies."

On the way to their future home, Immanuel Nobel's family may have taken the road across the Trinity Bridge, passing the foundations of Peter Paul's fortress and the Roman Catholic graveyard. The magnificent avenues might well have overwhelmed a little Swedish boy born in a small house on a back street in Stockholm.

From a watercolor by Immanuel Nobel we know that their home in St. Petersburg was a modest one-story wooden house on a canal. The fence was broken in places. Even though the family's standard of living was much higher there than it had been in Stockholm, every form of waste was forbidden. There is reason to believe that the cold-sensitive Alfred suffered as much from cold and drafty floors in St. Petersburg as he had in Sweden. Icy winds swept in off the tundras, sneaking inside through cracks in the doors and windows.

One tangible reason for the family's improved financial situation was Immanuel's strong contacts with the Russian general Ogarev. Through his influence, the war ministry had become interested in Nobel's land and sea mines. Immanuel also distinguished himself through his manufacture of weapons for the Russian army. Under his competent leadership, the weapons industry was transformed from an old-fashioned handicraft into a science. The Nobel success would be followed by an even greater involvement in heavy industry and finally be crowned by the oil empire Immanuel's son Ludvig established in Baku, on the Caspian Sea.

Less than a year after her arrival in St. Petersburg, Andriette gave birth to a boy, Emil. After that she had yet another son and one daughter, but both died as infants. Alfred's health remained frail. A chronic sinus condition gave him headaches, commentary on which, because he would never be rid of them, constitutes a kind of refrain throughout his correspondence.

Immanuel's activities resulted in a letter to the Russian minister of war from General Ogarev. Since this document is one of the few surviving from this time and throws some light on Immanuel's ingenuity, it is well worth quoting:

To Mr. War Minister:

Your Highness has in a written document of September 19, 1841, No. 597, informed me of His Royal Majesty's order to allow the Foreigner Nobel to conduct experiments with his invention to destroy the enemy at a considerable distance. Since that time, Nobel has unceasingly involved himself in preparations for such experiments, but the execution of the same has been delayed for specific reasons, the main being the fulfillment of another obligation Nobel had undertaken — namely to construct permanent sea mines, which, for the present, have provided very satisfactory results. Finally, at the end of the year 1844, Nobel has conducted, in my presence, an experiment to explode a piece of land with a powder apparatus of special construction, and this with total success. . . . In my written report of September 16, 1841, No. 2803, I informed Your Highness that Nobel, upon the acceptance of his system, wished to receive a gratification of 40,000 silver rubles, but he is declining the same — at this time — and asks only to be reimbursed once and finally for 3,000 silver rubles, to cover his expenses.

During the time of the Crimean War (1853–1856), Immanuel's sea mines were judged superior to the Russian versions and were used along the Gulf of Finland at Kronstadt, Sveaborg, and Reval. His son Robert was given the responsibility of organizing the laying of mines by the highest Russian commander, following a plan Immanuel himself had worked out. He was successful: the English fleet did not dare enter the Gulf of Finland. Although no enemy ship was destroyed, a contemporary newspaper account reports that "an unexploded mine became the object of such detailed scrutiny aboard the flagship *Duke of Wellington* that it exploded and killed a man, which gave the English deep respect for these small contrivances."

Immanuel recounted his experiences in a book bearing the weighty title *Système de défense maritime pour passages et ports sans fortifications dispendieuses et avec épargne d'hommes par Immanuel Nobel* [Sea Defense Systems for Passages and Ports without Ample Fortification and with a Saving in Manpower]. With its sumptuous colored illustrations the book bears eloquent testimony to its author's inventive spirit, energy, and talent for drawing.

By 1841, the payments from the Russian government had made it possible for Immanuel to open a machine shop as well as a foundry. He was receiving recognition and approval from every quarter and was soon considered one of Russia's most competent engineers. Success followed upon success. In 1848 he wrote to his now close friend, his brother-in-law, Ludvig Ahlsell: "Everything is running smoothly here: work up to my ears, irritations and discomfort in matching degree from the riffraff that want to get as much as possible while

doing as little useful work as possible." Calling some of his employees riffraff is typical of Immanuel's gruff straightforwardness
and stern Protestant work ethic.

Even at the peak of his success, he didn't seem to suffer much
from his lack of higher education. Not only did he pay his debts,
but he was able to help relatives and friends in Sweden. He writes
to Ahlsell: "If my sons get along and keep working together on what
I have started, I think that with God's help they will never want for
their daily bread, for there is still much to be done here in Russia."

Chapter 7

Immanuel Nobel's experiences had taught him that knowledge is the most valuable of all assets. One might lose one's money, but never what one knows. As soon as his personal finances improved, he was therefore eager for his sons to receive the best education available. He did not want them to be self-taught as he had been. Only with the greatest effort had he managed to acquire a credible grounding both in the natural sciences and the humanities. In his latter years, he would even study French and English literature, including the classic works, in his leisure hours. Immanuel's thirst for knowledge was inherited by his sons, who were not only trained as engineers but exceptionally well-read men.

From the very first Alfred was fascinated by the speculative and experimental elements of chemistry, and it became his favorite subject. His chemistry teachers were Professors Zinin and Trapp. Yuli Trapp (1808–1882) taught at the Technical Institute in St. Petersburg. He drew Alfred and Immanuel's attention to nitroglycerine, a heavy yellow oil produced by slowly pouring glycerol into a chilled mixture of nitric and sulfuric acids. Nikolaj N. Zinin (1812–1880) taught at the Academy for Medicine and Surgery and had himself studied under Alfred's future teacher in Paris — the celebrated T. J. Pelouze. Both Trapp and Zinin had become Immanuel Nobel's friends during his early years in St. Petersburg. Zinin's summer house was located near the Nobels' summer place outside St. Petersburg.

Among the boys' tutors there was one Swede: a language and history teacher named Lars Santesson, who had a master's degree in philosophy. Trapp, Zinin, Santesson, and a teacher named Ivan Peterov managed to impress upon their charges that there were no limits to what the mind could absorb, an insight that left a mark on their view of life. The brothers learned to make great demands on themselves and to be self-reliant. They were taught that one shaped one's own destiny and that industriousness was the foundation of success, so the days of study were long ones. Alfred in particular quickly proved capable of independent reasoning. He had a passion for learning, and his unusually good memory was a great help. As a student he toiled like a galley slave. The company of others interested him only when an intellectual contest was involved, an opportunity to trace a new thought. From an early age, every unsolved problem was welcomed as a tantalizing challenge.

The teacher Alfred grew most fond of was the wise Peterov, who showed fatherly concern toward Alfred. His favorite student drew immense strength from Peterov's praise, which spurred him to redouble his efforts. Alfred quickly and effortlessly caught up with his older brothers, and his teacher sensed his pupil's genius. How, he might have wondered, does one teach a genius?

Educators used to think one didn't have to worry about geniuses; they were assumed to be strong enough to fend for themselves. Others have found that nothing is further from the truth. Gifted individuals often have deficiencies for which they cannot compensate without assistance. Brilliance can be dulled by the endless hours in classes where there are few opportunities and little encouragement. If indeed Nobel had not been privileged enough to receive private tutoring of high quality, and instead been forced to struggle through a regular curriculum, year after year, would he have developed as he did?

During his life Alfred found only a handful of people with whom he could speak openly and honestly about issues of import: his teacher Ivan Peterov, Bertha von Suttner, Nathan Söderblom (who would become Sweden's archbishop, a leader of the Ecumenical Movement — whose goal was the unification of Christian churches — and win the Nobel Peace Prize in 1930), and Ragnar Sohlman, the executor of his will. All had in common an uncompromising love of the truth and a generosity of spirit, and these four were able to bring Alfred out of his shell.

With Peterov, Alfred would discuss the czar's oppressive politics. He had perceived that in his heart of hearts his teacher was hoping both for an end to serfdom and for freedom throughout his land, even if he dared only to hint at such thoughts. Peterov's caution may have inspired a passage in *Nemesis:*

> Even I weigh my words carefully, and know where I can speak freely, and where I cannot. When you live in a time such as ours, you smell a spy everywhere.

> [Act III, scene xi]

Police surveillance and censorship were constant realities in czarist Russia. Alfred turned sixteen the year Fyodor Dostoyevsky was imprisoned and sentenced to death, a sentence that was later commuted to four years in the penitentiary in Siberia and service as a soldier in a penal unit. The czar had toyed with him in a cruel fashion. Dostoyevsky and others were condemned to be shot, dressed in white shirts, and taken to a place of execution; there they were pardoned.

Alfred was no Dostoyevskian radical. Even as a young man, he placed little confidence in the political awareness of the masses. Only the educated and far-sighted elite, he felt, were fit to govern. He was repelled by the collective and could never bring himself to go along with the pack. One legacy of his Russian upbringing was that he was forever torn between sympathy and antipathy for the inhabitants of palaces and those of ghettos. Behind his lifelong rootlessness were feelings of alienation. Work was the only salvation.

When Ludvig went back to Sweden for a long visit, his father wanted him to hurry back. "I cannot let him stay," he wrote to Ludvig Ahlsell, "because, beyond the considerable cost to me, it does disrupt rather completely my other children's education; they are waiting for his return to go back to their studies." Ludvig returned in January 1849 and wrote his uncle a letter that gives a glimpse of Alfred at age sixteen: "Alfred has grown so that I hardly knew him. He is almost as tall as I, and his voice has become so deep and strong that I didn't recognize it."

At the end of 1849, Robert's formal education was finished, as we know from Immanuel's letter to Ahlsell the following January: "As a piece of news that belongs among the incredible I can tell you that I have become a merchant of the First Guild [a professional association of craftsmen or merchants created to uphold standards and protect its members]. The proverb is confirmed; nobody is too old to be scurfy. I had to take this step because of the volume of my business. Robert takes thorough care of the practical tasks, which is why he, with my partner's consent, is being paid 100 silver rubles per month — a tidy salary for a twenty-year-old lad. But I can say, God be praised, that he earns it." The partner Immanuel mentions was General Ogarev.

It was a time of expansion in Immanuel's foundry. Production was rising and so was the income. Besides steam engines, piping, and ironworks for the civilian sector, orders were pouring in from the defense department: repeating rifles, cannon mounts, and, of course, mines. Immanuel bought Ogarev's shares and the company name changed to Fonderies & Ateliers Mécaniques Nobel & Fils [Foundry and Mechanical Shop, Nobel & Sons]. For the sons this meant a step up; they were promoted to part owners following their apprenticeship. In his memoirs, Ludvig emphasizes the importance of the all-round education that he and his brothers received at their father's insistence. The results of that education were becoming obvious.

The transformation Alfred underwent during these years was remarkable. Out of a shy, brooding, sickly childhood arose an efficient and tough entrepreneur, interested in everything and surprised by nothing. His contributions were critical, and in just a few years the small workshop company developed into one of Russia's largest. With time, the assortment of products for the civilian market expanded to include heating units and piping conduits. Immanuel had invented and now was manufacturing Russia's first central heating systems.

Naturally, there were setbacks. For instance, Immanuel had constructed a new kind of wooden wagon wheel. The government showed interest, but customs regulations forced manufacturing to be halted, and considerable money was lost. Generally, however, everything went exceedingly well for the Nobels, and in 1853 Immanuel received an Imperial gold medal "for industry and artistic skill."

Thirty years of peace had led many Russians to believe it would last. At last, humanity seemed mature enough to solve its differences without resorting to violence. Czar Nicholas I had different aims, however. Wars with Persia (1826–1828) and Turkey (1828–1829) had helped his realm to grow. He wanted to continue his expansionist policies, even if it meant another war. The Russian war machine needed modernizing and, as a direct result, Immanuel's company received large orders. To fill them, he had to import not only munitions from Sweden but qualified foremen as well. Soon Nobel & Sons could deliver everything from rapid-firing guns to steam engines for Russia's first propeller-driven warships.

In 1853, the Crimean War became a reality. In spite of the advantages war meant to the family firm, Alfred viewed the war as a pure expression of personal lust for power.

Immanuel and his sons were now receiving one urgent government assignment after another. On September 15, 1855, they were in Kronstadt's fortress for the placement of mines. Alfred wrote that day: "This place is not providing me with any memories that will enlarge my soul . . . because in Russia, service to the Crown goes before service to God!" His principles did not, however, stop him from solving technical problems with such skill that Nobel's sea mines became the first ones truly fit for use.

Immanuel had to finance all the extensive and necessary experiments himself. He was becoming more and more unhappy about doing business with the czar. He was bitterly contemplating refusing a payment of 40,000 rubles, since it would cover only a small part of his expenses. In later years he wrote: "Never has greater energy and versatility been expended at a mechanical plant than here during the years 1854–1860, years of uninterrupted feverish work, and, in all probability, never has so much work been so little salaried."

Chapter 8

Thus I grew and developed into a thinking and feeling creature with an inner world of poetry that no tyranny has been able to extirpate. Our wonderful poets' songs to me were enchanting and soothing echoes from the spiritual world of emotion and thought. They were my faithful companions, when so often during starry nights I fell into a reverie at the edge of the Mediterranean Sea . . . then I dreamt myself, though awake, into a better world until sleep, this taste of death, erased the pictures of life and numbed for a while its bustle, its bruises, and its pains. . . .

Nemesis, Act II, scene ii

As a portrait of the inventor as a young man, this passage from *Nemesis* suggests that Alfred suffered all the torments of a struggling poet. Later, he looked at what he had produced with a twisted smile and burned all but one or two of his poems. But whether to choose the risky life of a poet or the no less risky life of an inventor was a real choice for Nobel in his youth. He had many qualities of a promising writer: a fertile imagination, a flair for style, and, not least, the capacity for disciplined philosophical reasoning. Two other eminent Swedes were serious poets in their youth and later abandoned writing — diplomat and council president Gustaf Philip Creutz (1731–1785), the author of *Atis and Camilla*[1] — and Sweden's secretary of state during World War II, Christian Günther. Günther, Creutz, and Nobel had in common youthful dreams of the arts and used their studies as camouflage for their writing. None had ambitions to attain a prominent position in society, and all had a keen sense of the vanity of human aspirations. "To reach one's goal is to see one's dreams disappear like mist; to stand there more empty-handed and alone than ever. Power, honor, riches — what are they other than rocks in a sea of hate and envy?" Günther is the author of that quote, but Creutz and Nobel might also have written it.

Alfred could write in five languages without difficulty and carried out his language studies with the greatest diligence and seri-

---

[1] Gustaf Philip Creutz, *Atis och Camilla* [Atis and Camilla] (1761), a pastoral poem about the love between the hunter Atis and the beautiful Camilla, one of Diana's priestesses.

ousness. He once translated a Voltaire text into Swedish but was not satisfied with it and translated the text back to French — after which he corrected his version against the original text. He had become convinced that his grasp of language was uncertain. More than anything else, this might be the explanation as to why, after the youthful attempts, he gave up writing altogether.

To Immanuel, his son's writing was only justifiable as a hobby. He refused to see writers as true professionals. It was therefore with the greatest concern that he noted signs that one of his sons was seriously considering becoming a "penman." Alfred ought to realize what high expectations were attached to him and outgrow such fancies. A wage-earning occupation and literature did not mix.

Purely practical reasons pushed Alfred into giving up his literary ambitions as well. In Russia of the 1850s, imprisonment threatened anyone unable to pay his debts. Though his father was enjoying considerable financial success, cancellation of payment was always a possibility. After the Crimean War, this threat would become a reality.

Since the family's finances had temporarily improved when Alfred was around sixteen, his father felt he could offer his son travel to other countries — on the condition that he give up any silly ideas about becoming a writer. Alfred gave in. He had seen how hard his father had to toil to keep the debit and credit columns equal while also developing his company. However, Alfred did pay a high price for his choice: his unsatisfied longing to write haunted him his whole life and left deep wounds, especially since he felt that he had the necessary courage and ability to live off his art. Alfred knew what he was giving up.

If his writing ambitions were thwarted, Alfred's hunger for reading was insatiable. In his letters he frequently quotes Shakespeare and, of course, Shelley, who had been the model for his own poetry. As noted earlier, his first poem especially shows Shelley's influence (he wrote it in English and afterward translated it into Swedish). The eighteen-year-old poet gave it no title but it is essentially an elegy that begins, "You say that I am a riddle." The subject of his tender feelings is a lovely Swedish girl working as a druggist's assistant in Paris, whom he met when he visited the city. He explains the story behind the poem in a letter:

I came to Paris — an ocean where Passion creates stormy weather and causes more wrecks than ever the salty waves did. Whoever is exploring this vast, boundless collection of sin and madness has to pay tribute to its false god, Sensuousness. My life, before then a desolate desert, came alive in felicity and hope. I had a goal, a heavenly goal: to win this lovely girl and to be worthy of her. I felt infinite happiness and we met again, and again and again, until we had become each other's heaven; and I became acquainted with the sweet compassion in her love and sealed it with a kiss, a chaste and holy kiss, of purest affection, even if no eye was there, except that of the Almighty, to watch over us. This could have ended in the usual way and provided joy and worry, but it was not meant to be; another bridegroom had a stronger claim — she is married until death.

The cryptic last line tells a tragic story. The young girl contracted tuberculosis and died while Alfred was still in the French capital. Her death, he claims, turned him into "a forsaken eremite in the world of the living, and I decided to consecrate my life to noble endeavors. From that moment on I have not involved myself in the pleasures of the masses. . . ."

During one of his trips to England, Alfred showed the poem to Reverend Lesingham Smith, an elderly English churchman with literary interests. Alfred was staying at a small hotel and happened to meet the clergyman, probably in 1868. Although Alfred was not religious, and normally reticent about discussing — let along displaying — his literary attempts, he asked Smith to read his poem. Smith took the time to write a lengthy response:

Notwithstanding some passages in it, which you yourself appear now to regret, I rejoice that it formed no part of the hecatomb which you made of your other compositions. The thoughts are so massive and brilliant, if not always true, that no reader can for a moment complain of dullness nor miss "the jingling sounds of like endings" any more than in the *Paradise Lost*. I have read not only carefully but critically, as you will see by the annexed remarks. I should have considered it as a marvelous production for an Englishman, but the marvel is increased hundredfold by the fact of its author being a foreigner. I have industriously hunted out every grammatical error and false idiom and you will see how small the amount of these is. There are not half a dozen mediocre lines in the whole 425. If you can write such a poem in the English tongue, what could you not do in your own, especially if you bide your time, as Milton did, till advancing years shall have enlarged your experience, shall have softened down asperities of thought and given you a perfect command over words.

The Reverend Smith wrote this letter in 1868, and in addition to its acuity, it tells us that Nobel had already burned all of his juvenilia, with the exception of that one poem, and another entitled "Night Thoughts," in which Nobel meditates on religion and does a credible imitation of the poets of the English Graveyard School, such as Edward Young and Thomas Gray. Nobel's "Night Thoughts" is again reminiscent of Shelley in the way that it combines the language of spiritual awakening with a decisive antireligious stance:

> The solemn silence of the midnight hour
> Unchains the fettered spirit, and the power
> Of reasoning takes a visionary flight
> Beyond the limits of defective sight
> Which may deceive us, yet attracts the soul
> Even with its wild and daring uncontrol.

Few Swedish poets have had the ability to write so effortlessly in English, and that fact ought to have strengthened the eighteen-year-old Alfred's self-esteem. Yet, as with the Voltaire translation, it seems to have reminded him that his poetry was derivative, and that he could only express himself through imitation.

Although Alfred's first love was poetry, in 1862 he also attempted to write a novel entitled *The Sisters*. Schück's opinion of the novel, published in that memorial piece for the Nobel Foundation, was clear-eyed in its assessment. "Utterly weak, especially in its language," he called the novel, and then went on to say that "This might have partly to do with the fact that the contemporary Swedish novel, which seems to have been his model, was appallingly poor. His characters are almost puerile and his dialogue unnatural. Nobel is no storyteller. . . ."

About bit-part actors it is often said that if nothing else they derive joy from proximity to the theater. In the same way, many a shipwrecked writing talent has found solace in a well-filled library. Alfred's library, which has been preserved at the Björkborn estate (where he lived part of the time during his last years) in the city of Karlskoga, Sweden, was well stocked. In a remarkably involved manner he followed contemporary literature. Outside of the great Russian authors, almost all the Nordic literature's finest are represented: Strindberg's *A Fool's Defense Speech;* Selma Lagerlöf's *The Tale of Gösta Berling;* Henrik Ibsen's *Peer Gynt* (upon which in letters to friends he comments enthusiastically); furthermore, there are works by the Norwegian writers Bjørnstjerne Bjørnson (winner of the 1903 Nobel Prize in Literature) and Alexander Lange Kielland, and, in a place of honor, the Swedish poet Viktor Rydberg. Surprisingly, Percy Bysshe Shelley is only represented by one work, *The Cenci.* Byron's *Childe Harold* is found in the library, as well as works by the English philosopher Herbert Spencer (1820–1903), whose belief in scientific progress Nobel shared. Judging from the worn appearance of the works by Spencer, Alfred seems to have read them closely.

With his Shelleyan taste for the idealistic excess, Nobel had difficulties appreciating works by naturalists like Strindberg and Zola. The latter he dismissed on one occasion as a "squalid writer." He preferred Rydberg's poetry, where "loftiness of soul" rather than the daily grind finds expression. When asked to donate money to build a monument to Rydberg, Alfred wrote: "As a rule, I am more concerned with the empty stomachs of the living than with memorials for the dead, for even if one believes in the soul as an independent entity, it is doubtful it has eyes. That said, I do not wish to withdraw, and therefore subscribe the sum of 300 crowns. There are writers whose very writings constitute a memorial. These need no other. Rydberg's writings, bearing witness to a loftiness of soul and beauty of form, belong in that class." Empty stomachs should be the concern of the businessman, not the poet.

This declaration is intriguing in view of the two most controversial words in Alfred Nobel's controversial final will establishing the Nobel prizes. One of the five awards, he stipulated, should be given to a writer "who has produced an outstanding work of literature in an *ideal direction* [my emphasis]." To Nobel, "loftiness of soul and beauty of form" were the artistic qualities most worthy of recognition.

In a letter to his brother Robert, Alfred characterizes himself as a "super-idealist, a kind of untalented Rydberg." The bitter word "untalented" indicates how much he still felt the thorn of his thwarted youthful ambitions. Henrik Schück for one believes that had "his poetic talent had a chance to develop, he would surely have been a poet whose strength would have been in the power of his thought."

Chapter 9

When Alfred made his first trip from Russia in 1849, he was, among other things, a trained chemist. A brilliant student, he had also done extensive studies on his own, and his laboratory skills were vastly superior to those of both his two older brothers and his contemporaries.

The self-awareness that would become so characteristic of him was awakening, and with it the determination to be the master of every situation. He was not going to throw himself into the world and let luck or chance lead the way. The way his first trip abroad was planned illustrates this. After a summer vacation in Dalarö with his uncle Ludvig Ahlsell and his cousins, he organized a trip to central Europe and England around his father's business connections. He went to Paris because he was invited to spend some time working in the laboratory of the celebrated Professor Pelouze. His trip to New York was planned around his meeting with the inventor and industrialist John Ericsson, a fellow Swede. Immanuel was experimenting with the theory that steam heat could be replaced by heated air and he wanted Alfred to find out what Ericcson thought on the subject. He also thought a long trip abroad would make his son abandon his literary ambitions.

A photo taken of Alfred at the time he left Russia shows him beardless and wearing bangs down his forehead. His shirt is stylish, and he is wearing a black, hand-knotted tie — a mixture of old and new. His mouth is wide and his eyelashes long. One might imagine that if he decided to smile, it would in all likelihood be a pleasant one.

It must have been with the greatest of expectations that Alfred arrived in New York to look up John Ericsson. Ericsson had come to the United States from England in 1838 (a year after his friend Immanuel Nobel had established himself in St. Petersburg) aboard the first propeller-driven oceangoing ship, *Robert E. Stockton,* which he himself had built.

When Alfred walked across St. John's Park toward a small three-story house at 36 Beach Street that morning in 1850, he intended to find out everything about John Ericsson's inventions he could, and in particular the warm air engine, or caloric engine, as it was also called. In the city of New York alone, twelve thousand of these warm air engines had been sold. Although the city had a widely developed water system, the pressure in the pipes was so low that it was only sufficient for the lower floors, and buildings were growing taller. Immanuel Nobel hoped to introduce this remarkable engine aboard warships.

Up until now Alfred had only read about inventors of genius, such as James Watt, the Scottish physicist who perfected the steam engine by separating the condensing chamber and the sliding vent; or Samuel Owen, the Swedish mechanic of English ancestry who had manufactured steam engines so successfully that they had made his adopted country a leader in this area. In 1818, the year the French Marshal Jean Baptiste Bernadotte became king of Sweden under the name of Karl XIV Johan, Owen launched the first steamboat in Sweden. Soon steam-driven paddle boats were common sights on Lake Malaren and the Salt Sea.

John Ericsson must have seemed the embodiment of success to young Alfred — although it would be another eleven years before Ericsson reached the peak of his fame with the construction of the iron-plated Union warship *Monitor*, which successfully challenged the Confederate ship *Merrimac* in a four-hour duel during the Civil War. Precious little is known about Alfred's apprenticeship with Ericsson. After his return to St. Petersburg, Alfred seems to have said very little about his stay in America. In a letter to his family, Alfred uses an expression that later stumped both Schück and Ragnar Sohlman. He writes about making "an agreement with a certain Captain Ericsson to send needed drawings that he had been unable to finish during the time I was in America. These drawings I am sending on to Mr. Arfvedsson in Stockholm." The phrase "a certain Captain Ericsson" led Schück and Sohlman to the conclusion that Nobel's acquaintance with Ericsson was rather casual. Yet Alfred had been sent all the way to the United States expressly to find out everything he could about John Ericsson's caloric engine. "A certain Captain Ericsson" may have been his way of downplaying how impressed he actually was by the man whose name was on everybody's lips in America.

When his stint with John Ericsson was ended, Alfred returned to Russia and went right back to work for his father. He wanted to give practical application to the ideas he had picked up. He was probably also tired of traveling, which, as his later letters attest, he never did much enjoy.

Alfred worked with such enthusiasm that by the summer of 1854 he became ill from overexertion. By this point his father's company employed more than a thousand men, and during the Crimean War the workpace was relentless. He was sent to a health spa to "take the waters," as was common. Following another visit to his relatives at Dalarö, he went to the Franzenbad spa. "I've been in Eger since the 4th of September," he wrote to his family, "and have begun my bath-and-guzzle cure (that's the correct term, because you guzzle enormous amounts of water here). The season is somewhat late but the cure is fine anyway." To show that he was not just lazing about, he gives a thorough account of what he has been doing for the family firm. Then he exclaims: "Enough about business. What fun to talk about memories of Stockholm and Dalarö. Ah, what pleasure they bring now! It is easy to see how much you lose when you trade relatives and friends for temporary acquaintances with whom you certainly can spend some pleasant hours, but with whom you can part, feeling about as much loss as you would for an old coat."

During his trip home, he writes his family from Berlin: "Finally, I begin to hope that my nomadic existence will soon come to an end and that I shall be able to turn to a more active life. High time, really, since it is beginning to bore me rather totally, not so much by its monotony — because you have to become accustomed to that sooner or later — but because of the thought that I am a burden instead of a contributor. Even though I have not been able to restore my health as fully as I had hoped (I believe that Stockholm and the time spent at Dalarö did me more good healthwise than Franzenbad), I am leaving for home as soon as I have finished with our business in Berlin. I long for home more than I can say. . . ."

In January 1856, Immanuel wrote to the Ahlsell family: "I can now also delight in the fact of Ludvig's recovered health, since this means I have a strong assistant in our many and toilsome duties. God grant that sweet, industrious Alfred be in as good shape as Ludvig. Then we would all be truly delighted."

Chapter 10

In 1947, the Swedish writer Sten Söderbergh wrote an unusual (and sympathetic) novel based upon Alfred Nobel's life entitled *Mannen som ingen kände* [The Man Nobody Knew]. In one section, when Alfred Nobel meets with John Ericsson, the older inventor says to his young countryman: "I once dreamt of putting all the ability fate has given me at my native land's disposal. But it has been for me as it was for your father — I have given my services to another country, and this other country has become my native land."

Both Ericsson and Alfred Nobel may indeed have had a patriotic streak in their nature, but that did not stop them from believing all inventions, as symbols of progress, belonged to all of humanity. They felt, as many artists do, that the work itself is the reward, and that one shouldn't count on any other. It was a belief Alfred had held to as a very young man. He had not forgotten the humiliation of poverty, and early on developed an interest in the financial side of his inventing activity. In addition to his technical creativity, he had a good head for business, and unlike most of his colleagues he understood how to make money from his discoveries.

After his return to Russia from the United States, Alfred found his father enjoying great success and earning a lot of money. Immanuel's pride had grown with his success, and he was boasting he was the first in history to construct an underwater mine. But Alfred had read about the American inventor Robert Fulton's experiments both at Brest and in the English Channel, and knew that experimentation with underwater mines had taken place as early as the American Revolution. He felt his father was laying claim to too much, and they quarreled over the issue. In this instance, at least, Alfred's criticism was somewhat unfair: Immanuel was the first to produce an underwater mine that actually worked.

There were other disagreements. Alfred worried about his father's taking out large loans. When the Crimean War ended in 1856, and Czar Alexander II was forced to sign a humiliating peace treaty in Paris, the Russian government stopped fulfilling its obligations. The situation became critical. Orders from the civilian market couldn't compensate for the loss of income from the military sector, and soon Immanuel was threatened by bankruptcy for the second time in his life. Desperate, he tried various ways of keeping the family company afloat. Alfred, now twenty-five, was sent to visit bank presidents in Paris and London. They turned him down. With the war over, Nobel & Sons was no longer considered a good risk.

The business struggled along a while by selling off different assets in order to pay the most acute debts. The once-successful Fonderies & Ateliers Mécaniques Nobel & Fils was irrevocably headed toward ruin. That Immanuel Nobel was deemed by the government as a "merchant of the first guild" and authorized to travel by four-in-hand (a carriage drawn by four horses) did not do anyone much good.

Once the bankruptcy was becoming hard reality, Immanuel went back to Sweden along with Andriette and their youngest son, Emil. Robert wrote this bleak analysis of the situation to his parents in Stockholm: "One can't stay afloat for long on the stormy sea. One labors to exhaustion, the water sogs our clothes, and, however much we struggle, we are sinking deeper and deeper. Who in hell would have believed we'd face such dismal prospects during the days of old, when our star was winking kindly at us in the East!"

In this desperate situation Ludvig was the one to show some mettle. With the consent of their creditors, he liquidated the family enterprise and attempted to save what remained of the trust capital they had created together. The result of his efforts — and those of Robert and Alfred — was that his parents could be guaranteed a small sum of seed money to start over in Stockholm. "The day a person doesn't work, he is not worthy of a piece of bread," declared Ludvig with puritanical fervor. While all this financial reconstruction was going on, the name of the company was changed from Nobel & Sons to The Brothers Nobel. Ludvig's letters give us an impression of a man of stature grappling with gigantic tasks and winning the admiration of his peers. He had a great deal of organizational talent. He also had a sense of social responsibility so highly developed that it sometimes bordered on pathos.

Two years after his father's business had failed, Ludvig, who had married his cousin Mina Ahlsell in 1858, had managed to save 5,000 rubles. Robert and Alfred were sharing a modest apartment, the kitchen of which Alfred had transformed into a small laboratory. His experiments there gave birth to his first patents: a gasometer, an apparatus for measuring liquids, and a "construction of barometer or manometer." Although neither of these inventions had any lasting

value, they show how active he was. The brothers got back in touch
with their former teachers, Zinin and Trapp, during this time of
strain, in the hope of finding fresh ideas. Zinin had already told them
about Ascanio Sobrero (formerly an assistant to Professor Pelouze
in Paris) and his observations regarding a liquid that had been shown
to be a powerful explosive: pyroglycerine, later called nitroglycerine.
Despite warnings from Sobrero regarding any attempts to find any
practical application for the discovery, Alfred became fascinated by
the substance and its remarkable and seemingly inexplicable behavior.
In front of his amazed students, Professor Zinin had poured a few
drops of the fluid on an anvil and then struck it with a hammer. The
result was "a report as from a pistol shot." The liquid exploded, not
the matter on which it was poured. The explosion did not "propagate," in other words.

For Alfred, this was the greatest challenge he'd ever faced: how
to detonate this explosive and liberate its awesome power? He carried
out one risky experiment after another. One day it occurred to him
to mix black gunpowder with the nitroglycerine and light the mixture with a regular fuse. The result was so promising that, together
with Robert and Ludvig, he executed several successful explosions
on the frozen Neva Canal outside St. Petersburg. Fired up by his
success, Alfred wrote his father about his progress. Immanuel soon
began experiments on his own with nitroglycerine mixed with gunpowder. Before long, he boasted to Alfred in an enthusiastic letter
that he had achieved "excellent results indeed," and that production
of the mixture could become big business in Russia.

Sensing that his father was jumping to conclusions, Alfred left
for Stockholm immediately. He found that his misgivings were well
placed. The measuring methods his father used were faulty and had
led to exaggerated results. The old tension between father and son
increased anew, culminating with Immanuel categorically insisting
that it was he, and nobody else, who had first conceived of the idea
to mix nitroglycerine with gunpowder.

His father was laying claim to his invention, and Alfred left
Stockholm in a fit of anger. Immediately upon his return to St.
Petersburg, to set matters straight, he wrote his father:

My dear Papa!

You were of the opinion that some explanation was necessary. I agree completely, all the more so as I would not

want to be again exposed to such imputations as last time, which are neither fitting to say nor to hear. I shall therefore review in detail our recent dealings with each other.

When you first wrote to me in Petersburg, you gave me to understand that the new explosive powder was a fully developed invention, and that it was twenty times as powerful as ordinary gunpowder. I was asked to go talk to General Totleben with that in mind, and I did, except that — as a cautionary measure — I declared it to be merely eight times as powerful. At your request, I came to Sweden, where I found that your figures were built on an inconclusive experiment using a lead pipe. The result of my visit was a complete fiasco and proved that by then you had given up altogether the idea of the glycerine powder, considering it impractical or not sufficiently developed. However, since I took Ludvig's sensible advice and decided not to bring discredit on me or us through a presentation of the chloroacidic powder, I began to work on my own with the pyroglycerine and actually succeeded in bringing about an astonishing effect underwater on a small scale. This was done, in the presence of Robert and Ludvig, by using glass pipes surrounded by powder, and was repeated in your and Emil's presence upon my arrival. Since the small-scale experiments had succeeded so well, it was my intention to invite Totleben to a demonstration of a large-scale explosion, whereupon the powder would probably have been accepted. But around that time another letter from you arrived with a new story about a shooting powder, twice as potent, and one that did not soil the guns even one-tenth as much as regular powder. You invited me to come to pursue the matter.

This idea was as poorly worked out as the first. Even before I'd left, Emil had discovered that granulated powder — since it did absorb pyroglycerine until dry — gave a better result in the powder tester than did regular powder. All I know is that at my arrival results fluctuated widely and that we wasted a whole summer with tests a competent person could have carried out in one day. Thereupon I returned to the rock-blasting method, which I had previously tried out in Petersburg, namely to use pipes surrounded by powder. Rather than regarding this idea as your own — far from it — you made a bit of fun of it at my expense. I decided then to take off the leash and find another way of reaching my goal without conflict or unpleasantness. Theoretical analysis of the course of events during an explosion led me to a completely different principle than the one that had been the basis for your use of the glycerine powder — namely that if one brings an insignificant amount of pyroglycerine to a rapid explosion, that explosion must be forced by means of a detonation accompanied by heat to propagate through the whole mass.

Everything I am setting down here is known both to Mama and Emil and would scarcely serve to deny the credit I deserve in the matter. I can hardly make myself believe that such would be your serious intent, but can only ascribe it to bad humor or ill health.

However, since Mama and Emil are familiar with the progress of the matter, it ought not to be difficult to trace our respective merit regarding it and, of course, decide upon our mutual share accordingly.

The only reason for indulgence on my part would be filial love, but in order to be maintained, it has to be mutual, and requires at least the same consideration as one owes to strangers. Your sudden departure from Petersburg at the moment when I — as you yourself expressed it — was on my deathbed was probably less a proof of love than of fear, but in you fatherly love seems to run aground on complacency or vanity. It should not seem strange that I, at the age of thirty, will not allow myself to be treated as a schoolboy.

It pains me to have to provide this whole long explanation, which ought to have been unnecessary. But, when it comes to serious matters, I have adopted the rule of acting seriously.

Your own
Alfred

When Alfred says that "another letter from you arrived with a new story," he is referring to a letter from his father, dated July 3,

1863, in which Immanuel wrote: "Now I can tell you that a truly successful result has been gotten using piece or cannon powder, which can be manufactured at negligible cost to be as good as the French hunting powder. The manufacture of this gunpowder could turn out to be an enormous business, especially in Russia. . . . It is therefore necessary that as soon as possible you return here to help your old father to pursue the matter."

Alfred's response was remarkably straightforward, a son's revolt against a father. Henrik Schück considers Immanuel's letter and Alfred's response "rather characteristic for both. Alfred's is very manly and honest and does not exceed the limits of filial duty."

Alfred's blunt language did not result in a breach with his father. Perhaps his letter helped clear the air between them. His mother played an important part, too. Thanks to her Alfred did not definitively break off relations with his father. "You did right," Andriette later wrote him, "to refute the accusations, which you least of all deserved. That was your thanks for so much effort and worry! The matter would still not be resolved, had you not taken it over. But my little Alfred will probably learn that the old man's sickliness is the true reason for his irritability."

After returning to Sweden from St. Petersburg, Andriette and Immanuel had settled in Stockholm, where they rented part of a run-down estate called Heleneborg, near Lake Mälaren in the south part of the city. Immanuel set up a small laboratory in a shed in the yard, a few steps from the half-timbered house that Alfred would later remodel for use as his laboratory. The discord between them ended, and Immanuel and Alfred, along with young Emil, began experimenting again with powder and nitroglycerine. They managed to pique the military authorities' interest and even received a grant — six thousand Swedish dollars — for a demonstration at Karlsborg's fortress. The demonstration was too successful. A newspaper account tells how Alfred loaded a pig-iron bomb half with black gunpowder and half with nitroglycerine, after which he urged the crowd to seek cover. When his charge detonated, it was with such force that even the military experts were frightened. They concluded, ironically enough, that such an explosive substance was too risky for use in battle.

The defense department sought no further contact with Alfred, who devoted all his energy to finding new ways to detonate nitroglycerine. Both his father's and his own experiments involved great expenses, and in 1861, for the second time, Alfred went to Paris to borrow money. This time he turned to Société de Crédit Mobilier, which specialized in financing railroad construction and other public works. Alfred figured that bankers there would be interested in an inexpensive but effective explosive, and he was right. They listened with interest to the young Swede's presentation. He provided an elegant account of his experiments with the nitroglycerine and the commercial advantages it would offer, and he was granted a loan of 100,000 francs.

His financial worries solved — at least temporarily — Alfred began to attack the real problem with nitroglycerine: how to produce a controlled explosion.

Chapter 11

The same year that Alfred Nobel successfully managed to detonate nitroglycerine for the first time, creditors in St. Petersburg sold his father's company. The buyer was a Russian engineer who changed the firm's name to Golubyev's Sampsonievsky Mechanical Shop.

Also in the same year, using his savings of five thousand rubles, Ludvig was able to buy a machine factory that followed the example of the defunct Nobel & Sons and produced heating units and pipe conduits. The purchase included a small amount of industrial space. On January 2, 1860, in a desperate attempt to save his father's company, he had tried to convince the Russian authorities to compensate for the ministry of the navy's failure to pay for its orders, orders that had led Immanuel to buy 400,000 rubles' worth of equipment. Ludvig's action was bolstered by diplomatic petitions from officials in Sweden, but they were of no avail. Ludvig was fully aware of the nightmare his father's second bankruptcy represented to him, and he redoubled his efforts to satisfy each and every creditor. He would later always be terribly proud — and rightfully so — for having managed to do this.

A silent agreement must have existed among the Nobels never to mention Immanuel's second failure. In the entire correspondence between him and his sons, there is not a single allusion as to why he was forced to leave the high life of the Russian capital for a modest life-style on the outskirts of Stockholm. The Swedish capital, though later called the "Venice of the North," contrasted starkly to St. Petersburg at the time: there were no sidewalks along the cobbled streets, which were strewn with stinking garbage and poorly illuminated. Few inhabitants dared to venture outside after dark. Unbowed, Immanuel was consumed by the desire to stage a comeback and with desperate energy started experimenting with nitroglycerine.

The hazardous qualities of nitroglycerine made it a fairly unknown commodity. It was only when the Nobels had managed to develop the so-called "explosive oil" that interest was aroused. Before then, blasting was done by powder charges, ignited using fire. Immanuel's original idea had been to replace the black powder in his mines with nitroglycerine, but he had not managed to solve the problem of how to make them detonate. For a long time mines were more dangerous to the manufacturer than to the enemy. About the time of his departure from St. Petersburg, Immanuel was inclining to agree with Ascanio Sobrero, the inventor of the explosive, that nitroglycerine would never be usable. Its capriciousness made it much too dangerous. Sobrero knew from experience how unstable the substance could be. His face had been badly scarred from glass splinters when the explosive oil exploded in a test tube in the 1840s. He saw no possibility of taming the unknown powers he had let loose.

A breakthrough came with Alfred's idea of mixing nitroglycerine with black gunpowder and igniting them by means of a fuse. On a memorable winter's day in 1862, when he threw the mixture into a water-filled ditch in St. Petersburg, the old thinking in the explosive-substance industry was detonated as well. Alfred had managed to unleash nitroglycerine's full power by finding a better — and relatively safe — way of making it detonate. Alfred and his teacher, Professor Zinin, had estimated the explosive strength of nitroglycerine to be at least fifty times greater than that of regular black gunpowder. The estimate turned out to be somewhat exaggerated.

When Alfred arrived in Stockholm in early 1863, he brought 1,209 rubles, which he had received from the Russian authorities to continue his experiments. The experiments did continue at Heleneborg, and the pile of bills to pay was growing. On several occasions, Alfred was so short of money he was forced to consider giving up. Instead, he took upon himself the entire responsibility of his family's finances, and Heleneborg. Astonishingly, he managed to scrape together enough for both household expenses and laboratory work.

Alfred's private correspondence indicates that he was constantly on edge during this period; his father's bitter fate was much on his mind. Every member of the Nobel family was acutely aware of how suddenly penury could kill dignity, but Alfred especially was haunted.

To Immanuel, Alfred must have appeared as a savior. Just when everything seemed lost, his son had managed to avert the disaster threatening to overwhelm them. Somehow, Alfred always seemed to find a way out. He was driven not by desire for fame but by fear. His feeling of responsibility toward his parents, his determination that they should not want for anything, was a powerful force.

Alfred never forgot poverty. When he became wealthy, he was generous almost to a fault toward those who were needy. On the other hand, he had no patience with careless borrowers. He writes to one business acquaintance: "There was a time when I had to fight against great difficulties . . . but in spite of this I have never, even by one day, exceeded a term of payment. This gives me the right to demand the same kind of punctuality from others that I myself have practiced." When a well-to-do borrower, who, after going through financial straits, had put his affairs back into order but still had not repaid his debt on time, Alfred's tone turned sharp: "Brother, since you have again forgotten my small claim, which, it seems to me, has been overdue long enough, I take the liberty of collecting it through the Embassy or the Swedish Relief Association to benefit our poor countrymen."

A study of his accounts verifies that Alfred's "small claim" consisted of 10,000 Swedish crowns (about $2,000 then) and was paid out to needy artists in Paris.

Chapter 12

In 1863 Alfred Nobel turned thirty. The young poet's passionate dreams had been replaced by the researcher's cool logic. Financial pressure was accelerating his development as an inventor. Yet his worries aside, the early period in his laboratory at Heleneborg was perhaps the happiest time of his life. The 775 Swedish dollars in rent was paid punctually by Alfred to the owner, a merchant named Burmeister.

Following his return to Sweden with only the modest capital that Ludvig had managed to secure on his behalf, Immanuel referred to himself, according to census rolls, as a "former merchant." Alfred could not have failed to notice his father's helplessness and self-pity. It was clear that both as an entrepreneur and as an inventor, Immanuel's desires exceeded his abilities. He was increasingly unable to sift through the unrealizable ideas for the viable ones.

Father and son had become reconciled after Alfred's "my dear Papa!" letter, but distance remained between them. The reasons for it would come to light in February 1868, when they shared the Letterstedt Prize, awarded by the Swedish Academy of Science "for original work within the fields of art, literature, or science, or for important discoveries of practical value to humanity." (The wording resembles remarkably Alfred's last will and testament.)

The Academy of Science had selected "Mr. I. Nobel and his son, Mr. Alfred Nobel, together — the former for his general services with respect to the use of nitroglycerine as an explosive, and the latter specifically for his invention of dynamite." The winners were given the choice of receiving either cash or a gold medal. They chose the medal, which remained in Immanuel's possession. When his mother died, Alfred relinquished his portion of the inheritance, with the exception of a few small things — this gold medal among them. That it still touched a nerve is evident from his words to the executor of her estate: "The Letterstedt medal should also be in my share. I understand very well why my mother bequeathed it to me by the annotation 'Belongs to Alfred Nobel.' My mother knew many things of which the public at large was ignorant."

A decade after the Letterstedt, Alfred chose the following words to describe his work: ". . . the real age of nitroglycerine began in

1864, when an explosion with pure glycerine took place for the first time with the help of a very small charge of gunpowder." The "age of nitroglycerine" is one way to express it — if like Alfred, one favors understatement. Another way is to say that Alfred had joined that group of human beings who extend the boundary posts of progress; his creative energy defined the development of the explosive-substance industry. Time and time again he bridged the gap between theory and application, thought and action. He was proving to be the inventor of the impossible. Scientists in the field have declared his work on initial ignition to represent the greatest progress in explosive-substance technique since the invention of black gunpowder. "The introduction of a detonating cap," writes the British historian F. D. Miles, "is without doubt the greatest discovery that has ever been made in the theory and practice of explosives. On this discovery all modern application of explosives is based." Ragnar Sohlman felt that the invention of the percussion cap and ignition devices "purely from an inventor's point of view as well as in light of the technical essence and importance, ought to be put far ahead of the dynamite." The consensus is that Nobel's artistry with nitroglycerine was unrivaled.

There is more kinship between the artist and the inventor than one might imagine. Both deal with the intersection of the experimental: between knowledge and intuition. Both observe, select, associate, and then test. Both are looking for the moment of creation. For Ingmar Bergman, such a moment is "magic." In his autobiography, *The Magic Lantern,* he describes a creative period by writing that "Grace had once more touched me, the desire was within me. The days were filled by the kind of secret joy that is testimony to an enduring vision." Such moments of "grace" almost never occur by chance. They result from focus and determined energy.

They can also have insignificant beginnings. Alfred conceived of the original idea for his blasting gelatin, one of his most important inventions, because of a cut on his finger. One night in the early 1870s Alfred couldn't sleep because of the pain and went down to his laboratory in his house in Avenue Malakoff in Paris. He put a little collodion on it, then went back to bed. An hour later, he was awakened by pain in his finger: the collodion coating had flaked off. He decided to go back down and apply some more. In his laboratory, at four A.M., he began to think about the chemical composition of collodion, a substance created by dissolving cellulose nitrate in ether and alcohol. The ether evaporates, and a gelatinous mass remains.

This mass became the object of Alfred's intense interest. He began by adding a few drops of nitroglycerine to it; they immediately dissolved. For hour after hour he varied the proportions and the ingredients until he had succeeded in forming a firm gelatinous mass. Blasting gelatin, or "rubber dynamite" as it would be called in Sweden, was invented.

He told his assistant, the French chemist Georges Denis Fehrenbach, that he had realized that even seemingly insignificant changes in the chemical proportions could give remarkably large variations in consistency. They immediately began a series of three hundred separate experiments. Only then would Alfred verify what he had suspected during his collodion night: a means of dissolution existed for cellulose nitrate that produced a material with the durability of leather and the flexibility of natural rubber.

What happens in the brain when one acquires a new insight, a new truth, sees a new connection? David H. Ingvar, a professor at Lund University's Institute for Clinical Neurophysiology in Sweden, says: "We walk around with a multitude of ideas, thoughts, conceptions, and 'pictures' inside our brain. We compare them to each other, and we test impressions of different connections. We attempt to understand the chaos our sense organs constantly subject us to. What happens then is a fabulous reduction — from our sense organs to our consciousness."

"Reduction" may be one way of looking at it — another is a "helicopter" feeling: one rises over a personal intellectual landscape and sees new contexts. Sometimes the miracle takes place while comparing pictures, thoughts, sentences, words, concepts, and different relations, then suddenly, instantly, one realizes how something should be done: the creative moment of grace arrives.

Chapter 13

Alfred felt at home in a laboratory, and all his life he saw to it that he always had one within reach. It was there he put his whims and notions — often scribbled on loose pieces of paper — to the test.

At Heleneborg in 1864, outside of Alfred and his father, the team consisted of an engineer, an errand boy, a servant girl, and the youngest of the Nobel brothers, Emil. The latter had passed his entrance exams in Uppsala at the end of the spring semester, and was planning to enter the Technical Institute in the fall.

Alfred worked feverishly in the small half-timber laboratory. Eighteen-hour workdays were commonplace during certain periods, and he constantly overextended himself. His already-frail health was exposed to constant strain.

As an organizer, Alfred was demanding because he was a perfectionist. Yet colleagues did not find him a tyrant, perhaps because he also inspired them. Some have testified that Nobel, even as an older man, was continually coming up with new ideas, many not limited to explosives. All his life he brimmed with ideas touching on mechanical engineering, optics, biology, and electrochemistry. Some ideas, like so many of his father's, were so farfetched that his colleagues must have wondered if he were serious. Alfred himself knew that many were dubious, but that didn't dampen his enthusiasm. "If I come up with 300 ideas in a year," he wrote, "and only one of them is useful, I am content." These words were echoed in Thomas Edison's comment on the praise he received for inventing the light bulb: "It isn't the discovery of the tungsten filament that is so important, but the 10,000 other things I tried that didn't work!"

Toward his employees Alfred was always considerate. Unlike many other driven men, he never became so obsessed by an idea that he forgot his concern for others. In a taciturn though highly efficient manner, he was always there to give colleagues the right word, and sensed the moment they needed encouragement. He urged them to follow developments in the field by studying scientific writings. On the other hand, in his own correspondence he rarely mentions someone else's advice to him. Perhaps he believed that if one was going to make a mistake, it was better to have only oneself to blame.

Alfred frequently locked himself up in his laboratory for days and worked nonstop. He could become so involved in a project that he would forget time and place, food, and sleep. Yet he seldom complained about ill health after these work marathons. Alfred would have agreed with Strindberg's declaration in *The Servant Woman's Son* that "work has given me such great pleasure that I found existence pure bliss while working and still do. Only then am I alive."

Alfred's method of research was helped by a well-developed intuition. The more than fifty experiments that preceded his invention of the patented igniter did not involve teamwork. Alfred rarely included colleagues in his preliminary work, so in all probability the direction of his project remained secret until the very end. He was a stranger to the kind of teamwork that modern research tends to favor. He worked alone in the Heleneborg laboratory during the first half of the 1860s, and until his death he never changed his habits.

During the summer of 1864, when he was experimenting with new methods of controlling nitroglycerine, one can sense Alfred's burgeoning self-confidence (and hear an echo of his father's pride) in the tone of his patent application: "I am the first to have brought these subjects from the area of Science to that of Industry." Before anybody else, Alfred had realized the commercial possibilities of his discovery, and he would not be shy about making that known. There were some who asserted that he was in too much of a hurry to exploit his invention, and like many trailblazers, he was discovering that some people automatically confuse being first with being wrong. He also discovered that the cost of being a pioneer could be tragically high.

September 3, 1864, a Saturday, promised to be a beautiful early autumn day. In Immanuel's and Alfred's laboratory at Heleneborg Emil Nobel was busy purifying glycerine. He and a friend, a fellow student named Hertzman, had been entrusted with manufacturing the explosive for an order from the Ammeberg and Northern Railways. The work was taking place inside the fenced yard. Alfred was extremely fond of his fair-haired younger brother, who was always quick to laugh. Under Alfred's tutelage, Emil was developing into a skilled lab worker.

A considerable stock of nitroglycerine had already been prepared. Eleven months earlier, on October 14, 1863, Alfred had received his first Swedish patent, having convincingly demonstrated how the explosive power of gunpowder could be increased by mixing in glycerine. During those eleven months, his neighbors felt, and not without justification, that they were living on top of a volcano. They had complained about this to the landlord, Burmeister. Both Immanuel and Alfred assured everyone that there was no reason to worry; their experiments were completely harmless.

That September morning, a large supply of explosive oil was being stored in the shed — according to Alfred's own estimates, 250 pounds [liquid measures will be given in pounds throughout — trans.]. Before being converted into a factory space, the building had earlier been used as coach house and was surrounded by a low wall. Immanuel and Alfred were unaware of the true potency of the nitroglycerine. They were concentrating on getting it to detonate and assumed it to be relatively safe. Beneath that assumption was wishful thinking: they did not want to believe that an accident could happen.

The yard outside the main building was deserted when catastrophe hit. The laboratory in the shed exploded with a thunderous roar. According to the report in the newspaper, the force was so violent "that the buildings shook on their foundations and windows in places around Kungsholm shattered."

The article continues:

We would learn later that the source of the blast was a building on the Heleneborg estate at Långholm Bay, where the engineer Nobel had constructed a nitroglycerine factory. In the capital people heard the violent sound of the explosion and saw a huge, yellow flame rise straight up in the air. It was replaced within moments by an enormous pillar of smoke that also disappeared so quickly that, with the exception of the abovementioned glass panes on Kungsholm and a few overturned hawkers' stands on the Munk bridge, one could see nothing further in the city. A much more terrible sight awaited one at the site of the accident. There was nothing left of the factory, a wooden building adjacent to the Heleneborg estate, except a few charred fragments thrown here and there. In the houses nearby, and even those on the other side of the bay, not only had the glass panes been smashed but also windowsills and molding.

Most ghastly was the sight of the mutilated corpses strewn on the ground. Not only had the clothes been torn off but on some the head was missing and the flesh ripped off the bones. These formless masses of flesh and bone bore little or no resemblance to a human body. The effect of the explosion could be judged by the fact that in a nearby stone house, the walls facing the factory had split open, and a woman who had been standing by the stove cooking had part of her head crushed, one arm torn off, and one thigh terribly mauled. The unfortunate victim was still alive and was carried to the hospital on a litter, looking more like a bloody mass of meat than a human being.

Mr. Nobel was not himself present, but one of his sons is said to be among the victims, and another son sustained major head injuries. Authorities fear another explosion, so no investigation can be carried out among the fragments of the factory. It is therefore unclear how many persons were killed in this terrible accident. At present, it is known that five or six mutilated bodies have been found.

Latest reports tell us that of the bodies recovered thus far, in addition to the corpse of Mr. C. E. Hertzman, positive identification has been made of a thirteen-year-old youth named Herman Nord; a girl who worked at the factory, Maria Nordqvist, who was the daughter of the night watchman at Bergsund; and the first-mentioned carpenter. No trace has as yet been found of engineer Nobel's youngest son. (Although some thought that they recognized the youngest member of the Nobel family among the corpses.) Further information will be provided as we receive such from the impending police investigation. . . .

Regarding the source of the accident, since the above was written we have managed to obtain the following information: The youngest son of engineer Nobel, Emil Nobel, and the technology student Hertzman were involved in preparing some experiments to make the glycerine liquid more explosive, when some carelessness must have triggered the explosion, which then spread to other nitroglycerine kept in open containers. Nitroglycerine is not combustible until heated up to 180 degrees or more, or through an explosion of some other substance on its surface.

Emil Nobel and Hertzman were killed instantly, as were the youth Nord and the nineteen-year-old servant girl Maria Nordqvist. The carpenter named Nyman, who had happened to pass by the factory, sustained severe injuries and died shortly thereafter. The engineer Blom and an older son of engineer Nobel, Alfred Nobel, were thrown to the floor by the violent pressure and severely injured in the face and head by fragments of wood and glass.

Nobody knows with certainty what Alfred thought and felt after this explosion, because he remained silent about the accident his whole life. Nowhere in his vast correspondence does he analyze the tragic event in any detail. Perhaps he believed, once he realized the scope of the catastrophe and its tragic outcome, that his future was destroyed forever, that everything he had been secretly fearing had come true.

Only two months earlier, in July 1864, full of confidence, he had written in his patent application for his igniter: "If the heat of the gunpowder can be imparted to the nitroglycerine with the speed necessary for an explosion, then, with the assistance of the impact and the pressure of the developed gases, the even greater heat developed in the nitroglycerine, will, after a detonation impulse has been obtained, be able to sustain its own explosion."

But the fatal Saturday in September did not destroy Alfred. Even his father admired his composure. Two days after the accident, faced with a thorough police investigation, Immanuel was able to write a factual and utterly detailed account for the police in Stockholm.

The newspaper *Stockholms Dagblad* of September 6, 1864, tells us exactly what had taken place:

The police conducted an examination yesterday to find out the particular circumstances surrounding the tragic event at Heleneborg last Saturday. To this examination the police commissar of the area had called both the owner of said estate, the merchant Burmeister, and engineer Nobel, the owner of the factory, which the explosion totally destroyed, as well as some relatives of those who perished.

The wholesale merchant Burmeister was asked to account for reasons why Nobel had been permitted to establish and carry out dangerous experiments at that location. Mr. Burmeister said that about three years before Nobel rented the larger dwelling house belonging to Heleneborg, and that he and his family have been living there. It was not until the spring of this year that Nobel was given permission to use an adjacent building, which had formerly been used as coach house, and the right to fence in part of the yard. The experiments Nobel had been carrying out lately were on a larger scale and involved preparing explosive oil; they had frequently been the subject of conversation between them. Nobel always assured him that there was no danger to persons living close by, and with that assurance Burmeister had attempted to calm the worries of his other tenants, who were concerned about the proximity. The buildings on the estate damaged by the explosion, Burmeister declared, were insured by the City of Stockholm's Fire Insurance Office, from which he intended to seek compensation for his loss.

The story in *Stockholms Dagblad* continues with Immanuel's detailed account of the nature of his manufacturing. His statement reads as follows:

Since none of those directly involved with preparing the explosive oil, or nitroglycerine, have survived, naturally no complete explanation as to the cause of the explosion can be given.

All I am able to conclude from some remarks made by my son before the accident is that the explosion took place when he was trying to simplify the method of making the explosive oil.

Because nitroglycerine is innocuous even when directly ignited — even the greatest carelessness with fire hardly would cause an explosion — and because there was no fire to begin with, there remains as the only possible explanation that the tests my son was doing brought about a reaction that increased the temperature of the mixture to a temperature (around 180 degrees Celsius) at which nitroglycerine explodes.

In other words, the cause of the accident was negligence, in the form of not using a thermometer during a new experiment in order to read the temperature before it rose too rapidly.

Nitroglycerine is normally prepared in two ways:
1) Through the so-called warm method, in which the temperature rises to around 60 degrees Celsius and never higher. This methods has been used hundreds of times and is without the slightest danger.

2) Using cool temperature, by means of a frozen mixture, at which the temperature is not allowed to rise above the freezing point and therefore no danger can exist. The reason why I have not prepared the explosive oil outside the city is that under normal circumstances no danger has ever been foreseen, and for the following reasons:

a) Because nitroglycerine is ignitable without explosion and burns like oil — but with less danger because it extinguishes itself.

b) Because I have heated large quantities of it in glass beakers in order to learn the effect thereof and have found that even then only a very small amount explodes and the rest is scattered.

c) Because unless it is heated to 180 degrees Celsius and in a strong container, it is nearly impossible to bring about a total explosion — as can be proved by the number of rock blastings that failed to ignite nitroglycerine during the early stages of development.

The reason that the preparation of the explosive oil has not been registered is that, until these last few days, manufacture has taken place on a very small scale and been more intended for experimental development than for commercial purposes, as is obvious by the fact that there has been no advertising in the newspapers.

In order to avoid misunderstanding, I must also add that although the refinement of glycerine, which I believe my son to have been occupied with at the time of the accident, does not need to have the slightest association with the preparation of nitroglycerine, it ought to be possible to do this purification in the same factory where the glycerine is prepared. An accident of this nature should not occur again during nitroglycerine manufacture.

Heleneborg, September 5, 1864
I. Nobel

Immanuel Nobel himself may not have been injured in the explosion, but the accident took its toll one month later. On October 6, he suffered a stroke that impaired his ability to move. His condition was to improve somewhat, but until his death eight years later, he remained physically a shadow of his former self. A letter that he managed to write in pencil in April 1865 — a little more than half a year after the accident — has been preserved. In it, he tells Alfred that he has recovered the mobility in his right hand. In the same letter, his wife writes that though he cannot walk or even stand "the little old man has already begun to fantasize, and who would blame him, given the monotonous and anxious life your poor daddy leads. To lie in bed for four months, not able to move at all without the help of others — that is a hard test of the patience of a poor old man."

In other letters to Alfred, his parents lament the fact that they lack "means for a sustained care at some bathing establishment." Alfred responded to their pleas for money, even though at this time he found himself in financial straits. His mother's gratitude was unbounded: "Next to God, we have little Alfred to thank for our being here taking the baths. Little old papa is still not able to walk a single step, but he feels stronger, and I feel so much better."

Immanuel continued to work on his drawings, his unquenchable energy remaining undiminished until his death. During seven endlessly long years he "fantasized," as Andriette put it. Among other things, he obsessed about an invention that would give him "dictatorial powers in matters of war and peace in the whole world for at least several centuries." Andriette reported that he was spending his time "speculating about all kinds of affairs, involving lots of people, but in my opinion without a purpose — they are of course a result of the dear old man's former activities trying to reassert themselves."

Not all of his ideas were unrealistic, however. For instance, in 1870, two years before his death, he published a small booklet with the lengthy title, "An Attempt to Create Employment to Check the Emigration Fever Now Caused by the Lack Thereof." He had in mind finding some raw material available in rich quantities in Sweden and so inexpensive that even those with small resources could acquire it. Immanuel writes: "During five years of suffering from the effects of a stroke, with pains causing many and long sleepless nights, I have succeeded in coming up with a raw material that I am convinced would be the best and most suitable for arriving at the solution of this problem."

The material that Immanuel had in mind was wood shavings still covered with bark, created during the sawing of timber and then burned, "for no other reason and purpose than to get rid of the nuisance." From this refuse, he insisted, "one could acquire eminently suitable material for smaller woodwork, and thousands of those now unemployed could earn their livelihood through it, especially those seasonal workers who are almost totally without daily bread during the long winter." Besides being useful for woodwork in the home, wood scrap, Nobel thought, could be used for "building large and small ships and also mobile houses; the latter could become an invaluable export article to countries with warm climates, especially those plagued by earthquakes." He suggests manufacturing of "a kind of cross veneer of laminated wood or thin sheets of wood, one put on top of another so that the grains in the different layers cross. . . . One might wonder as to the feasibility of manufacturing objects out of shavings and thin slices of wood. But the slabs should be manufactured with special steel that would both plane them and cut them to the exact thickness." It was no senile Utopian who wrote these lines; Immanuel seems more like a visionary who foresaw what would later become a huge industry, the manufacture of plywood (also called cross veneer in Sweden).

While some of his suggestions later realized commercial success, others were simply whims. For instance, he proposed, with complete seriousness, that one should "manufacture pipes for the transport of coffins from the cities to burial sites outside them." He also proposed an idea of "coffins that were so constructed that someone apparently dead but actually in a state of suspended animation could himself from the inside lift off the lid, which would be provided with necessary air holes for breathing and connected by way of a pulling cord to a signaling bell."

With Poe-like eeriness, Immanuel's ideas evoke what was to be one of his son Alfred's lifelong phobias: being buried alive. Alfred's phobia is well documented in both his letters and in his last will and testament. In 1887, when his brother Ludvig asked him for a biographical self-portrait, we might remember Alfred answered: "Greatest single request: not to be buried alive. . . ."

Immanuel remained a dreamer his whole life, less interested in financial results than in the research work itself. In spite of his occasional entrepreneurial successes, he had a kind of *l'art pour l'art* attitude, and it was that attitude that got him into trouble economically. A contributing factor was his lack of formal training. Had he received as solid an education as he had provided for his sons, who knows how far he might have gone. As it was, he was a man whose talent showed itself in fits and starts.

His last letter to Alfred is dated December 26, 1871:

Our own Alfred!

Your loving telegram arrived exactly as we were ready to enjoy our morning tea and all your sweetmeat gifts were brought by our kind Liedback at five o'clock on Christmas Eve itself, which was livened up by old Ahlsell's visit — he has not been seen in our house since my birthday — to the great pleasure of your sweet Mama, to whom you have brought joy by not only remembering Pauline and the children, but by remembering Lotten Henne and her children.

My New Year's gift to old Mother Svea's [Sweden's] defense in its present defenselessness is so close to finished that it can be turned in as a suitable New Year's present at the beginning of the year. Let's see how it will be received by our Parliament. A hearty hug is sent to you, the last one this year, from your old parents, who take great gladness in having such sons who only give us joy and never sorrow.

"Old Mother Svea's defense" dominated the aging Immanuel's interests. Three drawings illustrate his mines and his repellent defense system. To use his own words, they concretize his "thoughts regarding the means of defending our beloved homeland against a superior enemy now and in the future, without costly fortifications or great sacrifices of manpower and money."

These illustrations were found in a book fifty years after Alfred's death, hidden away among the belongings of one of Immanuel's great grandsons. What makes the book interesting is less the fifty pages of text than the colorful drawings, done in India ink and pastels, which depict dramatic mine explosions, and are labelled as follows:

Inexpensive Defense of Archipelagos (floating mines)

Inexpensive Defense of the Country's Roads (land mines)

Suggestions for the Defense of the Nation. New Year's gift to the Swedish People, 1871.

Chapter 14

The explosion at Heleneborg reverberated in the minds of Stockholm's citizens for decades. People often referred to events as occurring before or after "the Nobel bang."

Sometimes it takes a serious trial for a person's character to take shape. Such was the case with Alfred after the accident and his father's stroke. In spite of his grief over the death of his youngest brother, the animosity of the general public, and the careful scrutiny of the authorities, he was able to carry on and handle the cleanup. Incredibly, he went back to work the day after the accident.

Alfred's life was not made easier by all the well-meaning advice he received, especially advice offered in agitated letters to the newspapers. Advice also came from closer to home. In May 1864, eight months after the accident, his brother Robert wrote from Finland that he had little confidence in Alfred's invention involving nitroglycerine. He offered his brother some advice that Alfred, fortunately, did not heed: ". . . leave the damned invention profession as soon as possible: it only brings misfortune. You have such great knowledge and so many outstanding qualities that you need to break more serious new ground. Had I your knowledge and your ability, I would flap my wings rather high, even here in wretched Finland, but now I have to flap moderately. . . ."

During a visit to Stockholm after the accident, however, Robert realized that nitroglycerine had a future. In a generous gesture, Alfred gave him the right on his own behalf — but in Alfred's name — to seek the patent for the invention in Finland. Robert's patent application was approved on December 9, 1864, and by the following spring he had established a small nitroglycerine factory near Helsinki. He took rather well to marketing. The following advertisement appeared in *Helsinki Daily* on September 21, 1865:

At the request of the undersigned, the foreman for Ska-
tudd's canal and bridge construction will employ a few
sizable test shots with nitroglycerine and, for purposes of
comparison, some with gunpowder at Skatudden below the
Russian church toward the north harbor, tomorrow
Wednesday September 27 at 5 P.M. All interested parties are
invited. The most suitable and safest place to witness the
effect would be the corner of Kyrkogatan and North Pier.

The signal for the detonation of the nitroglycerine shots
will be a red flag and for powder a white flag.

R. Nobel
Manufacturer of nitroglycerine.

According to a follow-up article in the *Helsinki Daily*, the effect
was "astonishing."

The Heleneborg accident and the ensuing storm of controversy
surrounding his work had not changed Alfred's goals. He was determined to use — in the most efficient and safest possible way —
nitroglycerine as an explosive substance. Nothing would make him
give up the practical application of his invention. From his letters it
is evident that he had coldly calculated that the task he had set before
him might involve the ultimate sacrifice.

Since Alfred continued to receive proof that Stockholm's inhabitants disapproved of his occupation, it must have been encour-
aging that the mines in Dannemora and Herräng ordered considerable
quantities of nitroglycerine. Furthermore, on October 10, 1864 —
only five weeks after the explosion — a representative of the state
railroads declared that they would use Nobel's explosive oil exclusively during their construction of a tunnel that would connect the
northern railroad lines with the southern. To Alfred, this represented
an official sanction of his work.

Behind his back, however, people gossiped cruelly about how,
yet again, the Nobels were ruined. Alfred responded with deeds,
not with words: he began planning a company for the manufacture
and sale of nitroglycerine. Given the public-opinion climate, finding
the initial capital was not easy, but one financial backer remained
steadfast from the beginning: Captain Carl Wennerström of the Navy
Mechanical Corps (1820–1893). He had firsthand experience dealing
with the hazardous explosive oil as supervisor of tests with it in the
mines of Herräng and Vigelsbo.

Now Alfred had to find someone with great financial resources. Ragnar Sohlman recounts in *The Legacy of Alfred Nobel* how Alfred managed to find the right person:

I've known the name Nobel all my life. In the early 1860s, through her social and cultural educational work in the Swedish capital, my mother met and developed a friendship with a sister of Immanuel Nobel, Alfred's aunt, an active and energetic lady by the name of Mrs. Elde. At this time Immanuel and Alfred were busy experimenting with nitroglycerine, which they manufactured in their small laboratory at Heleneborg. The responsibility of bringing their innovations to reality came to rest squarely on the shoulders of Alfred. Both he and his father lacked the means necessary for actual manufacture and were, in addition, threatened by large compensation claims. After the accident, convincing people to risk their money in such a perilous undertaking was not easy.

Through the intermediation of my mother and Mrs. Elde, Alfred Nobel was able to get in touch with the man later known as "the King of Kungsholm," J. W. Smitt, a cousin of my mother's, and managed to interest him in the Nobel invention. Smitt went on to finance the newly formed Nitroglycerine Company — one of the best investments this successful businessman ever made.

J. W. Smitt (1821–1904) had made his fortune in South America and was one of Sweden's richest men. Persuading him to invest was no simple matter. Several factors argued against an investment. For one, it was far from certain that Alfred would get the permits to build a nitroglycerine factory at Winter Bay as he planned. For another, Smitt was keenly aware of how the general public felt about the Nobels and their work. Besides, Alfred could not claim to be the original discoverer of nitroglycerine. Nor could he guarantee that there would never be another accident.

Other than Alfred's straightforward manner and passionate enthusiasm, which impressed Smitt, it was probably the state railroad decision to use nitroglycerine for the construction of the south tunnel that helped him make up his mind. Once he'd gotten a positive answer from "the King of Kungsholm," Alfred, along with his father and Carl Wennerström and, of course, Smitt, formed Nitroglycerine

Aktiebolaget on October 22, 1864. It was the world's first company in this line of business.

The introduction to the founding charter reads as follows:

> We the undersigned, through our company Nitroglycerine Aktiebolaget, have agreed to buy and, within Swedish borders, to utilize the patent for the preparation and employment of nitroglycerine, granted on July 15 of the present year to civil engineer Alfred Nobel by the Royal Commerce Collegium. Furthermore, after the bylaws of the intended company have been drawn up, we make the following agreement:
>
> Of the joint-stock company, one hundred and twenty five shares:
> Subscribed by Mr. Alfred Nobel . . . . 62 shares
>   *of which Mr. Immanuel Nobel takes 31 shares*
> Mr. Carl Wennerström . . . . 31 shares
> Mr. Johan Wilhelm Smitt . . . . 32 shares
>   Total   126 shares

According to the charter, Alfred would receive 38,000 Swedish dollars for transferring his patented right to manufacture nitroglycerine to the company. To this day it is not clear if he was actually paid this sum. With the exception of Norway, Alfred Nobel never sold the manufacturing right to any country for a set sum. Rather than being content with his license yields, he preferred founding his own companies with himself as director.

The new company faced considerable problems from the outset. One was the ailing Immanuel's demand to be the company's managing director. During a visit to Stockholm following the creation of the company, Robert wrote to his brother Ludvig in St. Petersburg on the subject (December 8, 1864):

> I have tried my best to convince the old man to renounce his wish to be director. I pointed out his limited ability as writer, speaker, and chemist, and he agreed that I was right and promised not to take this post, but let it go to Alfred. Papa can be terrible when he wants; he could make rocks shake, and I could not stand it for as long as Alfred has. In spite of this, I do not really like Alfred's

line of conduct either. He is too fierce and despotic, and the two of them are heading for a collision. To give in totally to the old man cannot be done, because financially he would ruin the whole thing. Alfred's position is indeed tricky, and yet Mama is to be pitied most of all because she has defended Alfred and must therefore take all kinds of abuse from Papa.

It was more than sad to leave Stockholm, where my presence might have kept a balance between Papa and Alfred, who are rapidly reaching a point where a reconciliation is impossible.

The family dispute was calmed through a compromise: Alfred relinquished the post of executive director and Carl Wennerström was elected as such. Relenting, but still hotheaded, Immanuel was offered a deputy position on the board of directors. Since Alfred only attended the first shareholders' meeting, his father later became a full director.

Another problem was that filling the company's orders for explosive oil was hindered and nearly prevented altogether by the police prohibition against the "manufacture and storing of nitroglycerine within a residential area." Backed into a corner, Alfred proved his abilities as an entrepreneur. He found and bought a covered barge, which he anchored in Bockholm Bay. Using primitive equipment, he manufactured "Nobel's Patented Explosive Oil" on board, selling it for 2.50 crowns (about fifty cents, at the time) per pound. The industry that within a few years would span the world was started on the water outside Stockholm.

Alfred had less than 25,000 crowns in working capital, and this forced him to do most things himself. He did all the work of a managing director, as well as that of head of production, financial manager, and, not the least, director of publicity. He mailed advertisements to prospective buyers that included detailed instructions for use. Under the heading "Necessary Tools" one reads: "A long pipe through which the oil is poured into the hole in the rock, so as not to waste any part thereof which could stick to the sides of the hole." These instructions, and Alfred's igniter in particular, were much discussed in professional circles and in the pages of technical magazines.

Alfred traveled to stone quarries and mines, demonstrating the superiority of his manufactured nitroglycerine compared to the old powder. Because of its greater explosive power, he could promise and deliver substantial savings: blasting work could proceed faster and require fewer workers.

Alfred dominated the activities of the company during the first few months. One of his first and most important decisions was to hire his childhood friend, the engineer Alarik Liedbeck (1834–1912). In Liedbeck Alfred had found a person with the same unshakable confidence in his inventions as he himself had.

Carl Wennerström retired early as managing director, in November 1865, and was succeeded by J. A. Berndes. Berndes died the following month (having managed in that short time to embezzle more than 2,000 crowns). The minutes of the board of directors meetings of February 17 and March 28, 1866, show that the mood was agitated, to put it mildly. The usually hotheaded Immanuel kept quiet when majority shareholders Smitt and Wennerström awarded themselves 1,500 crowns each "as compensation for their trouble as members of the board of directors during the past year." Immanuel was hoping that Robert would be selected as the new head of the company. He wrote to Alfred on April 7, 1866: "I give in to their pressure, but only to facilitate a good end result for Robert."

Immanuel got what he wanted: Robert was called home from Finland to become managing director. Since Alfred had declared himself content with a deputy position, Robert also became a member of the board. Alfred had his sights set on greater things.

Chapter 15

Twenty-five years after the founding of his company, Alfred Nobel wrote a letter to an acquaintance. At the time he was visiting his brother Robert in Getä, outside the Swedish city of Norrköping, a seaport at the head of a narrow inlet of the Baltic Sea. Written with great precision, the letter tells us a great deal about his activities as an inventor between 1862 and 1875.

Getä, near Norrköping, the 28th of August 1889

My dear Sir,

Due to my recent extensive travels I have not until now been in a position to reply to your letter of August 7.

Below, you will find answers to the four questions you had directed to me:

1. I started my work with nitroglycerine in 1862.

2. Mass production began at the end of 1863.

3. In June 1862, for the first time, I managed to make a load of nitroglycerine packed in cannon powder explode underwater during an experiment in St. Petersburg.

Toward the end of 1863, I was regularly detonating nitroglycerine with the help of a small load of hunting powder (about one gram). Soon after I was using detonating powder attached to the end of a slow fuse — the first step toward the employment of a stronger detonator, which I later used for dynamite.

I invented dynamite November 1863. In my first patent application, dated January 10, 1864, I laid claim to the originality of using "nitroglycerine absorbed in highly porous coal or in any other very porous substance." But since I was not yet familiar with the serious risks inherent in the transport of liquid nitroglycerine, I did not occupy myself with the completion of dynamite. Though I didn't turn back to it until 1866, I prepared and detonated the first dynamite charge (nitroglycerine absorbed in porous

coal) in an iron pipe (blown to bits) in November 1863.
The explosion took place without a detonator.

4. I invented the blasting gelatin in 1875. Experiment
and research were carried out without mishap. I ought to
add that as early as 1866, I had attempted to gelatinize nitroglycerine but without success. However, I had nearly
succeeded with a similar method, because I tried to dissolve trinitrated cottonpowder in nitroglycerine and it did
not dissolve. However, at this point the matter was of no
special importance. My research was guided more by curiosity than by serious interest.

> With friendly greetings,
> A. Nobel

Alfred also displayed his marketing skills when he invited Prince
Oscar — later King Oscar II — to a demonstration in the Tyskbagar
Mountains, showing what explosive oil could do. A thirty-foot hole
was drilled and the explosive liquid was poured into it. A newspaper reporter in attendance noted that "the mountain seemed to
rise up, and an enormous mass of rock was loosened." Thirty years
later, King Oscar II would also honor Alfred Nobel's company by
a royal visit to the Bofors works. Alfred was no passionate royalist
himself, but he fully appreciated the publicity value of royal patron-
age. His father had invited the Czar to various blast demonstrations
as well.

Once Alfred's company had received permission from the
county administration, on January 21, 1865, to build a factory on
land located at Winter Bay outside Stockholm, the manufacture of
the explosive oil began. After only a month, nearly a hundred pounds
of it was produced; by August they had reached two tons. Production proceeded at a dizzyingly rapid pace after leaving the barge
in Bockholm Bay. Ragnar Sohlman remembers how as a child he
heard J. W. Smitt talk about his visits to Winter Bay: "Perhaps his
stories were the reason I decided to become a chemist. I worked as
an apprentice a couple of summers at Winter Bay, the oldest of
Nobel's explosive substance factories, when I was a student. Alfred
Nobel's meteoric visits to his native country and his factory struck
awe into us."

So it would anyone. As he was wont to do, Alfred worked with inflammable agents and highly explosive substances late into the night, so the lab was always brilliantly illuminated. Outside the glassy walls hung kerosene lamps with reflectors. To someone passing by in the dark, the laboratory, bathed in light and nestled in sparkling snow, must have seemed like an unworldly sight: a worthy setting for the first land-based nitroglycerine factory.

Chapter 16

Alfred Nobel was first to solve the problem of detonating nitroglycerine in a practical, useful manner. Nitroglycerine's true value was its fearsome power; the problem lay in detonating it. As we have seen, Alfred had begun by mixing the liquid with gunpowder and lighting it with a quick-match fuse, which was invented in 1831. He worked from the theory that somehow the nitroglycerine had to be heated very quickly, and that one way to do that was to push a pressure wave through the liquid. This was the theoretical basis for the blasting cap. (Blasting cap, percussion cap, explosive capsule, and detonator are all synonyms for the same thing, though Alfred's working name for the prototype was "initial igniter." In his patent application in 1864, he employed the term "percussion cap," but it was not long before "blasting cap" was more common; today, "blasting cap" is used when speaking of cartridges.) Alfred would later change his explosive capsule so that it could be ignited by an electric spark. The blasting cap created the foundation for the modern explosive substance technology and was used without any major alterations into the 1920s.

The prototype Alfred developed from his experiments consisted of a test tube containing a compressed powder mixture, to which, through a piece of wood at the other end, was attached a quick-match cord thread. The method worked, but didn't provide enough of a pressure wave for larger amounts of nitroglycerine, so he replaced the powder with mercury fulminate. Mercury fulminate is highly explosive, but, with great caution, could be used in small doses while damp.

Alfred then had a brilliant idea: first he put a few milligrams of fulminate into a small copper capsule, then he squeezed a quick-match fuse cord into it. This simple but revolutionary invention opened the door to make the practical use of all new explosive substances possible. Combining nitroglycerine and an explosive capsule produced the first new form of explosive since the fifteenth century, when gunpowder was first becoming known in Europe.

You cannot begin a revolution and expect an easy life. By the mid-1860s, Alfred was already pitted against the two forces that he would battle all his life, the bureaucracy and the press — the bureaucracy for refusing to accept change, and the press for holding him personally responsible for the accidents that accompanied it. There is no shortage of invective in Alfred's letters for bureaucrats and patent officials. Yet the epithets he earned from the press — "devil in the guise of a man," "traveling salesman in death," and "mass murderer" — wounded him deeply.

To calm public opinion, Alfred was spending a considerable amount of his time lecturing, visiting mining villages, giving demonstrations, and writing explanatory letters to the newspapers. But because he was invariably honest about the risks involved with explosives, Alfred's public appearances did not always quell fears. "Nobody should expect," he wrote, "that an efficient blasting substance will become available to the general public without loss of lives."

By the end of the 1860s, Nobel had opened nitroglycerine factories in Sweden, Germany, Norway, Finland, and Austria (England and France followed suit not long after), and the legal disputes that Alfred was pulled into were a constant drain on his strength. It is in the letters dated after this time that he talks about being pursued by those "spirits from Niflheim." He often sought solace in solitary work or travel. To find some measure of anonymity, he would suddenly disappear for a day or even a week without warning even his closest colleagues, reappearing when one of his many patents drew him into fierce negotiations with the world's foremost attorneys. These negotiations took up most of his time. Nobel's inventions were not only sought after but copied. An extract from a letter to a friend shows how exasperated he was:

In most countries one is not allowed to refer to the use of analogous substances, which is why, in order to have a halfway decent patent, an invention frequently demands that one must have at least two dozen in the same country. If, for instance, you seek patent protection in the British colonies and other major countries, you have to figure on about 40 states: 40 times 24 = 960 patents for one invention! Even with the luxury of a patent, protection in most cases is illusionary. I therefore suggest giving the patenting of chemical improvements the name "Taxation of inventors to encourage parasites." One

becomes a revolutionary when examining all these
worm-eaten, monstrous, and stillborn laws. It should be
any newspaper's mission to end such misery.

Being a revolutionary was not easy, and an end to misery was
not in sight. As late as the 1880s, Alfred was still having to claim
his due, continuing to deny vehemently that his discoveries were the
product of dumb luck rather than hard work. Many were ready to
deny Nobel his due; others were anxious to cut themselves in for a
share.

A man by the name of Taliafero Preston Shaffner (1818–1881)
was one of the first, and for a number of years he became Alfred's
nemesis. Soon after his explosive oil became a success, Alfred was
courted by profit-hungry quacks. But nobody would give him more
trouble than Shaffner.

Shaffner called himself "Colonel," but the rank was self-
bestowed. Immanuel and his sons did not know this when they were
first contacted in St. Petersburg by the Colonel, a self-taught American attorney from Virginia. Shaffner was frequently involved in
gigantic projects: at that time he was enthusiastically promoting a
transAtlantic telegraph cable that would stretch from the Labrador
peninsula in northeastern Canada to St. Petersburg by way of Green-
land. He had heard about Immanuel's underwater mines and set out
to learn in detail how they were constructed. Upon his return to
America, he passed himself off as "the world's leading expert on
military underwater mines."

The next time Alfred came face to face with Shaffner was in
September 1864, immediately after the tragic Heleneborg explosion.
The cleanup work was in progress when Shaffner appeared and began
to nose around among the still-smoldering ruins. Alfred was so
shaken by the accident that he had no strength to keep the meddle-
some adventurer at a distance.

They arranged to meet at the Hotel Rydberg in Stockholm,
where Shaffner declared that he wanted to acquire the explosive oil
patent for the United States. Alfred suggested $200,000 as a reason-
able remuneration. The Colonel's counteroffer was an insult —
10,000 Spanish dollars of little or no value. Learning that Shaffner
had been invited to visit by the Swedish defense department because
he was "an expert on mines" did nothing to lessen Alfred's outrage.
(The Swedish authorities were researching the possibilities for re-
ducing the costs of the country's defense.)

Shaffner was forced to return empty-handed to America, but what he couldn't get through legal means, he tried through illegal means. He wrote to the American diplomatic representative in Stockholm, asking him to obtain as much information as he could on the Nobel method of detonating nitroglycerine.

When Alfred received the American patent for his invention on October 25, 1865, Shaffner, with unparalleled effrontery, insisted that he had made the discovery first. His protests were loud enough to cause the American consul in Hamburg, James H. Anderson, to ask Alfred to answer some questions, which he did on January 22, 1866. Witnesses were called in (at Alfred's expense), among them his co-financier and temporary managing director of the Swedish company, Carl Wennerström. Another was a mine worker named Pehr Wilhelm Jansson. After being sworn in, Jansson made this declaration:

"In December 1863, I was present at the Ämmeberg's mines when experiments were being done with Nobel's nitroglycerine. . . . I'm familiar with blasting with gunpowder, and an explosion made by nitroglycerine is about twice as large." Wennerström testified that "Mr. Nobel has time and again improved upon his invention." Thereafter, according to the official record, there was "cross examination through Colonel Shaffner with Mr. Alfred Nobel, age 32":

Question 1: What day, month and year did you first succeed in detonating nitroglycerine using the method described in your American patent?

Alfred Nobel: My original idea goes way back, as is the case with most inventions. But my first success with the detonation of nitroglycerine occurred during experiments at the beginning of the summer of 1863, whether May or June I cannot recall with certainty. [Actually, the first attempt took place in 1862.] With my brothers Robert and Ludvig watching, the nitroglycerine was detonated under water.

Question 2: Where and under what circumstances did you conceive of the idea?

AN: Many years ago, Professor Zinin in St. Petersburg drew my father's and my attention to this substance. He demonstrated its tremendous power by detonating a few drops of nitroglycerine on an anvil and demonstrating that the explosion occurred only on the precise spot where the hammer had struck. No practical use for the nitroglycerine had been found up to that point, but he added that it would be of the greatest importance if one could discover a practical method for its preparation and, most of all, how to make larger quantities of it to explode. This happened, I believe, twelve or more years ago, but I have never forgotten it. Since my father invented and manufactured underwater mines, it is only natural that I would turn my attention to explosive substances, which is what I have done.

Question 3: Which were your first experiments? Describe them in detail and name those present.

AN: My first attempt at rock blasting took place at a quarry at Huvudsta near Stockholm in the presence of several workers. I had brought along a fully loaded cartridge of lead plate. Then I improved the invention, and in the fall of 1863, it was tested for the Swedish government for possible use in grenades. In December 1863, experiments to use it for rock blasting were made at Ämmeberg's mines before witnesses. The tests done on behalf of the government were performed before a large number of people. Present at the Ämmeberg test were the chief mine engineer, Mr. Turby, engineer Beck, and several workers.

Question 6: How long have you been manufacturing and selling nitroglycerine in Sweden?

AN: I have sold nitroglycerine in Sweden since the beginning of 1864. I cannot recall with certainty what month it was, but regular manufacture for the purpose of sale was begun in May or June of 1864.

Question 7: Did you personally direct production and who assisted you?

AN: At first, I manufactured the nitroglycerine personally. Later I was assisted by a young man by the name of Hertzman and a few workers; all of them perished in the explosion that destroyed the laboratory on September 3, 1864.

Question 8: How much of the invention for which you have applied for a patent originates from your father's or your brothers' ideas or suggestions?

AN: Help from my father and my brother Robert was a great benefit to me, but the best proof that they consider the invention mine is my name on the patents. My father experimented with nitroglycerine long before me, but the actual invention was mine, and he makes no claims to it.

Alfred, like his father, was impulsive, but at no time during this examination did he vent hostility toward Shaffner. He was commendably matter-of-fact, unpretentious, and controlled.

The examination ended in an unqualified victory for Alfred. The report of the proceedings verifies that he, not Shaffner, was the rightful owner of the American patent. Colonel Shaffner refused to give up the fight, however. The possibilities for making a fortune with the help of an effective explosive substance with low production costs were unlimited. Construction was booming. Transportation networks were now being expanded. Railroads and new harbors were being built in most countries. In the mine excavation field, the need for a new, powerful explosive was greater than ever, since the mineral supply in the colonies had but begun to be exploited.

Shaffner had influence in his own country. When Alfred sailed for New York at the end of March 1866, he was probably considering some kind of compromise agreement with him. A need for local capital creates strange bedfellows, and no break had taken place between Alfred and Shaffner on a personal level. At least not yet.

Chapter 17

By the time Alfred landed in New York for the second time, on April 15, 1866, he was an international industrialist who viewed the whole world as a market. His professional contacts had multiplied and his self-confidence had grown. He was ready to take on America.

For anyone with initiative, post–Civil War America seemed promising beyond one's wildest dreams. The country was entering into a phase of wild capitalism. The newspapers were filled with reports about new constructions and building projects. To someone like Alfred, conditions could hardly have seemed more propitious, even though the Shaffner affair had given him a taste of how business got done in the New World. But a problem for Alfred was that word that his nitroglycerine was unreliable was spreading. It was felt — rightfully so, by the way — that transporting Nobel's explosive oil in canisters of leaded plate in wooden crates was dangerous to life and limb. In spite of Alfred's booklets and lectures, the public remained ignorant of nitroglycerine's properties. He himself did not set the best safety example. He routinely traveled with a couple of bottles of nitroglycerine in his luggage, even though he must have been conscious that it would not take much for the fluid to ferment — and leak, were the corks pushed out of the bottlenecks.

In anticipation of his arrival, the number of newspaper reports about accidents involving nitroglycerine seemed to jump sharply. They made for very good copy. For instance, a German guest at a hotel on Greenwich Street in New York had been given permission to store a wooden crate behind the reception desk. He never came back to claim it. Employees began using the crate as a bench, or for polishing their shoes. One day, somebody noticed that wisps of smoke were leaking from the crate. To be safe, a porter carried it out into the street. He had barely returned to call the police when a violent explosion blew out the hotel windows and ripped a hole a yard deep in the pavement. Nineteen persons were injured, some seriously. Experts concluded that what had happened was "a spontaneous combustion of nitroglycerine."

Less than two weeks before Alfred's arrival, what the *New York Times* termed "one of the most horrible accidents in history" occurred when a steamship exploded near Panama's Atlantic coast. Forty-seven persons were killed. The ship was loaded with war materiel and a large quantity of explosive oil. Shortly thereafter, the newspapers reported yet another devastating explosion aboard a large ship. The German ship *Mosel,* bound for New York, was completely demolished before it left Bremerhaven when a consignment of nitroglycerine detonated. Eighty-four persons were killed and 184 were injured.

From Sidney, Australia, came the news that a large number of persons had perished when a warehouse and some adjacent buildings were leveled in an explosion. An investigation revealed that two crates with 350 pounds of nitroglycerine had been kept in the storage building. In San Francisco a warehouse exploded, taking fifteen lives. Finally, while he was crossing the Atlantic, Alfred's factory outside Hamburg exploded.

Linked as he was with nitroglycerine, Alfred became an object of fascination to the American general public the moment he stepped off the boat, particularly since the newspapers were by that point explicitly warning their readers about his deadly explosive oil. As the scrutiny intensified, Alfred decided on the direct approach: he requested and received an audience with New York's mayor, John T. Hoffman, who granted him permission to demonstrate — with fully adequate measures of safety — his explosive substance in the city. Alfred wanted to prove to the American public, once and for all, that he had invented a method making it possible for nitroglycerine to explode in a risk-free manner, and that his invention would be of incomparable assistance in the realization of all of New York's magnificent building projects. He believed in what he said.

Directly after his meeting with the mayor, Alfred went to his hotel room and wrote a letter to the editor that the *New York Times* printed the next day:

> Since my arrival in this city, I have, with the deepest regret, learned that two accidents involving nitroglycerine have recently occurred in this country. Even if the causes of the explosions are not known, it is my hope to be able to convince competent and scientific authorities that nitroglycerine is a substance that is less dangerous than gunpowder to handle and store. For that purpose I intend to undertake a series of experiments within the next few days, hoping these will be convincing. Time and place

will be announced in your worthy newspaper. Until
then, may I most respectfully petition the general public
to defer their opinions since these experiments will make
it possible for each and every one to make a factual
appraisal.

On April 25, 1866, Alfred was summoned to Washington, where
he was received by a civil servant to whom Congress had given the
task of collecting background material for their decision regarding
nitroglycerine. Alfred admitted that his explosive oil could be un-
predictable, a fact that certain accidental explosions verified. He was
unable to point to any concrete cause for the latest accidents. On the
other hand, he could certify that neither friction nor impact — however violent — would cause it to detonate. He cited an experiment
that had been carried out in Hamburg. A load of nitroglycerine had
been shot a thousand feet into the air and still did not explode when
hitting the ground. Overheating, however, would cause an explosion.

His arguments fell on deaf ears. Congress later passed an anti-
glycerine law with wording that sensationalized the subject. Even
though he had not won over the lawmakers in Washington, Alfred
went ahead with his New York City demonstration. Nobel's American "premiere" took place on May 4, 1866, at a quarry in upper
Manhattan. The *New York Times* coverage is worth quoting at length.

With some trepidation, we accepted yesterday an invitation
from Professor Nobel to be present during a gathering of
scientists at the mountainous slopes between Eighth and
Ninth Avenues, near 83rd Street, in order to witness a series
of experiments with the exciting substance that is com-
monly known as nitroglycerine. The professor was
equipped with an abundance of the substance in crates and
bottles as well as with matches, fuses, and quite a bit of
courage. He opened a bottle and poured a small amount of
its contents on a rock. He brought a match to it, and it
burned like pitch. Unpunished he threw a canister and a
bottle, both filled with the explosive substance, from a high
cliff down to the ground, which demonstrated that impact
alone could not make it explode. When it comes to transportation, he said that the correct type of packaging guarantees complete safety. The substance will only explode if

the temperature is increased to 360 degrees Fahrenheit, a heat that cannot be generated during normal conditions, and his theory is therefore that the explosions that have occurred were caused by the material in which the canisters were enclosed — material saturated with leaking oil from the canisters and then ignited by some kind of spark.

In a variety of entertaining and graphic ways, he kept experimenting with the explosive and convinced those present that, during the conditions there presented, nitroglycerine is safer to handle and transport than both gunpowder and cottonpowder, but its explosive force is considerably greater.

If Alfred's purpose was to get attention, he succeeded. Editorials in newspapers across America were commenting on his experiments with the explosive oil and overexcited readers flooded editors with letters. The overwhelming majority portrayed Alfred as a trafficker in death and horror.

While in New York, Alfred again met with his countryman John Ericsson, who had remained one of his few supporters. Ericsson had also been summoned to give testimony before Congress because one of his cannons on the warship *Princeton* had exploded, and several well-known politicians and military officers had perished. Ironically, Ericsson had called his cannon "The Peacemaker." Not only was he convinced that his propeller would some day drive all ships in peaceful trade, but that his cannon, if maintained and used correctly, would serve peace through its deterrent effect. The two inventors had much in common: they were both blamed for accidents involving their inventions.

The letters Alfred wrote following the congressional inquiry show how hurt he was by the attacks against him. He was terribly disappointed when even the *New York Times* ended up censuring him in no uncertain terms, concluding in an editorial that the inventor was evidently not familiar with all the risks involved in the handling of nitroglycerine.

In the face of all this American resistance, Alfred's confidence began to waver, and his assurances regarding the safety of his explosive oil were no longer as categorical. He knew that if he did not somehow manage to gain full control over the "extraordinary circumstances" under which spontaneous explosions could occur, his original invention would not be worth much. A great deal was at stake. His competitors were smelling fresh hope for their business. General Henry Du Pont, the head of Du Pont de Nemours, which manufactured gunpowder, declared that "it's just a question of time how soon a man who uses nitroglycerine will pay with his life." (Ironically enough, the same Du Pont factory would later contribute actively to making Alfred's inventions known and utilized throughout the world.)

Alfred had to do something about the distorted image his explosive oil had in the public's imagination. Continued debate in the press was futile; it was meaningless, he felt, to discuss scientific questions with persons who had "suspended all logic" in advance. He had no choice: stranded in a foreign country and without access to his own laboratory, he needed to find a solution that would make it possible to transport nitroglycerine safely.

He performed some experiments while in New York and discovered that through the addition of methyl alcohol — wood spirit — the sensitivity of the nitroglycerine was lessened to such a degree that the mixture could be transported in total safety. Methyl alcohol had yet another advantage in that it prevented the explosive oil from freezing. Nobel's Swedish patent application for this method is dated "New York, the 20th of May, 1866."

On May 12th, when the legal process regarding his American patent began, he had no patent for his solution to the safety problem, a fact that would turn out to be unfortunate. During the course of the patent process, Alfred increasingly suspected that his case was not receiving a fair and impartial trial. It was evident that the court was being influenced.

Alfred began to understand when he saw members of the court listening with rapt attention to what Colonel Shaffner, who had been summoned as a witness, had to say. Taking advantage of the unstable public opinion, Shaffner maintained that the public must be calmed at any cost. He was no longer pressing his claim to Alfred's invention; instead he was pushing his claim that he himself had invented a method to package the risky explosive.

That the court finally rejected Shaffner's claim regarding the priority right to the patent came somewhat as a surprise to Alfred. But he also sensed that Shaffner's comments about his packaging method had not fallen on deaf ears. It would later become evident that the lawmakers in Washington had indeed paid attention.

Another Shaffner-like figure was Otto Bürstenbinder, an acquaintance of Alfred's German partner, Dr. Bandmann. Without

Alfred's knowledge, Bürstenbinder had sought to introduce Alfred's explosive oil in the American marketplace. When the patent case was decided in Alfred's favor, Bürstenbinder began offering the public a chance to buy shares in a company called United Blasting Oil Company. Bürstenbinder had lined up a few financial backers in New York and had a planned share capital of a million dollars. He offered Alfred a fourth of the shares free, plus $20,000 in cash compensation in exchange for the patent rights. Taken aback by the boldness of his enterprise, Alfred accepted almost without thinking.

Before long, however, he would withdraw his promise to Bürstenbinder. Shaffner was now offering Alfred his cooperation. He wanted to establish United States Blasting Oil Company and demonstrate the product during an extensive tour across America. He described his newly invented package method: a canister of metal plate with double walls; the space between the walls was filled with water. Alfred was less impressed by this invention than by Shaffner's influence in Washington, from which any day he expected new legislation against nitroglycerine. As certain state legislatures already had, the federal government might very well decree that "every death, directly or indirectly caused by transport of his blasting oil on ships or conveyances of any kind, is to be considered murder of the first degree and is to be punished by death."

At the worst possible moment came word that Alfred's factory in Germany had blown up. The Winkler brothers were pleading with him to return without delay. Alfred was under tremendous pressure: Congress would be making up its mind at any moment. He needed to use Shaffner. Despite deep misgivings, he agreed to a partnership. Their agreement made no mention of Shaffner's packaging method, which Alfred did not consider viable, but Alfred's American patent rights were transferred to the Colonel — with the proviso that they be used exclusively for military purposes. As compensation Alfred requested the token sum of one dollar.

The anti-nitroglycerine law was passed on July 26, 1866, although essential parts of the original proposal had been altered. Punishment for those responsible for an explosion accident was prison, not death. Furthermore, transport of blasting oil was permitted under the condition that shipping crates be prominently labeled "DANGEROUS." Finally, the new law expressly required that the explosive liquid be stored in those containers Shaffner had invented, and for which he had been granted a patent. The Colonel's lobbying efforts had paid off.

One day later, United States Blasting Oil Company was registered in New York. At the inaugural meeting, Israel Hall, an elderly acquaintance of Alfred's from St. Petersburg, was elected chairman. He had been persuaded to buy 1,625 shares, and so, apart from Alfred, he was the largest shareholder in the company. Since Shaffner lacked economic resources, Alfred gave him ten of his own shares, so that the Colonel could formally be elected a member of the board. This proved to be a mistake. Before long, Shaffner was traveling across the country as a commercial salesman in explosive wares, boasting that he had "fired ten thousand blasting shots." The U.S. Blasting Oil Company received some publicity, but mainly Shaffner was lining his own pockets at the company's expense and appropriating the lion's share of the compensation for every demonstration.

When the Colonel's shadowy manipulations came to light and the share capital was not met in full by subscription, Alfred's American patent rights were transferred to a hastily formed company in San Francisco, the Giant Powder Company. California gold miners had termed the new, efficient, and inexpensive explosive "giant powder," hence the name. The new company took off quickly and a factory was soon built on the Hackensack River in New Jersey. When Shaffner, who had succeeded the aging Israel Hall as the head of U.S. Blasting Oil, got wind of what was going on, he pulled off a coup. With a few strokes of a pen, he and a few co-conspirators transferred the company's patent rights to their own company in New York, the Nitroglycerine Company. The idea was that this company would sell licenses for both Alfred's blasting oil and Shaffner's own transport crates. Shaffner had set himself on a collision course with Alfred, who was still the largest shareholder in the U.S. Blasting Oil Company. In a letter to his brother Julius in San Francisco, Dr. Bandmann captured the situation in a nutshell: "For a song those rogues have transferred the profit possibilities inherent in the patents to others. The shares will of course not yield any dividends, but Shaffner and his partners have charge of all the money."

Alfred wrote Shaffner a letter whose rancor makes it unique in his correspondence: ". . . I am very surprised, so far as anything that comes from your direction can surprise me any more, at your doings right now. If you consider yourself able to afford to belittle my services, let us have a try at what antagonism on my part can accomplish. For a start, since you write that you are going after my shares, I am going to make yours worthless by letting loose a competition that lies beyond both your and the law's possibilities to prevent."

Alfred backed up his words with action. A new company was formed, the Atlantic Giant Powder Company, with three million dollars in share capital. When Shaffner realized he was being excluded, he sued the U.S. Blasting Oil Company, but his shady maneuverings meant he had lost his influential contacts and his desperate action produced no results.

A few sentences from *Nemesis,* written in the fine tradition of the revenge tragedy, provide an appropriate epitaph to the Shaffner episode, since it is not inconceivable that Alfred had Shaffner in mind when writing them:

BEATRICE: Some devilish plan, if possible more cowardly than all preceding abominations!
CENCI: Stop right there! You are the first who with impunity dares to insult me, but you could have to pay dearly for it.

[Act II, scene iii]

Alfred's American adventure was finally over when he landed in Hamburg on August 10, 1866, if not wealthier at least more experienced. His expectations of the trip to the United States had been met in part: he had successfully defended his right to the blasting oil patent against Shaffner's claims. Whatever the difficulties that remained, the American market still promised to be extremely lucrative.

On August 14, 1866, Alfred was granted a patent in the United States — number 57175 — for his blasting oil. Letters of interest and orders soon came pouring in to the Alfred Nobel & Company office in Hamburg. Not only had America's interest in the revolutionary and safe explosive awakened — but so had the world's.

Chapter 18

Back in Hamburg, Alfred summed up his experiences in America in a letter to a friend: "If you need to put new lining in an old overcoat, let me offer you my shares in 'Blasting Oil.' Their color is beautiful."

Alfred never returned to the United States. A letter to a colleague provides one reason why: "Life in America was not pleasant to me in the long run. The exaggerated stress over money destroys too many of the pleasures of society and ruins the sense of honor for the sake of imaginary needs."

Alfred felt he had seen enough of unscrupulous fortune hunters, cheating "colonels," and corrupt legislators to last a lifetime.

Besides, he had plenty to occupy him at home. Faced with a grave economic crisis at the Krümmel factory outside Hamburg, Alfred proved again his ability to act. Shortage of working capital was what had forced him to go to New York in the first place. Though the debts amounted only to 7,000 German marks and assets were worth around 25,000 marks, the assets consisted mostly of unsold blasting oil (15,000 marks) and raw material (6,000 marks). Luckily, the plant had not been included as an asset — since it was destined to be blown up twice.

In an amazingly short time, Alfred managed to reorganize the business, concentrating on making the sales organization as efficient as possible. He attracted a large number of skilled foremen and workers from Winter Bay. (A reminder of this small-scale Swedish emigration is seen today in many of the store signs in the area, featuring names such as Andersson, Johansson, and Pettersson.) Crop failures in agrarian Sweden had spurred a labor movement south. That a large number of Swedes went specifically to Krümmel may have had something to do with Alfred's reputation as employer: he paid well and took care of his workers.

The credit for the Krümmel factory's model organization and efficiency has to go to Alfred's childhood friend, Alarik Liedbeck. Together the two established factories around the world. Liedbeck, one of the foremost technical experts in high explosives, had begun his career as factory foreman at Winter Bay. From the beginning, Alfred relied heavily on him whenever he encountered technical problem with his inventions or when a new factory needed building. Over the course of thirty years, Alfred grew so dependent on Liedbeck that he rarely made a final decision on a technical matter without first having discussed it with him. Liedbeck's work was crucial to the development of dynamite presses and air injectors for the nitrating of glycerine, as well as presses for smokeless powder. Liedbeck was the grandson of the man who had pioneered gymnastics in Sweden, Pehr Henrik Ling, and had on numerous occasions demonstrated rare physical courage. He personally carried loads that threatened to explode at any moment out of the factory. During his time as engineer at Winter Bay, two large explosions occurred — one in 1868 and the other in 1878.

Alfred returned from America keenly aware that blasting oil had a fundamental flaw, and that that flaw had to do with its consistency. "As early as 1863," he later wrote, "I had arrived at an understanding of the disadvantages with the fluid form of nitroglycerine." Accidents were occurring even when the explosive was being used by mining experts and construction engineers. The experienced building contractor O. Bergström had a theory about what was wrong: "Despite all the necessary cautionary measures we have taken, constant accidents occur during the blasting of nitroglycerine. In most cases this is because some is left over after the explosion and it gets squeezed down into fissures in the rock."

Alfred kept his head during it all, even when he realized that his blasting oil had yet another drawback: its tendency to become solid at several degrees above the freezing point of water, which necessitated melting the oil down. That meant additional hazards.

Having mastered the detonation process, Alfred now needed to find a foolproof way to transport his oil safely but without diminishing its blasting power. A new mixture was needed. Returning to experiments he had done three years earlier, Alfred took advantage of the unlimited quantity of infusorian earth, or kieselguhr as it is called in German, that could be found along the banks of the Elbe River and its tributary the Alster. Kieselguhr consists of hardened algae and is as fine as powder. Alfred could not have found a more suitable matter than this for the absorption of nitroglycerine. He mixed 25 percent kieselguhr with 75 percent nitroglycerine and produced a highly effective explosive substance in solid form. It was easy to handle and almost risk-free, and its explosive power remained enormous.

Alfred's Swedish patent (dated September 19, 1866) reads: "My new explosive, called dynamite, is simply nitroglycerine in combination with a very porous silicate, and I have given it a new name, not to hide its nature, but to emphasize its explosive traits in the new form; these are so different that a new name is truly called for." "DYNAMITE OR NOBEL'S SAFETY POWDER" was the full trademark name that Alfred formulated, deriving "dynamite" from the Greek *dynamis,* which translates as power. His choice of name may well have been influenced, too, by the name given to an electric generator — dynamo.

Dynamite was described as a "reddish-yellow, soft and plastic mass that is pressed into cartridges of a certain thickness and then enclosed in paper wrappers." Today dynamite usually consists of 50–70 percent explosive gelatin kneaded together with 24–45 percent ammonium nitrate and 2–5 percent wood flour into a plastic mass. For rock blasting, cylindrical dynamite cartridges, which are placed into drilled holes, are used. Except for a few minor alterations, the method has remained largely the same as it was in Alfred's time.

This time nobody could dispute that Alfred was the inventor. Soon he was known across Germany as *"Der Dynamitenkönig"* (the Dynamite King) and it was obvious to everyone that he had laid the foundation for a world industry.

Although Alfred intended dynamite for peaceful uses exclusively, many thought — not the least in despotic Russia — that it made it much too easy for revolutionaries to commit terrorist acts. It was considerably more difficult to attempt assassinations with gunpowder than with dynamite. August Strindberg paid homage to Alfred as "the deliverer of ammunition to assassins." In a poem written in 1883, Strindberg elegizes the inventor of dynamite as a man who has given the masses a chance to pay back the creator of gunpowder, Barthold Swartz, who had made it possible for the aristocracy to maintain power:

> You Swartz, a small deluxe edition, finely bound
> just for the nobles and the princely houses meant!
> Nobel! A budget-priced paperback, easily found
> since hundreds of thousands into the world were sent!

Assassins did indeed make use of this new and manageable explosive. Czar Alexander II barely escaped certain death in February 1880, when a load of dynamite exploded beneath his dining room in the Winter Palace. A little more than a year later, he lost his life during a drive through the center of St. Petersburg. The weapon was a dynamite-filled bomb.

Chapter 19

GUERRA: *Are you in pain?*
BEATRICE: *. . . Yes! I have been defamed.*
GUERRA: *You, defamed? Impossible! Who would dare . . . ?*

Nemesis, Act III, scene v

While Alfred went on researching and inventing, creating companies and building factories, malicious rumors were circulating behind his back. Alfred was "decking himself out in borrowed plumes," they went. The slander that Alfred didn't invent his inventions was beginning to stick, perhaps because it contained a grain of truth — about the two-year period when Alfred had studied with the chemist Pelouze in Paris. During his time in Pelouze's private laboratory, Alfred shared his workspace with Ascanio Sobrero. In 1846, Sobrero, by combining nitric acid and sulfuric acid, had created an oil with highly explosive qualities. The sulfuric acid was necessary to prevent separation, while the nitric acid constituted the foundation for his experiments. Through Professor Zinin, Alfred had heard about Sobrero's "pyroglycerine" in St. Petersburg, although it was thought to have such an enormous blasting effect as to be totally impractical.

Alfred realized the practical implications of nitroglycerine, which Sobrero had not. When the Swede took his invention as his own by introducing it on the world market Sobrero was mortified. It should also be noted that other chemists before Sobrero had been on the same track. Besides Pelouze, the Russians Zinin and Petrusjevski, the Frenchmen Bracconneau, Chevreul, and Berthelot, and the Swedish chemist Carl Wilhelm Scheele had all made preliminary experiments some years before. For his part, Alfred never hid his admiration for Sobrero's talent and always freely acknowledged Sobrero to be the discoverer of nitroglycerine.

Yet dynamite's success made Sobrero feel that he had suffered an injustice. He expressed his bitterness in a paper to the Scientific Academy in Turin in which he stated that in 1865, before the French Academy, Alfred had given an account of the explosive power of nitroglycerine without mentioning Sobrero's name. "It is not ambition now driving me to speak up," he added, "but love of justice."

The genesis of nitroglycerine was purely the result of "tenacious Italian work." In the debate that followed, it was suggested that Sobrero's discovery had saved the Nobel family from impoverishment after their financial fiasco in Russia.

Ascanio Sobrero was born in Caseale Monferrato, located between Turin and Milan, and originally hoped to become a doctor. When his doctoral thesis in medicine was not accepted, he changed course and studied chemistry, first in Turin and then with Professor Pelouze in Paris. When he discovered his nitroglycerine, he did what chemists often do — he tasted it: "The substance has a sweetish taste, strongly aromatic, but its exploration must be done with the greatest caution. . . ." For a long time, his discovery was considered a scientific curiosity because of its dangerousness.

Sobrero knew from personal experience that his warning about nitroglycerine's explosive qualities was not exaggerated. He writes: "It splits asunder at high temperature. One drop heated on platinoid metal ignites and burns violently. Under certain circumstances, it may detonate with enormous violence. Once a small quantity of pyroglycerine ether solution evaporated in a glass bowl. What remained of the pyroglycerine was certainly not more than two or three centigrams, but when the bowl was heated over a spirit lamp, a violent explosion occurred and the bowl crumbled into small bits."

During an experiment with "a drop in a test tube," the mixture exploded and Sobrero's face was severely injured. The Italian chemist finally abandoned work on nitroglycerine after an explosion that took place at the armory in Turin, when four hundred grams of mitromannite — a compound like nitroglycerine, the only difference being that glycerine had been replaced by mannite — detonated with devastating results. All work was stopped while Sobrero attempted in vain to decide the chemical composition of nitroglycerine.

To get as full a picture of Sobrero as possible, we might consider his own words: "When I think of all the victims killed during nitroglycerine explosions, and the terrible havoc that has been wreaked, which in all probability will continue to occur in the future, I am almost ashamed to admit to be its discoverer. One and only one consideration can give me solace: If I hadn't discovered nitroglycerine, it would have been discovered sooner or later by some other chemist. . . ."

Alfred never entered into public polemics with Sobrero; his

contact with him was always deferential, as the following letter shows:

Paris

May 25, 1879

Dear Highly Esteemed Professor!

Allow me to take the opportunity as a consequence of your utterly friendly letter to give expression to the admiration and great respect I have always felt for you. I am envious of Mr. Duchene for having the good idea of having a statue of you done for general exhibition in Avigliana. The whole world owes you a debt of gratitude for your significant invention.

Your affectionate

A. Nobel

Some speculation surrounds this letter. Did Alfred feel pangs of guilt? Did he want a reconciliation with Sobrero while time yet allowed it?

The marble bust of Sobrero that Nobel refers to represented public acknowledgment of a scientific pioneer. It was unveiled in 1879 at the annual meeting of Nobel's Italian company. The factory at Avigliana still has today a few hundred grams of nitroglycerine that Sobrero had prepared in 1847, and turned over in 1882, when he retired. The man who took over his professorship had not dared keep the risky explosive sitting around in the university's laboratory.

The difficulty of correcting a historical account once it takes hold is apparent in a booklet published in connection with the one-hundred-year celebration of Sobrero's birth in 1812. The author, a chemistry professor by the name of N. Guareschi, doesn't mince words: Sobrero was unjustly treated and the Nobel Foundation ought to call their award the Sobrero-Nobel Prize. Nobody else picked up the cause, however. Others point out that today Sobrero's chemical synthesis of nitroglycerine would hardly be called a discovery or an invention; if anything, Nobel was generous in his praise. Sobrero may have known this, but that didn't prevent him from making larger claims. In his speech to the Turin Academy, he said he considered himself "to have the right, on behalf of my country and myself, to demand recognition for a discovery for which others now are taking partial or even complete credit."

Sobrero did indeed discover nitroglycerine, but it was Nobel who succeeded in putting it to work. Alfred not only tamed it, he marketed it. Not for the first time in history has an invention proven it needed two talents: that of the creator and that of the exploiter.

Chapter 20

His dynamite patented and his customer list growing daily, Alfred was rapidly becoming financially independent. Between 1866 and 1872, he traveled constantly, spending countless hours in cramped train compartments that in his letters he called "my rolling prisons." He was restlessly active during these journeys, as if the changes of scenery infused him with renewed energy. It was work therapy: diligence kept his depressive tendencies at bay.

He was determined to conquer the British market. "England," he wrote to J. Norris, the British financier with whom he collaborated, on September 1, 1868, "is a jewel worth the rest of the world. A dynamite company there would have the entire Empire as its market." Off he went to Aberdeen, Glasgow, Middlesbrough-on-Tees, and Bristol, dragging a suitcase filled with his new explosive, weighing more than twenty pounds. By so doing, the normally law-abiding Alfred was knowingly disobeying current ordinances. Had the content of his suitcase become known to the authorities, he could have ended up in prison for two years.

Alfred was becoming not only an adept salesman but a skilled businessman. When it came to defending his own interests, he could show an unbending will, as the following rather threatening letter to the Scotsman John Downie attests: "Formerly I sought your friends; they will have to seek me now. If we agree, well and good; if not I shall before spring start a factory in England without the aid of capital. Your friends are much mistaken if they think that it is their funds I value. I need only say a word and the capital will be placed in Germany at my disposal. What I want is good and commercial ability to overcome the prejudices which will act as a stumbling block on our first start. To these my concession will be made, not the capital."

By the beginning of the 1870s, Alfred had financial dealings in practically every European country. His traveling tempo picked up speed: "My country is wherever I work, and I work everywhere." That slightly boastful formulation doesn't mirror the whole truth, for his roots in Sweden ran deep — it was where his beloved mother lived and where he would return when older. He never gave up his

Swedish citizenship. But it is also true that the city in which he felt
most at home was not Stockholm but Paris. To him, the French
capital was the center of business and cultural life.

In 1873, once Alfred's most hectic years of travel came to an
end, he settled in Paris, where life seemed to shimmer. He had developed that impression as an enamored seventeen-year-old, and it
stuck. Paris, he felt, was the stage on which the big events were
being played out, an ideal base of operations.

Ever since his youth in St. Petersburg, Alfred had spoken French
"à la perfection." He was also an admirer of French literature, which
would lead to a close friendship with Victor Hugo. The year Alfred
settled in Paris, Emile Zola published *Le Ventre de Paris* [The Un-
derbelly of Paris]. Zola was the foremost practitioner of naturalism
and a journalist by training. He was therefore well acquainted with
Alfred's life. *Le Ventre de Paris* depicts an idealistic French chemist
named Froman, whose energies are devoted to inventing a fright-
eningly effective explosive.

Over time, Alfred became increasingly influenced by everything
French: his letters often mingled French words and Swedish, and his
gestures became Gallic in their animated scope. He was also able to
express himself so articulately in the language that it impressed native
speakers.

As soon as he decided to settle in Paris, Alfred began looking
for a comfortable dwelling, where he could spend time undisturbed
between his many journeys.

He began his search in the area near the Arc de Triomphe and
Bois de Boulogne. Having spent most of his life in drafty laboratories
and Spartan offices, he wanted a patrician house surrounded by high
fences. From there he would plan dynamite's continued victory
march through Europe.

When Alfred and his father were involved in mine placement in
the Finnish Bay during the Crimean War, the city of Sevastopol on
the Black Sea had been reduced to ruins. One of its most famous
fortresses was called *Malakov*. Eighteen years later, standing outside
number 53 Avenue Malakoff, the new owner of an impressive building must have found the coincidence and irony inescapable.[1]

Counting his parents' homes in Stockholm and St. Petersburg,

[1] In 1892, the street number was changed to 59. In 1936, the stretch of Malakoff he
lived on was renamed Avenue Raymond Poincaré, and Alfred's house was given
the number 74. Today it serves as the embassy for the People's Republic of Laos.

this was Alfred's third permanent residence. The contrast between the dilapidated house at Heleneborg and this luxurious dwelling could hardly have been greater. The house was located close to the green pleasures of the Bois de Boulogne, to which Alfred would walk or take a carriage pulled by a couple of his imported Russian horses. Through the magnificent windows of the second-floor parlor, passers-by could catch glimpses of festively dressed guests whenever his residence was lit up for a banquet.

To the right of the front entrance was a door leading into a yard where Alfred had immediately built a small but well-equipped laboratory. The left side of the house contained the library.

The first impression the house gave was of being overwhelming rather than inviting. The glass roof and the glass wall made the winter garden's atmosphere like a hothouse's. Behind the flower-covered tables hung heavy velvet drapes; only the drawing room furniture and a piano reminded a visitor that this was a private residence and not a hotel.

Located on the mezzanine level, the winter garden was illuminated by a large crystal chandelier whose pieces sparkled like ice. Besides the musical scores of *Carmen, Mignon,* and other operas, testifying to Alfred's interest in music, there was hardly anything to give a homey touch. The dining room was different, however. Two paintings by the Swedish open-air painter Alfred Wahlberg, which Alfred had personally selected, hung there along with the French artist Gustave Courbet's *Waterfall in the Mountains.*

In the greenhouse grew orchids, one of Alfred's passions. Horses were another. Alfred wrote to his brother and asked him to find a pair of the finest horses in St. Petersburg, saying that he would find several thousand rubles a reasonable price to pay. In his youth in St. Petersburg it was a natural thing for wealthy people to use horse and carriage even when traveling very short distances. Having a carriage pulled by two or even three horses was a sign of status. Alfred remained a devoted lover of horses all his life.

Most of his time at Avenue Malakoff was spent in his laboratory with his assistant Georges Fehrenbach, who would be his valued partner for nearly two decades. When Alfred found it necessary to seek a more suitable location for his experiments, he found Sevran-Livry, northeast of Paris. There, in 1881, he bought an estate, situated at some distance from other buildings. It would become routine for him to take the train to Sevran in the morning and stay overnight whenever his work kept him there.

A manservant and a housekeeper — an *ekonomka,* to use the Russian — took care of all his personal needs. As his "dynamite travel" — Alfred's own favorite expression — diminished, his life became orderly and predictable. When he did come home from a trip he would always find his desk piled high with letters, invitations, and the endless requests for donations. Success brought an unending flow of letters begging for money, and from every corner of the world. Requests for gifts or donations mounted into the millions. "Each day the mail brings at least two dozen applications and requests for money amounting to at least 20,000 crowns (then about $4,000). That makes seven million crowns annually, which is why I must state that it would be better to have a reputation for being miserly than for being generous."

There are exceptions. When a woman who took care of his household was getting married, Alfred asked her what she wished as a wedding present. The quick-witted young woman astonished him by replying without hesitation, "As much as Monsieur Nobel himself earns in one day." Impressed and amused, Alfred agreed, without giving the matter further thought. The girl received a monetary gift of such size that she and her husband could enjoy it as long as their marriage lasted. The bank draft Alfred signed was for 40,000 francs (approximately $110,000 today).

Still, Alfred developed a remarkable ability to separate the wheat from the chaff among those entreating him for money. He often helped desperate individuals who without forewarning turned up at his doorstep, despite his own strict orders that nobody should be let in. He nearly always got involved — though with great discretion — when he saw an opportunity to assist diligent and sincere young people; he remembered his own youth and those memories for which, as he later wrote Bertha von Suttner, ". . . there exists no eraser as for blackboards. I don't ask where their fathers were born, or what Lilliputian god they worship; helpfulness — the right kind — recognizes no national borders and seeks no confessions."

Once his daily mail was opened and answered, Alfred would glance through the world's papers: *Le Figaro, Le Matin,* the *Times,* and, after 1877, the *Times Literary Supplement, B.Z. am Mittag,* and more. Although he devoured them, his newspaper reading left few traces in his letters and notes. Indeed, he considered it of rather slight importance to know and comment upon the latest "journalistic thinking" about the most recent theatrical success or political scandal.

For long periods, Alfred's house was mainly used for entertaining. Financiers and industrial giants; company heads in different countries, such as Gustaf Aufschlager in Hamburg and C. O. Lundholm in Ardeer; relatives from Sweden and Russia were frequent guests.

His visitors have provided a clear picture of Alfred's habits. Between work shifts in the laboratory and at the conference tables, he liked to stroll the boulevards, enjoying the lively street life and the boisterous ambiance of the sidewalk cafés. He felt a refinement of mind could exist in Paris, and it had nothing to do with belonging to a certain social class. "Even the mongrels smell of civilization," he wrote to Ludvig. When the loneliness in his house became too much to bear, he could walk to the bistro down the block and eat a simple dinner, musing over his problems and listening to the sounds surrounding him.

Physically, Alfred was very unobtrusive and unathletic. Fairly short to begin with, by forty he had already begun to walk with a slight bent. Some said it was difficult to imagine he had ever been a young man. He walked with small, quick steps, which caused Ragnar Sohlman to remark that he "went tripping along." His hair was dark brown but turned gray fairly early on. Bushy eyebrows shadowed blue, deep-set eyes. Like most men of his time, he had a beard, which was always neatly trimmed. His complexion was pale, since he preferred to remain in the shade during sunny days. He always dressed in a dark suit with a white shirt and carefully knotted necktie.

He was not a vain man, illustrated by a comment he made to the editors of an anniversary booklet, who wanted to include his picture. "When my assistants and every worker here have been asked to submit their portraits," he told them, "I will send the depiction of my pig's-bristle bachelor snout, not before." He had difficulty keeping his body still, as if afflicted with some nervous condition. In fact it was rheumatism that plagued him, forcing him constantly to seek new, less excruciating body positions.

His letters give testimony to growing melancholy. "I am two steps ahead of my competitors," he writes in one, "[but] the accumulation of money and of praise leaves me totally indifferent." Whatever his tendency toward misanthropy, however, he refused to give up his hope for a better future. Increased wealth, he felt, could be accomplished by spreading knowledge and information. Once again, an exchange in Act II of *Nemesis* illustrates the point:

GIACOMO: But don't you think it could be a danger to our
social order to spread knowledge among the crude mob?

GUERRA: What can be cruder than the mass of evildoers and
madmen who govern the world and give it its spiritual
direction? Believe me, excesses of the rabble — however loathsome they may seem — are children's games
compared to the organized abomination under which the
people sigh, suffer, and decay morally!

The bitterness here doubtless reflects Alfred's experiences with judicial authority. The courts, he felt, were subject to inappropriate
influences by politically powerful men. Such misuse of power could
only be prevented if, in the spirit of Montesquieu, impermeable walls
were built between the executive, legislative, and judicial powers.
Since in Alfred's eyes the guardians of law and order were ambitious
and corruptible, their authority had to be limited. That would only
be possible through education of the masses.

Chapter 21

When Alfred turned forty, he felt that he had passed the meridian of life. Sitting alone in his dining room, quietly eating his dinner, he was subject to attacks of ennui, as his letters attest. He told friends and family that his existence was dismal and that he had begun to shun society. Invitations were not lacking, but he most often turned them down, citing urgent travel as an excuse.

When France's heads of state invited him to a banquet, however, Alfred felt it his duty to be present. Patrice Maurice de Mac Mahon was president of the Republic between 1873 and 1879 and marshal of France. He had also masterminded the conquest of Sevastopol during the Crimean War, and subdued the Communard insurrection in Paris in 1871. Jules Grévy was one of the Republic's progressive leaders and president between 1879 and 1887. Alfred was often given a conspicuous place of honor: the government considered him to be a person of highest importance.

The construction of a modern laboratory in Sevran marked a turning point in Alfred's inventing activities. From now on, he could dedicate himself to experimenting with new types of explosives, including those that might have military use. An arms race was taking place in Europe, demanding ever more effective weapons and ammunition. The French government gave Alfred permission to experiment at their nearby shooting range with both cannons and army rifles. He would later discover that the French felt that this gave them the right to his inventions.

During these extremely busy years, Alfred was concerned about not trifling away his time socializing. A fundamentally considerate person, who did not want to reject elementary etiquette, he still accepted some invitations. Upon his arrival at an event, he became the object of great curiosity or an overly exuberant welcome, to which he would always respond with a stiff bow. He felt flattery was a tempting bait that hid the hook. He would then quickly retire to a corner, where he remained, deftly refusing to let himself be drawn into the limelight.

From his temporary lookout, he would silently make the observations and reflections that fill his correspondence. Conversations seldom had the power to involve him. Alfred did not do this purely out of arrogance; it was as much from self-criticism: he was well aware that he could dampen the merriest mood if he were not amused. That was why he would often keep in the background until everybody was called to the table.

Being seated at a festively set table in a dining room bathed in strong white light (as was the fashion), he would quite often have an attack of migraine. He found that drinking a couple of glasses of wine very quickly gave him temporary relief. *Nemesis* touches on Alfred's cure:

> CENCI: What after-effects does the drink have?
> CANTARIDINA: One usually spends the whole next day feeling enfeebled and attacked by severe migraine; but easily digested food and a few glasses of fiery wine will soon repair the damage.
>
> [Act III, scene vi]

Alfred was not unaware of the risks he ran by isolating himself. "Unfortunately, it is true," he writes in a letter to Sofie Hess, "that in our life one who withdraws from educated society and neglects the interchange of ideas with thinking human beings finally becomes incapable of such interchange and loses respect for himself as well as the respect of others, which he had formerly earned and enjoyed."

His view on French women's roles in social life is reflected in a not altogether gallant passage in a letter to his brother Robert: "Personally I feel that the conversation of the Parisiennes is among the most insipid there is, while the communication with educated and semi-emancipated Russian women is exquisitely pleasant. Unfortunately, they have an antipathy to soap, but one cannot ask for everything!"

Why Alfred did not marry remains something of a mystery. Our meager understanding of Alfred's love life comes mainly from the two women he was closest to — Sofie Hess and Bertha von Suttner (née Kinsky). Neither provides any dark, speculation-rich secrets about his sexuality. Letters from both women, different as they were from each other, portray him as a shy and rather awkward beau. From Alfred's own notes we know that he thought himself too unattractive to arouse feelings of passion in a woman. He seems to have wanted to avoid placing himself in a position of emotional dependency. If anything he was dependent upon a romanticized image of himself as a loner. In that letter to his sister-in-law Edla quoted earlier, he describes himself as "a nomadic condemned by fate to be a broken shipwreck in life" who had voluntarily excluded himself from "love, happiness, joy, pulsating life, caring and being cared for, caressing and being caressed. . . ."

Though he never states it outright in his letters, he hints at his belief that marriage would hinder his ability to run the Nobel enterprises. He was prepared to pay the high emotional cost of solitude. He called his life "half a life." Yet, as we shall see, his celibacy was not entirely by choice.

At this time, there was animated discussion about the risks versus the advantages of sexual abstinence. In England, an organization to abolish prostitution was formed, and in Sweden *The Friend of Morality*, published in 1878, campaigned for the same thing. Perhaps these inspired the following lines from *Nemesis*, in which Alfred seems both to be praising and condemning those who practice "unbridled fornication," as well as those who militate against it:

> Those stupid moralists who preach about improving people hardly succeed with one in a thousand, while tempting virtue into the wildest and most unbridled fornication is the easiest thing in the world. And what fun it is! What would life be worth if immorality with all its variants didn't exist?

> [Act I, scene viii]

Chapter 22

Whatever his private struggles, Alfred's capacity for work did not diminish as he approached middle age. After one feverish period, he created a new explosive gelatin (92 percent gelatinized glycerine, 8 percent nitrocellulose) that combined the potency of nitroglycerine with the relative safety of dynamite. The blasting gelatin was not only safe against explosion from impact and friction, but could be used underwater, which dramatically increased its utility.

Alfred had come a long way from the barge in Bockholm Bay to the laboratories at Avenue Malakoff and Sevran. After days of nonstop work, he had managed to concoct what was from several points of view the ideal explosive — in the unanimous opinion of experts in the field, at least. Alfred himself felt that not only was blasting gelatin an improvement on dynamite, but it was an improvement based upon an absolutely original combination of compounds.

A letter to Archibald Shaw, a member of the board of directors of Nobel's Scottish company, reveals Alfred's acute awareness of the market value of his new invention. "It is certain," he writes, "that at the time of the formation of the Co. neither they expected to acquire nor I to cede, free of charge, a patent of such importance."

At first Alfred hoped that his blasting gelatin would find a military use in grenades, cannons, or handguns. After many time-consuming experiments, he and Sir Frederic Abel in England concluded that the blasting gelatin was too powerful to be of service.

The success he anticipated was therefore long in coming. In France, England, and Germany, the development was slowed because the blasting gelatin was more expensive than dynamite and riskier to produce. It was, however, proving perfect for blasting through hard rock. During the work on the nine-mile St. Gotthard tunnel, blasting gelatin proved just how much better it was than dynamite. In a letter to Alfred dated February 27, 1880, his French partner Paul Barbe tells him that they were able to blast seventy to eighty feet per month, as compared to only forty to fifty when they were using dynamite.

A patent was sought first in England, where the head of the

government's explosive-substance division, Vivian Majendie, threw so many problems in the way of the blasting gelatin that an exasperated Alfred complained of that country's ". . . restrictive rules, bureaucracy, pedantry, arrogance, and other unpleasantness."

In 1879, the English explosive inspection office had forbidden the manufacture of gelatinized explosive substances, and it would be another five years before that ruling was changed. Alfred started an investigation to find out what might lie behind the foot-dragging of the British authorities. He found out that they had relied upon the expert advice of Sir Frederic Abel, and Abel had discovered a way to produce guncotton that had a smaller risk of chemical decomposition. Being called upon to judge the blasting gelatin clearly created a conflict of interest for Abel, who in 1870 Alfred had called "the distinguished advocate for guncotton." The real reason for the ban on the gelatin, as we shall see, was that Abel knew it would pose serious competition to his own guncotton.

The resistance in England to Alfred's blasting gelatin turned out to be an isolated phenomenon; it was more appreciated in other places, and royalties came pouring in. The businessman in Alfred was evidently gratified by this success, but, to judge from his letters, it did nothing to disperse his darker thoughts.

In his letters Alfred describes himself as an interloper in his own house, and not just during those intense periods of travel. Again, *Nemesis,* though written twenty years later, provides the best mirror of his thoughts:

> MADONNA: My life is woven out of torment. All the incomparable splendor that surrounds me is more likely to increase than to alleviate my sorrow.
>
> [Act II, scene viii]

He wrote Alarik Liedbeck: "Like others and perhaps more than others, I feel the heavy weight of loneliness, and for years I have been seeking someone whose heart could find its way to mine."

It was while he was visiting Vienna that he decided to look for someone to help him with organizing his life. He had come to feel affection for this city, older than both Austria and the Habsburg monarchy, and he spent a great deal of time there. Up to this point he had employed a housekeeper to assist him with simple chores,

such as copying letters and filing. Now Alfred needed a highly qualified private secretary to help him with his letter writing and records.
He placed an ad in a Viennese newspaper: "Wealthy, highly educated,
elderly gentleman seeks lady of mature age, versed in languages, as
secretary and supervisor of household."

The "elderly gentleman" was not yet past his forty-third year,
and the lady he was seeking would need to be able to write letters
in five languages as well as be versed in history, literature, and preferably music. She should also be able to cook.

One of the many responses drew his special attention, since both
the handwriting and the elegant choice of words indicated an unusually qualified applicant. She was none other than the Countess
Bertha Sofia Felitas Kinsky von Chinic und Tettau, who stated that
she was presently employed as governess for the daughters of the
Baroness von Suttner. She was thirty-three years old and unmarried.

The Kinskys were one of the most aristocratic families in Austria, and though Bertha's father was a poor military man in Vienna,
her way of expressing herself and her bearing were characteristically
upper class. Accustomed as she was to move in Vienna's finest drawing rooms, she was well suited to take care of necessary entertainment
duties as well.

After a brief exchange of letters, in which he explained that he
was looking for someone willing to live in Paris, Alfred was convinced that Bertha Kinsky's qualifications were indeed more than
adequate. The image he had formed of her seemed to match some
ideal (an ideal which Russian women, as we have seen, lived up to
more than women of other nationalities). The eagerness with which
Alfred answered Bertha's letters shows he had a premonition of what
she would come to mean to him.

Aristocratic or not, Bertha Kinsky had not led a life of ease, as
she states with complete honesty in her memoirs.[1] After a difficult
childhood, necessity forced her to enter into service with the wealthy
von Suttners. The family's young son, Arthur, fell deeply in love
with Bertha, seven years his senior, but his mother opposed any
thought of marriage between them, not only because of their difference in age, but because of the meager dowry Bertha would bring.
When the Baroness read Alfred's advertisement in the Vienna news-

---

[1] Bertha von Suttner's *Memoiren* [Memoirs] were published in 1909; an English
translation appeared a year later.

paper, she immediately saw a way of resolving conflict, and convinced Bertha to apply for the position. Once Alfred and Bertha had agreed on her salary, she left for Paris without further delay.

When Bertha arrived, she knew little more about her new boss other than that he was wealthy and had invented dynamite. From their correspondence, she had also learned that he had substantial literary and philanthropical interests and that he led a secluded and lonely life. What he said about loneliness seems to have struck a chord in her.

Alfred met her train at the Gare de l'Est, and as they climbed into his carriage he told her that his house at Avenue Malakoff was being remodeled. He had therefore taken the liberty of reserving her a suite at the Grand Hotel on the Boulevard des Capucines.

Bertha was pleasantly surprised by her new employer. "Alfred made a highly agreeable impression," she wrote later. "The 'elderly' gentleman the ad had prepared me for was nothing like the man I met: born in 1833, he was then forty-three years old, somewhat under average height, with a dark full beard, his face animated only by a mild glance from his blue eyes, his voice showing more melancholy than cynicism. Alternately sad and humorous — that was his nature. Little wonder Byron had become his favorite poet."

Their first meeting delighted them both. In her employer Bertha encountered a polite and witty escort, and Alfred saw she was as beautiful as he had imagined. From existing photographs of Bertha we know what he saw: an oval face with classic features under a broad-brimmed hat; her dark, thick hair wound into a bun. Her expressive eyes sparkled with humor and life. She wore her dresses tight, emphasizing the slimness of her waist.

It is tempting to speculate that he wrote the following passage from *Nemesis* based on his first meeting with Bertha:

> CENCI: There is something magnificent in that girl's nature.
> An aristocrat from the top of her head down to her toes,
> with a latent passion in her soul that could drive her to
> limitless love or limitless hate. Captivating in both her
> proud defiance as well as her gentle humor.
>
> [Act I, scene viii]

According to Bertha's diary, they had breakfast in the dining room of the hotel, after which they set out in Alfred's carriage toward

Avenue Malakoff. Bertha also described the drive to Alfred's house: "We drove along the Champs-Elysées — it was the time of day when people went for walks . . . a multitude of carts with fragrant violets whose aroma filled the air. The sun's rays played with *Rond Point's* shimmering fountains and made the carriage's lanterns and harnesses sparkle."

How much Alfred would be paying Bertha as a salary is not known, but it was probably considerably more than the parsimonious wages usually paid in the Germanic countries at this time. The house at Avenue Malakoff also pleased her. She wrote in her memoirs that she especially liked his well-stocked library that catered to the most varied tastes.

After visiting the house, they went toward the Bois de Boulogne, where their conversation became more lively. Bertha later wrote to her mother in Vienna: "Because of all the letters we had exchanged, we did not at all feel as though we were strangers to each other."

The normally taciturn Alfred began a spirited conversation with Bertha, describing to her in detail his present experiments. For once he did not have to force himself to sound light-hearted. In Bertha he had found an inspiring conversational partner.

Bertha was still some years away from the crusading work for peace that would later earn her both world renown and a Nobel Peace Prize, but she doubtless listened very closely when the "dynamite king" shared his views of the "wretched trade" that the production of war materiel constituted. Moral considerations, he declared, would always be subordinate to national interests.

He also told Bertha that the art of war was just beginning. Only when it had reached its completion would the deterrent elements be such that all nations would be forced to live in peace. On another occasion, according to Bertha's diary, Alfred expressed something similar: "I would like to invent a substance or a machine so frightfully effective and devastating that it would forever make wars altogether impossible." Such were Alfred's thoughts seventy-five years before the nuclear sword of Damocles would hang over the world.

Bertha notes in her memoirs that much of Alfred Nobel's conversation centered around means of destruction — despite the fact that the latter part of the nineteenth century, with the exception of the brief Franco-Prussian War, was a peaceful time in Europe. Alfred firmly believed that while dynamite and blasting gelatin might have military uses, their true function was in peaceful endeavors. Another decade would pass, however, before the two of them would begin a serious and involved exchange of opinions on these questions.

From that first day, Alfred was convinced that in Bertha he had at last found an intellectual equal; Bertha, for her part, was deeply impressed by her employer's serious manner and articulateness. After she had bid Alfred good night, she wrote in her diary: "To speak with him about the world and people, about life and art, about problems of the moment or eternal problems, was an exquisite pleasure."

Sometime over the next few days, Alfred handed his new employee the poem he had written in his youth that began, "You say I am an enigma." He did so mumbling apologies about it being the result of "a lonely man's hobby." Bertha was bewildered. One moment he played the part of a moody poet, the next he was an energetic industrial leader with grandiose plans for the future. He tried to explain the contradiction by saying that he was a pessimist who viewed "the future of mankind with hope."

From the beginning it was clear to Bertha that he needed someone to care for him, someone who would be much more than a skilled secretary. She cannot have been totally unprepared when a day or two later, during a lunch in the Bois de Boulogne, he asked her if "her heart was taken."

As tactfully as she could, Bertha revealed that she was actually engaged to Arthur von Suttner, and had only temporarily broken off with him because of pressure from his mother. She had responded to Alfred's ad, she said, because she needed to be financially independent.

Bertha had been in Paris only a week when urgent business forced Alfred to leave the country. He was gone from May 9 to May 30, 1876. On his return, he found that Bertha had packed her things, paid the hotel, and left. He realized that it had been a mistake to leave her alone in a hotel suite. Bertha had followed her heart and returned to Arthur in Vienna. She had sold a diamond pin she'd inherited from a relative to pay her hotel bill, despite the hotel manager's assurances that Monsieur Nobel had given orders that the bill be sent to him. Bertha describes what happened in her memoirs: "I was acting as if in a dream, as if guided by an irresistible inner compulsion." She sent a bellboy to the station to buy her ticket, and an hour later she was aboard the express to Vienna.

Bertha and Arthur von Suttner were married on June 12, 1876, in a small parish church outside of Vienna, without his parents' knowledge. Ten years would pass before Arthur and his family were reconciled, making it possible for the couple to move into the family estate at Hartmannsdorf.

Alone again, Alfred was convinced he would never be able to awaken tender feelings in a "woman of the world." He was even afraid that he had appeared ridiculous to Bertha. Such was his state of mind when he met the beautiful and charming Sofie Hess, with whom he would begin a long relationship. He was prepared to seek solace wherever he could find it.

Chapter 23

CENCI: *I advise you to comply with my will, without any sign of resistance, yes, even that you meet it half-way. Lengthy experience has taught me that from a girl's resistance to a woman's devotion there is only one step. . . . My recent little admonition did not have the proper effect; but if you think that I don't have other means at my command, you are underestimating me. Blind obedience, which is where you will end up anyhow, could save you from a great deal of pain.*

Nemesis, Act I, scene x

Alfred met the twenty-year-old Sofie Hess late in the summer of 1876, at the health resort Baden bei Wien near Vienna. She was working as a salesgirl in a florist's shop. Alfred was immediately attracted to the coquettish girl, and before long a relationship began. In spite of countless ups and downs, it would last almost two decades.

In the beginning Alfred was so taken with Sofie that he would return to Baden bei Wien whenever his business allowed him to do so. His feelings toward Sofie seem to have vacillated between fatherly tenderness and sexual desire, the latter once he had overcome his apprehension about initiating a relationship with a girl twenty-three years his junior. He found Sofie's obvious interest in him touching and somewhat flattering. This was his first intimacy with a woman since his tragic love for the pharmaceutical assistant in Paris twenty years earlier.

Alfred's letters to Sofie constitute one long, continuing document, and the portrait they provide of her is of course highly subjective. Her handwriting by itself reveals that Sofie was unschooled, a fact Alfred does not hesitate to point out time and time again. Her letters were written hurriedly and mostly involve her need for money or her health. The ingratiating tone of her letters (particularly when they were requests for money) must have bothered Alfred, for she wrote as she spoke, thoughtlessly, but with a nimble tongue and an ear for gossip. His desire to educate her, to broaden her views, created an embryo of conflict that grew: Sofie detested his superior and patronizing tone.

It would be a long time before Alfred realized that his efforts to make Sofie feel at home in the world of arts and letters were wasted. His admonitions became increasingly stricter and were increasingly more resented. The relationship between Alfred and Sofie brings to mind Shaw's *Pygmalion* — except that Sofie Hess lacked Eliza Doolittle's capacity to transform herself. Alfred still dreamed of a woman who would be his equal and with whom he could exchange thoughts and impressions. Bertha Kinsky would have filled that role brilliantly. His female ideal, a woman carrying herself with easy confidence in refined milieus and conversing knowledgeably with intellectuals and artists, was so strong a conception that he did not want to be seen publicly with Sofie, a form of hypocrisy that fit well within the boundaries of acceptable conduct for powerful men of the era.

His brother Ludvig, one of the few people close to Alfred who had met Sofie, asked if Alfred had picked her up in the street. Ludvig saw her as an adventuress hoping to snare Alfred in marriage and ruin his life. In a letter dated November 8, 1878, he explains why, on a certain occasion, he had not wanted to meet Sofie: "Happiness . . . will not be found where you are now seeking it. True happiness is found only among respectable women from good families. Misfortune does demand compassion, but only womanly virtue and dignity will awaken the respect we are so willing to dedicate to a woman. Forgive me, dear Alfred, for touching upon a subject on which you have not sought my advice, but since you might find it strange I have not visited your lady friend, even though I do know her, I have refrained from doing so in order not to nourish her hopes and ambitions to bind you to her for life."

We can only speculate why Alfred didn't marry Sofie. One reason might be that he felt it wrong for an aging misanthrope to tie down a young person with an appetite for life. Another — incredible as this might sound — was that severe financial setbacks during certain periods made him feel insecure about his ability to afford her life-style. The main reason must have involved the differences in their education. When Alfred writes about Sofie's inability to raise herself up, his words are venomous — the tone of an intellectual aristocrat. Alfred was a snob in the original sense of the word, that defining someone from the middle class aspiring to a higher social or intellectual circle.

Still, between spats, their relations were warm and intimate, and when things went sour, the fault was mostly Alfred's. His letters testify to his inability to establish intimacy with more than a few people, such as his colleagues Alarik Liedbeck and Ragnar Sohlman. As he got older, Alfred increasingly isolated himself, entrenching himself more and more in his library at Avenue Malakoff.

Protective urges are sometimes an expression of the displaced need for affection. Someone as introverted as Alfred Nobel is seldom capable of giving of himself completely, or of expressing feelings of love. In fact, Nobel was generally suspicious about that which is called love. His diligent letter writing stemmed less from a need to express his tender feelings than the compulsion to hush his own anxiety about Sofie.

The ten-year period between 1883 and 1893 was his most strenuous. It is clear from his letters that Alfred was near exhaustion from all the legal battles and accidents. Sofie's extravagances were becoming increasingly a source of irritation. Ludvig died in 1888 and his beloved mother the following year. Alfred felt more rootless than he ever had. Sofie might have compensated for his sense of loss and become his life companion, but instead she begins to complain more. In letter after letter, Alfred wrote of injustices, real or imaginary, and Sofie quite reasonably tired of the subject. No longer does she bother to reassure him that he is the only one for her. She was tired of being courted by correspondence. He had denied her virtually any chance of having her own social life, since her *mode de vie* — despite Alfred's supposedly enlightened views about education for women, and his hopes that Sofie would refine herself — was essentially that of a kept woman. With a few notable exceptions, she was only permitted to see servants and her own sisters. It is hardly surprising that she grew restless and resentful.

In his letters to Sofie, Alfred expresses in great detail all that occupies and interests him: accounts, experiments, legal controversies, and so forth. Sofie's letters usually ask for money. He replies by admonishing her for her wasteful nature but continues to pay for her carriage, jewels, and expensive clothes.

Although for quite some time Alfred suspected that Sofie was not faithful to him, her cry of distress in the spring of 1891 when she learned she was pregnant with another man's child was a shock to him. His dignity was deeply wounded. With great effort of will, he managed to keep his agitation under control. In a friendly but forced tone, he even tried to console Sofie. But her pregnancy was irrefutable proof of Sofie's betrayal of trust, and Alfred felt he had no choice but to break off relations with her.

Chapter 24

The following sections contain excerpts from some of the 218 preserved and numbered letters Alfred wrote to Sofie Hess from 1878 to 1895. From a strictly biographical point of view, they are priceless, but they raise a specter that faces biographers: does anyone have the right to publish correspondence that was obviously never meant to be made public? The dilemma is complicated by the fact that Alfred expressly requested Sofie to destroy his letters immediately after reading them — a request she did not heed. Meanwhile, Sofie kept copies of all her letters to Alfred, but the only ones that still exist today date from early 1891, soon after Alfred had learned of her pregnancy. Not long after Alfred's death, the Nobel Foundation came to an agreement with Sofie, exchanging a sum of money for the letters. Sofie did not hand all of them over, however, hoping to extract more money from the foundation later — a ploy that was not successful. For its part, the foundation kept the letters a secret until 1950, when it permitted scholars and historians to view them. The day was long past when they might have harmed Nobel's name or the mission of his final will, and the view they give of his life and times is invaluable.

In the early days of their relationship, Alfred rented a villa for Sofie in Ischl, a small, attractive health resort known for its waters, in Salzkammergut, about fifty miles from Salzburg. Built in the 1870s, it was what today we would call a cultural center for theater, concerts, and literary gatherings.

Later, Alfred bought Sofie another house in Ischl, and beginning July 1, 1880, and for six years thereafter, Alfred also rented an apartment for her on Avenue d'Eylau in Paris, within easy walking distance of his residence at Avenue Malakoff. As in Ischl and Vienna, it was unthinkable for a gentleman in Paris to live openly under the same roof as his mistress. It is therefore surprising that occasionally Alfred brought Sofie not only to visit some of his acquaintances but also to visit his brothers.

Everything was arranged for Sofie's pleasure and comfort. In her Paris apartment, she had a maid, a cook, and a French companion. Alfred had employed the latter in the hope that his protegée would learn to speak French fluently. An unsigned report in the Nobel Archives reveals that the concierge of the apartment building had been questioned about Sofie's habits and life-style, most likely at the request of the jealous Alfred.

During the summer months, Alfred paid for Sofie's stays at health resorts such as Schwalback in Germany and Trouville in France. He sometimes wrote to her every day from Paris. Sofie calls him *"Der Brummbar"* (the Grumble Bear); Alfred calls her "the Troll." That pet name is also found in his private account book, in which Alfred would enter (in Swedish) all expenses large and small.

Here is one page from it:

Hats for the Troll	Frs.	300.00
Gloves for me	"	3.75
The new horse	"	8,000.00
Flowers to Madame R	"	40.00
Cloakroom attendant	"	.25
Sent to Ludvig	"	2,300,000.00
Auguste (the man servant)	"	52.00
Wine, the Troll	"	600.00

In one letter Alfred surprised Sofie by offering to take her to Stockholm with him to visit his mother. Sofie's insecurity about this got the better of her, and she developed a stomach condition. Alfred realized this was an excuse and may have decided that it was for the best.

Sofie would return to Vienna whenever her tendency to make new young male acquaintances became too irritating to Alfred, which it increasingly did. His tone grew successively sharper each time as he wants to know if the gossip he has heard about her is really just gossip. Cenci in Act II of *Nemesis* may reflect his dark thoughts:

> CENCI: I have not his young years but I don't believe that the female heart is a closed book to me. . . . If an intelligent girl must choose between a youth and a mature man, she will always prefer the older one. Her instinct tells her that the man's experience of a woman's nature is an invaluable treasure. Young women do not thrive in inexperienced hands. The love of a young man is clumsy. . . . Crazy girl! You believe that you can defy me. I have tamed wilder natures than yours, but today I wish to be gentle.

As Sofie continued to go in and out of the grandiose health resort hotels, her waste took on proportions that disturbed Alfred. His letters show his mood did not improve when she began to use the title "Mrs. Nobel." Actually he himself was the original cause for this, since he would frequently address his letters to Frau Sofie Nobel or Madame S. Nobel. An embarrassment occurred when Alfred received a congratulatory telegram from Bertha von Suttner. In a florist's shop in Vienna, the new Baroness had heard that flowers had been sent to a Madame Nobel in Nice from a Monsieur Nobel in Paris. She assumed that Alfred had married and wanted to congratulate him. Alfred lied very uncomfortably in his response to her:

> Paris
> November 6, 1888
>
> My Dear Baroness and Friend!
>
> What an ingrate this old Nobel is! Only in appearance however — because the friendship he harbors for you actually grows increasingly warmer. The closer he approaches his grave, the more he values the few human beings — men or women — who have shown him a crumb of genuine interest.
>
> How could you seriously have believed that I would have gone ahead and entered into matrimony — and done so without informing you? That would have been double high treason — against our Friendship and against Courtesy. The old bear is not yet so far gone as that.
>
> When the lady in the florist's shop made me into a married man, she did so with flowers. As for "Madame Nobel" of Nice, it was doubtlessly my sister-in-law. So there you have the explanation for my secret and mysterious marriage. Everything in our sordid world will be explained sooner or later except that magnetism of the heart, to which the same world is indebted for its life and continued existence. This magnetism is precisely what I must be lacking, since there is no Madame Alfred Nobel and since in my case Cupid's arrows have been inadequately replaced by cannons.
>
> You can see in other words that there is no *"jeune femme adorée"* either — I am quoting you literally — and it is not in that area that I believe myself able to find a remedy

for my *"nervosité anormale"* — again I am quoting — or
for my melancholy thoughts. A few delicious days at Har-
mannsdorf might possibly liberate me from them. If I
have not as yet responded to your so excellently amiable
and friendly invitation, this is for a thousand different reasons, which I would like to attempt to explain in person.
Whatever happens, I must absolutely see you very soon,
because if it doesn't happen momentarily, one never
knows if I will ever again have the pleasure and the solace
of doing so. Fate, alas, is unwilling to be transformed into
an insurance company, even though we would be willing
to offer her temptingly high premiums.

My hearty greetings to your husband! So far as you
yourself are concerned, I do not need to tell you once
more that I

remain your affectionate and brotherly friend
A. Nobel

Sofie's recklessness with money forced Alfred to intervene on
several occasions in order to prevent seizure of her goods but did
not lead him to break off his relation with her. But in his letters he
continues to call her alternately *"liebes Sofferl"* and *"liebes, süsses
Kindchen."*

Chapter 25

The first in the collection of Alfred Nobel's letters to Sofie Hess was sent from Vienna sometime in the beginning of 1878. Pressburg, where Alfred is headed, was the German name for Bratislava, the city in eastern Czechoslovakia, known for its important riverport and its chemical industries. The correspondence between Alfred and Sofie will be presented in chronological order throughout the text.

[n.d., 1878]

My dear, sweet little child,

It is already after midnight, and the directors have finally finished today's third meeting. What is occupying us to such a lively extent is the old story with which you are familiar. Tomorrow, off to Pressburg, where my presence is required. Everything has been terribly neglected, and, if it weren't so repugnant to me, I really ought to stay here even longer. But I am not comfortable in the company of these gentlemen. I long to be off and back with you. As soon as possible, I will send you a wire or write to say where and when we can meet; until then I send you a thousand hearty greetings and wish you all good things.

Your most affectionate friend
Alfred

London, Westminster Palace Hotel
May 16, 1878

Dear child,

It is one-thirty at night and the company executives have just left me, having tormented me all day with negotiations. Never have I had such need for peace and never have I longed more for such than today. Write me, if you

wish, a few calming words about your health and give me
thereby great and true joy.

Your most affectionate
Alfred

P.S. I have such a headache that I can hardly see to write.
I hope to be more fit for work tomorrow. Good night!

London, Westminster Palace Hotel
May 17, 1878

Dear child,

. . . It is only with great difficulty that I manage to find a
few free moments to write to you. Conferences with lawyers, negotiations with the Minister of the Interior, scientific debates plus consultations regarding the rebuilding of
factories take up my whole day. We begin at eight in the
morning, and I cannot go to bed until about two o'clock
at night.

Tomorrow night I hope that the negotiations here will
finish as quickly as possible. Unfortunately, this morning
I received a message about an explosion at the factory in
Scotland, which is why I have to go there.

Time passes very slowly, especially as my headache
worsens from the poor food and the putrid air. I am already rejoicing in the moment when I will be able to return. When I write that, you do understand that I say so
for totally different reasons as well.

Take good care of you, dear child, and most of all, do
not worry.

A hearty *"lebe wohl!"*

Alfred

Ardeer [Scotland]
May 17, 1878

Dear little Sofie,

Here I am sitting in my little nest with winds howling
from every direction, and my thoughts go back to our
pleasant time together recently in Paris. How are you,

dear little child, far away from your old grumbling bear?
Is your imagination spinning golden threads of the future
or does your young soul stroll through her little treasury
of memories? Or perhaps your delight in the present
cheers your day? My thoughts vainly attempt to penetrate
this riddle, but from distant lands I whisper my wish,
filled with longing, that you be well. Good night!

Alfred

Paris
August 24, 1878

. . . So many unresolved matters await me here that I
have not yet had the strength to think of anything else.
Work, work, and more work is therefore the order of the
day. . . .

Paris
August 25, 1878

. . . It does not take much acumen to guess who put together the French telegram you sent me. He writes rather
well but makes some mistakes anyhow.

I am spending almost the whole day at home, working.
Time passes slowly because I feel very lonely. I have gotten out of the habit of participating in society life and am
more and more shying away from contact with people.

You will probably not believe me when I assure you
that yesterday I sat at my work table all evening and will
do the same today. If you don't believe I am telling you
the truth, it might do your conscience good. I have never
pretended to be a seeker of hearts and have therefore no
obligations. You on the other hand give so many assurances that one could almost believe them to be true, if it
weren't for that somebody who writes your French
telegrams. . . .

Paris
August 26, 1878

. . . Enlighten me — if you can — as to who wrote the

first French telegram for you. This is a sore point between us which has strongly affected my trust. Honestly speaking, my dear child, you ought always to be completely truthful with me, even when you find it difficult.

Now I don't want to say anything that could dampen your good spirits. I do not have anything cheerful to report since I feel very lonely and am brooding a great deal. The fact of the matter is that I have a feeling that all your thoughts remain in Wiesbaden.

Your latest letter — written after midnight since you obviously could not find time before then — gave the impression of having been written in remorse after some injustice you had done me. But I hold you dear in spite of your not liking me anymore. I also wish you a quick and complete recovery. In your pursuit of joy, do not forget the decency and dignity without which no woman can be a good wife or a true mother.

From your second letter I can clearly read between the lines that things are going well for you and that my absence seems to give you more happiness than sorrow. For me it is the other way around. Life here seems very dismal to me, and I feel more lonely and abandoned every day.

P.S. My brother-in-law and my sister-in-law's sister have arrived. I think I have to undergo the torture of having them stay with me. There is nothing more repugnant on earth than uninvited guests. . . .

Paris
August 28, 1878

. . . Today it has been three days since I had a letter from you and because of that I am not without anxiety. But perhaps you are having such a good time that you cannot find time to write. In that you are not totally wrong, because one must enjoy life in one's youth. Later come the sorrows and the broodings. Just see to it that, despite your pleasures, you take care of your health because without it life has little value.

[Alarik] Liedbeck arrived a few days ago. He sat beside

me from morning to night, forcing me to holler until I go deaf myself. Today, for instance, he arrived at eight-thirty in the morning and not until a short while ago — at nine o'clock at night — could I get rid of him. Perhaps you can imagine how tired I am. Still, I have to go on working since a lot of unanswered letters have been accumulating. . . .

Chapter 26

After several years of searching, Alfred thought he had finally found the right person to introduce his inventions in France: Paul François Barbe. Barbe had contacted him in Hamburg as far back as the fall of 1867. Together they formed a company in France. Alfred received his shares free of charge against the transferral of his patent, and a contract between them directed that he would receive half of the company's profits.

Alfred was anxious that his new partner understand that delay-causing accidents sometimes occurred, and that, in most instances, they were due to human error. Diplomatically, he also let Barbe know that before every important decision, he must first acquire Alfred's approval. The Frenchman did not always keep to this part of their agreement. "A nimble man," Alfred once described Barbe, "with excellent capacity for work but whose conscience is more elastic than rubber. It is a pity, since his combination of sense and energy are so rare."

When the Franco-Prussian War broke out in 1870, Barbe alerted French authorities that this new explosive called dynamite could be of great military use. As a consequence, he argued, the right to manufacture it ought to be approved quickly. Barbe had good connections with some influential deputies in the Assemblée Nationale and his request was granted almost immediately. He was even able to procure a promise of sixty thousand francs in government money toward the establishment of a dynamite factory, even though the government had a monopoly on the manufacture and marketing of explosives.

During neither the Crimean War nor the Franco-Prussian conflict did Alfred ever — publicly or privately — give any hint as to what he thought of his inventions' wartime use. Yet we know from Bertha von Suttner that he thought about their destructive capacity. Perhaps during actual wartime these thoughts were so frightening that he suppressed them.

Under Paul Barbe's forceful management, the manufacture of dynamite was begun in Paulilles near the Spanish border, an isolated spot chosen for security reasons. In spite of difficulties created by the French authorities, business was good. By the summer of 1872,

Alfred had collected 189,283 francs in profit — even after 10 percent went toward construction costs, and 6 percent was paid out as a return on invested capital. From his portion of the profits Alfred gave 25,000 francs to Barbe to show, as he said in a letter to Alarik Liedbeck dated August 10, 1872, his appreciation for "the immense work Barbe has done at the expense of having to neglect his other business." He continues: "The marketing is going very well here. We are hoping to collect even larger profits this year unless something totally unforeseen happens. The governmental problems go on but do not hinder us. They will have to give in."

Alfred was forced to admit an abominable war had facilitated his successful debut in France, but he hoped dynamite would soon be used for peaceful purposes. Reports of more and more sales were coming in from one country after another. Scotland in particular was contributing considerably to Alfred's coffers. The value of the shares therein had multiplied tenfold in less than four years.

On the heels of Barbe's success with French authorities, he and Alfred planned to expand operations, not only in France but in the rest of Europe. Experts considered their factory in Paulilles to be a model operation. A saltpeter (nitric acid) and sulfur factory (which in 1880 would be supplemented by a nitroglycerine plant) was built after lengthy consultations between Alfred and Alarik Liedbeck. To prevent any more accidents, they were determined to take full advantage of all their dearly bought knowledge.

As soon as all formalities had been taken care of, Barbe began to launch Alfred's inventions in his own country with matchless energy. He was well prepared for the job. He had first read about Alfred's demonstrations in the German mine districts and had taken notice. His own family business consisted of a mechanical shop, a foundry, and, not the least, iron mines. Alfred's explosive oil and dynamite, Barbe knew, would be invaluable. He was an ambitious engineer, and his experience as an officer in the French army had given him extensive knowledge of cannons, howitzers, and mortars.

Barbe's organizing skill and administrative talent were also extremely useful. The French market would be significant first and foremost because of the high price of gunpowder. Due to the state monopoly on manufacture and sales of explosives in France, gunpowder was three times as expensive as in Germany. Alfred therefore knew that the prospects for the considerably less expensive dynamite were very promising. Emperor Napoleon III had appointed a commission to ascertain the advantages and disadvantages of the new blasting substance. Alfred knew from experience that nothing better proved the efficiency of dynamite than a single demonstration. Before long Barbe and Alfred began concentrating on their strengths: Alfred focused on the technical development while Barbe undertook the administrative guidance of the company and cultivated his good contacts in the government.

Their success was greater than they could have imagined. Not only did they receive permission to manufacture dynamite but also the right, despite the state monopoly, to sell it. Alfred must have felt that at last a partnership was working out well — Barbe was doing in France what Colonel Shaffner had done in the United States — using connections — but this time the results were profitable.

Alfred may have found a competent business partner in Barbe, but the two men never did become close friends. Alfred was full of respect for Barbe's professionalism and industriousness, yet he kept his distance. He wrote Robert: "[Barbe] has a sharp technical overview, is an excellent businessman and a clear-sighted finance person, and understands how to use people and get out of them all the independent work of which they are capable. He himself has a capacity for activity and work that is unbelievable." What Alfred goes on to say may explain his reservations: "On the other hand, he is not trustworthy, except when his own interests coincide with those of the other side. This is not a pretty character flaw but, in spite of it, I do not know anybody I would rather see as co-executive, with Ludvig, of our Russian oil company. If he were, all its financial difficulties would disappear. *C'est un géant* [He's a giant] — that was said recently about him by one of the most respected bankers and businessmen in Paris. It is true."

Describing Barbe as a "giant" might be true, but since his business ethics did not measure up to Alfred's strict standards, Alfred never brought him fully into his confidence. His letters always began "Mon cher Barbe" or "Cher Barbe" — rather than "Paul" — and his closing phrases are impersonal and conventional. In short, Alfred tolerated his business partner's manipulations and greed. It was the latter that would in time lead to Barbe's downfall.

Paul Barbe was not the only person to whom Alfred would delegate financial responsibilities. He also valued highly Dr. Gustaf Aufschlager, who had made sizable contributions to the main company in Europe as well as to the business in other parts of the world. He especially won praise for his achievements in the increasingly important South American market. Yet another adviser was Julius

Bandmann in Hamburg, until Bandmann disagreed with Alfred's decision in 1873 to move his main office to Paris. Bandmann had been determined to make the Krümmel factory the main supplier of dynamite to the whole world and insisted, with a stubbornness that Alfred did not care for, that the explosive was now safe enough to be transported practically anywhere on earth. Bandmann opposed manufacture in other countries.

A third adviser was an old friend of Alfred's father, Nils Adolf von Rosen, who had vast and valuable international contacts. There were others, such as the Winkler brothers in Hamburg and Alfred's first financial backer, John Wilhelm Smitt, but as time went on he consulted with them less and less.

The most influential adviser of all was Alarik Liedbeck. Alfred honored only Liedbeck and two other persons by calling them "friend" in his letters: the technical consultant Isidor Trauzl and the factory head at Ardeer, George McRoberts. Alfred looked upon technicians and researchers as his equals. Financial bigwigs and stock exchange magnates would never be afforded the same intimacy.

During the years 1873–1885, Alfred and Barbe were actually laying the foundation for a multinational empire. Because Barbe was playing an increasingly central part in the planning, Alfred asked him to move from the south of France to Paris. Once in Paris, he would be able to keep an eye on him.

Corpulent and charismatic, Paul Barbe had an almost square face with a drooping moustache and always wore a pince-nez on a black cord. Barbe's work methodology was to concentrate on what we today call profit maximizing; caring about the needs of those working for the company was secondary at best. But Alfred would never renounce his concern for the individual, and increasingly the difference between how they treated employees became more glaring.

It is clear from Alfred's letters that he had trouble following Barbe's quick shuffles between truths, half-truths, and untruths. What worried him most was Barbe's indifference to what people might think of his methods. Contempt for others, Alfred felt, often points to contempt for oneself. Alfred would eventually keep his personal contacts with Barbe to the absolute minimum. He did not want to be sullied by his unscrupulousness, even if he found that it suited his purposes. It didn't. Without informing Alfred, Barbe was speculating with huge sums belonging to the company (just how he was able to do so wasn't clear until immediately after his death).

Examples of Barbe's manipulations abound. In 1881 Alfred was offered the opportunity to buy a smaller competitive firm, Société Nationale des Poudres et Dynamite. The owner, Geo Vian, had offered Barbe a generous compensation if and when the business was completed. Barbe consequently pretended neutrality when the question of whether or not to buy the company came up within the Nobel board of directors. For a number of reasons, the deal never went through, though Barbe's game of intrigue did become known. Another time, Alfred discovered that some engineers at the Italian-Swiss dynamite company Barbe ran had been allowed to moonlight at a competitor's company. Alfred never forgave Barbe for the betrayal.

Before Barbe's death, the rift between him and Alfred had become unbridgeable. By 1882 Alfred had seen through Barbe's double dealings. On April 15 he wrote him: "You have recently originated a system which by necessity will lead to the impoverishment of most, if not all, of the dynamite companies. . . . When honesty disappears, good relations die . . . and all that remains is a fight to the finish."

Barbe escaped his creditors by taking his own life.

CENCI: Nothing can be truer than that the end justifies the means.

BEATRICE: Or that abominable acts unjustify the man.

[*Nemesis*, Act III, scene vii]

Chapter 27

Alfred began his European empire in Germany because he deemed the economic situation for his blasting oil to be especially favorable. For one thing, German mining operations were extensive; for another, railroad construction was just beginning. In Hamburg he had come in contact with the Swedish-born brothers Wilhelm and Theodor Winkler of Winkler & Company. Times were bad and trade with Sweden was becoming less profitable, so the brothers were searching for a new product. In Alfred's blasting oil they had found what they had been seeking. They introduced Alfred to Christian Eduard Bandmann, a business lawyer in Hamburg who had good connections in the German mining industry. Alfred registered Alfred Nobel & Company in Hamburg's trade register on June 20, 1865. This was his first foreign company, and the brothers Winkler, along with Bandmann, were his partners. Bandmann invested 25,000 marks; the brothers Winkler apparently did not contribute any venture capital.

The Krümmel factory was situated near the Elbe River in an isolated hilly section very similar to the environment of Winter Bay. The ground consisted largely of the sterile sand called kieselguhr that would prove so valuable to his blasting oil a year later.

It would take several months before Alfred received all necessary permits; on November 8, 1865, he received a list of the conditions. He was asked to ensure that the nitration-producing process be conducted at an adequate distance from the manufacture of the ignition caps. Moreover, the factory premises needed to be "surrounded by natural or artificial earth mounds at least fifteen feet high and at least twenty feet wide at their base." If the conditions were met, "the manufacturer Alfred Bernhard Nobel of Hamburg" could assume that his application had been granted.

Originally, it had been Alfred's resolution never to risk any of his own money over and above what it cost for the acquisition of patent rights, but in Krümmel he was forced to bend his own rule. To start production, he had no choice but to invest. After just a month in Germany, he pledged his shares in the Swedish nitroglycerine joint-stock company to J. W. Smitt in Stockholm. By so doing, he freed up 25,000 marks, which constituted his only working capital during the early period.

The Winkler brothers rented him a warehouse in Hamburg's harbor and there Alfred set up a primitive laboratory. He prepared a small quantity of blasting oil and took it around to the mine districts, where he attempted to convince management and personnel of the superiority of his new explosive. His demonstrations at Dortmund, Klauthal, and Köningshütte were written up in the local papers.

The authorities in Ratzeburg (in the royal Prussian duchy of Lavenburg) were familiar with nitroglycerine's properties. One reason they had given approval was Krümmel's isolated location. The high sand ridges together with the artificial walls were thought to offer satisfactory protection. Alfred thought Krümmel's location ideal because it was located only a few miles south of Hamburg, Europe's largest port.

In a letter to Smitt dated January 9, 1866, Alfred writes: "I arrived today at Eisleben, where I have carried out large blasting demonstrations to the open-mouthed astonishment of the German *Herren,* who at first were stiff, but then soft as candle wax." In another letter to Smitt, Alfred writes that one person had declared himself willing to invest half a million marks, but that his conditions were unacceptable. Alfred wanted a free hand to run things, whatever the cost. He had opened an office in Hamburg besides establishing his private laboratory close to the factory facilities in Krümmel. The factories were rebuilt after the explosions that would occur in 1866 and 1870, and greatly expanded.

Alfred received his patent for dynamite in England, and on September 19, 1867, Sweden granted one. The American patent was granted on May 26, 1868.

Alfred's letters from around this time are filled with an uncustomary vivacity concerning the strategic plans for his dynamite empire. Few inventions have had such practical importance as dynamite. Between 1871 and 1874 production quadrupled. In a lecture to the Society of Industrial Arts in London in May, 1875, Alfred made the exact figures available:

1871	785 tons
1872	1350 tons
1873	2050 tons
1874	3120 tons

With the precision that was so characteristic, Alfred compiled a list of all the factories he had established or helped to establish between 1865 and 1873:

Winter Bay, Sweden 1865
Krümmel, near Hamburg 1865
Lysaker, near Oslo 1865
Little Ferry [New Jersey], USA, destroyed 1870 . . 1866
Zamky, near Prague 1868
Rock Canyon, near San Francisco 1868
Hangö, Finland 1870
Ardeer, near Glasgow 1871
Paulilles, near Port-Vendres, France 1871
McCainsville, now Kenvil, USA 1871
Schleebuch, near Köln [Cologne] 1872
Galdacano, Spain 1872
Giant Powder Works, near New York City 1873
Isleten, Switzerland 1873
Avigliana, near Turin, Italy 1873
Trafaria, near Lisbon, Portugal 1873
Pressburg, now Bratislava 1873

The largest, and for a long time most profitable, enterprise in his group of companies was the Krümmel factory. When in 1875 he made a sales projection for 1877, he estimated that 1,200 tons would be sold, 400 tons through export. By comparison, the English dynamite company that year was projected to export only 58 tons.

As a concession toward the Austro-Hungarian clientele, the German company was called Deutsch Oesterreich-Ungarische Dynamit-Actien-Gesellschaft. But soon, Austria and Hungary were dropped from the company name, and it became Deutsche Dynamit-Actien-Gesellschaft, or DAG for short. As they had agreed, Paul Barbe (who spoke German surprisingly fluently) kept a watchful eye on the company for Alfred. Barbe reported to Alfred that the competition had become stiffer now that their own companies were competing with each other. This would bring the prices down. In November 1878, Barbe wrote to Alfred suggesting that he merge the English company with the German, thereby increasing the dividend from 15 to 20 percent. "That way you would prevent hidden competition."

Alfred's worries increased when the competitive situation intensified at the beginning of the 1880s. In Germany alone, three new
dynamite companies were established: Dresdner Dynamit-Fabrik,
Kölner Dynamit-Fabrik, and Deutsche Sprengstoff. In 1886 Alfred
was again having to demonstrate both his financial talent and his
knack for diplomacy. He managed to unite his three competitors
with his German and English companies in a cartel. Their agreement
included a division of the markets, and Alfred guided the complicated
negotiations through to their conclusion.

Twenty years after inventing his initial igniter, Alfred laid the
foundation for what he himself christened the Nobel Dynamite Trust
Company Ltd. The dynamite companies included within it would
in time each become highly successful and, one after another, important parts of chemical conglomerates such as I. G. Farben in
Germany, ICI in England, and Du Pont in the U.S.

During the years of transition, the German company was called
Dynamit A/G, vormals Alfred Nobel & Company. The share capital
would rise from 5 million marks in 1888 to 36 million by 1918. In
1926, the German Nobel group merged with the English company
and I. G. Farben Industrie A/G, and the main office was moved from
Hamburg to Cologne. By the time World War II broke out in 1939,
more than three thousand people were employed by the company,
and the share capital was valued at 47 million Reichsmarks. (The
foreign exchange market stabilized after the the post–World War I
inflationary period.)

The Krümmel factory was leveled during an air attack toward
the end of the war, with bombs that ironically were loaded with
Alfred's explosives. Krümmel was then one of Germany's largest
ammunition factories, with more than nine thousand employees.
How many were killed during the raid is not known; all that remained
after the massive air strike was the administration offices and a bronze
bust of Alfred.

After the war, there were attempts to establish a paper factory
on the site of the ruins, but the Allied military command vetoed the
idea. Three decades later, Krümmel became the site of Germany's
largest atomic reactor. It was chosen for the same reason Alfred had
first been attracted to it: the isolation and the high sand ridges.

Chapter 28

August 29, 1878

. . . I am hard at work on the projects we spoke of before I left. All the people running in and out of here make it hard to concentrate, however. I have to go into town to attend a meeting at the French company. But immediately upon my return, I will write to you. . . .

P.S. A propos: "Monsieur" is written with an "n" and not "Mosieur," as you write.

Paris
August 29, 1878

. . . So it was a lady who wrote that French telegram for you. Well, that's men, men, men for you! . . .

I am busier than ever but hope in the future to organize my business so I will have more free time. . . .

If you are a good girl and get well quickly, I will try to arrange for you to accompany me on my trip to Stockholm. But in order for you to do so, the main condition is good health, which I wish you with all my heart.

Your old Grumble Bear

Paris
August 30, 1878

. . . As my thoughts are flying to you, I would like to do the same. How much more pleasant the peace and quiet of the country than this city life, where one runs into people for whom one has not the least sympathy but whom, for the sake of convention, one must greet courteously. This makes me exceedingly nervous as it impedes my work. I am devoting much time and energy to modernizing the

business and hope that the result will be quickly forth-
coming. But every improvement takes time-consuming
work, which is why you have to forgive me if these next
few days I will write only little brief letters. . . .

Day in and day out people come and go as if my house
were a hotel and this gives me too little peace for
work . . . .

Today again I only have time to write you a few words
since I have been outside the city for some explosion experiments. I just got back and must go without delay to
the theater with my brother's relatives. . . .

Paris
September 1, 1878

. . . What a pity you were not with me at the theater last
night. It was an excellent play and masterfully performed.

I need to know what you have decided, and it is urgent,
since I am just about ready to leave for Stockholm. Otherwise the work goes well, and it would proceed even
better were I not constantly disturbed by people demanding my attention.

A letter just arrived from my brother Robert. He is in
Petersburg and may come here for a visit. You would like
him because once he trusts someone, he can be most
warm and friendly. He will probably come here with
Emanuel. . . .

Paris
September 2, 1878

. . . Yesterday's letter from you worried me because you
seem to be feeling really poorly.

As for me, I am preparing for my trip to Stockholm.
While I am gone, I suppose you will be courted a great
deal. That has probably been happening for some time,
but like the wise child you are, you keep quiet about it. I
don't want to be a pest, but I would very much like to
know who has taught you the elegant expression "dar-
ling." An English lady, or perhaps an English gentleman?

Or have you learned it from a German who speaks English?

In spite of it being Sunday yesterday, I stayed at home, working all day. Today I actually already have a few sketches of the new machines ready, but such things are hardly of interest to you. I am absolutely convinced that my life is enormously more tedious than yours. My brother's relatives are pure torture, and it will be good to have peace and quiet around me again. . . .

Take care so you don't catch a cold and think at least once a day of your affectionate

Grumble Bear

Chapter 29

England, Alfred wrote Robert, was "a jewel worth as much as the rest of the world." As the most industrialized country of that era, the potential market for new cost-saving explosives was extraordinarily large. For that reason, even though he was constantly traveling during the second half of the 1860s, overseeing the establishment of new enterprises on the continent, he kept visiting England regularly. His "dynamite travel," which entailed demonstrations, was written up in detail in the trade press. On July 14, 1867, in Merstham, Surrey, his demonstration was as dramatic as any of his "performances" in New York. A crate with several pounds of dynamite was thrown from a high ledge down into the quarry where he himself stood; then he placed a crate with the same contents onto a bonfire. Nothing happened, of course.

Alfred had already received his English patent for dynamite in May 1867, thanks to the superb work of his attorney Robert Newton, whose specialty was patent cases. Alfred was so impressed by Newton's ability to move things along through the British bureaucracy that he began an alliance with him that would last many years.

His meeting with Newton had been arranged by a business lawyer named Orlando Webb, an import agent and chairman of the board of directors of a Welsh mining company. Webb had become so convinced of the new explosive's commercial potential that he started an import company. Before long Alfred hired him as his representative in London. Webb repaid Alfred's confidence in him by suggesting he turn British Dynamite into a limited liability company. Together they struggled to overcome obstacles put in their way by Parliament and the bureaucracy.

In December of 1867, Alfred wrote an article in the *Times* in which he emphasized again that the true causes of almost every explosive accident were carelessness and ignorance. To be safe, people simply needed to be informed. He also pointed out that his explosive substances were far more effective than gunpowder. What was most controversial about the article, which received wide attention, were Alfred's insinuations about who was really behind the British protectionist attitude.

That person was Sir Frederic Abel (1827–1902), chief chemist of the war ministry, who ten years earlier had been granted a patent for a manufacture process of guncotton (or cottonpowder), and saw in dynamite a potential competitor.

England's protectionist legislation had delayed dynamite's victory march and led to a most curious state of affairs. Orlando Webb was forced to import blasting oil in wine bottles packed in wooden crates bearing the label "light wine from the Rhine country." To get around the transport prohibition, Webb asked friends and acquaintances coming to his quarries in Wales to bring along cartridges of dynamite in their luggage. Alfred did the same when he visited the mining districts. Had they been caught, they could have spent up to two years in prison.

Then on August 11, 1869, the British parliament passed the Nitroglycerine Act, which prohibited the "manufacture, import, marketing, and transport of nitroglycerine and all substances of whatever kind that might contain the same within Great Britain." (Before this, it had mainly been transportation of nitroglycerine that was illegal.) This law effectively halted any plans for expanding manufacture of dynamite in England, which Sir Frederic Abel had correctly feared that Alfred would do. With mounting anxiety, doubtlessly, Abel had noted that more and more foreign explosives were making their way into England, not only by way of London but through Glasgow.

Alfred was in Glasgow meeting with mine owners and interested financiers when the new law was passed. Having had trouble finding willing investors in London, Alfred was concentrating his efforts on attracting enterprising Scottish industrialists, such as Charles Tennant, who later became his partner.

Alfred felt that the new law was nothing less than a bull of excommunication against his explosive, since it banned any product that used nitroglycerine as an ingredient. However, a colleague, John Downie, found a loophole: dispensation might be granted in a few cases following a direct appeal to the minister of the interior. With the help of the experienced Webb in London, Downie wrote a clever petition to the home secretary. He soon received a terse and somewhat curious answer: the explosive substances might be permitted if they were manufactured at the site where they were to be used. It was the transport that was deemed too risky.

When Alfred set out to discover what or who might lie behind this strange reversal, the name of Frederic Abel came up. Alfred learned that Abel owned shares in a company that was manufacturing explosives using Abel's own patented process, a blatant example of conflict of interest. He decided to look up Abel, since he was obviously directing the explosive-substance policies in England and Scotland from behind the scenes.

The details of their meeting are not known, but a short truce followed until Abel again betrayed Alfred's trust over a patent question. This time Alfred took off the gloves. In a letter to the minister of the interior, he went after Abel:

> The eminent advocate for guncotton in England and the foremost adviser to the House of Commons in dynamite questions seems to have exaggerated the dangers of this explosive. If it were as tremendously risky as he insists it is, it must be noted as a wonderful coincidence that no accident has occurred with such large quantities as have been employed. And if guncotton is as harmless as he believes, how come the insignificant amounts of this substance that have been used have caused (in Austria and other places) accidents of such great numbers and seriousness?

On May 20, 1868, during one of his visits to English mining districts, Alfred wrote to J. W. Smitt that with sufficient capital behind him, he would "knock the guncotton off the British market in two years."

Not long after Alfred had delivered his letter, Sir Vivian Majendie was named Inspector of Explosives. Lengthy negotiations with Majendie followed, and Alfred and Downie were granted permission to start production on the condition that they adhere to a long list of precise and rigorous safety rules.

After four long years, the road to the English market was finally open: the long-planned British Dynamite Company Ltd. was founded in 1870, with John Downie as managing executive. Alfred relinquished the chairmanship of the board to the shipbuilder Charles Randolph, part owner of the company at which Downie had begun his career.

During the negotiations that preceded the founding of the company, Alfred engaged in a few controversial moves. In two letters, dated June 17 and June 20 respectively, he suggested to Downie two production scenarios. The first involved producing 200 tons per year and allocating 15,000 pounds in share capital; the second involved increasing annual production to 500 tons and the amount of share capital to 20,000 pounds. That Alfred was tightening the screws or raising the ante became obvious when he presented his ultimatum: either Downie would find financiers willing to invest 20,000 pounds, or Alfred would pull out.

Moreover, should Downie raise the capital, Alfred outlined precisely how the money was to be allocated: 8,000 pounds for the building of a factory; 5,000 for dynamite storage; and 2,000 for storage of raw materials. The remaining 5,000 pounds would be working capital. For his own part, Alfred wanted eventually to be paid 11,000 pounds for the use of his dynamite patent. As usual he did not want to risk his own money but still demanded half ownership. He would also demand another 1,000 pounds as compensation for costs incurred in obtaining his English patent. Alfred also made it clear that his commitment was not binding. He reserved the legal and moral right to make an agreement with another willing and financially secure partner if he should so choose.

Despite the rigors of Alfred's conditions, Downie was enticed by the 10 percent commission he would draw from Alfred's share. He understood that Alfred was trying to find the price for dynamite that the market could bear.

Alfred and his Scottish partners formed the British Dynamite Company Ltd. in 1871 with 24,000 pounds in share capital. According to the "Prospectus of Dynamite Manufacturing Company of Great Britain, Ltd." that John Downie sent out, it was proposed that the capital be divided into 900 A-shares and 1,500 B-shares, each in the amount of ten pounds. The 900 A-shares would go to Alfred for the patent rights he was putting at the company's disposal. The A-shares would yield 6 percent in dividends, and at first Alfred wanted half of the profits, but he finally agreed to three-eighths. The Scottish partners received five-eighths — on the condition that he would be assured the right to buy shares under the same conditions as the financiers.

The original proposal also contained a passage Alfred found unacceptable: the Scottish financiers wanted to place an embargo on Alfred's future patents having nothing to do with explosives. Annoyed, Alfred wrote to Downie: "Why not on the patents of my children also? Of course I would not dream of doing business on such terms."

Such declarations of independence were becoming a common

theme in Alfred's financial negotiations. He wanted at all cost to avoid becoming dependent on other people's money, hence his insistence that his economic obligations be strictly limited to his part of the share capital. The financial structure of British Dynamite bears Alfred's imprint, and there is good reason to remember it. In none of the dynamite companies did Alfred own a majority of the shares, and with time his share in each different company dropped to between 3 and 10 percent.

When the formalities had been concluded, a suitable site for the dynamite factory needed to be chosen. Alfred and Downie found it in Ardeer, on the Firth of Clyde on Scotland's western coast. The location was as secluded as Krümmel and Winter Bay. Virtually without vegetation, Ardeer was a windy, rainy place hidden behind tall sand dunes. As Alfred wrote to Sofie: "If I had not my work here, Ardeer would certainly be the most disconsolate place in the world. Picture unending bleak uninhabitable dunes. Only the rabbits find sustenance here, by eating a substance that quite unjustifiably goes by the name of grass, and of which one sees only a few traces. It is a sandy desert, where the wind always blows and often howls, filling one's ears with sand which also drifts about the rooms like a fine drizzle. The factory is like a huge village, and most of the buildings have concealed themselves behind the sandy hills."

Under Alarik Liedbeck's experienced guidance, the new factory was constructed in Ardeer with machinery designed by Liedbeck himself. When this model industrial complex was completed (it eventually consisted of forty-five buildings and employed hundreds of workers) 5.5 million pounds of explosives would be manufactured per year, 2.2 million of which consisted of different kinds of dynamite, and 1,500 tons of nitroglycerine.

John Downie noted with justifiable pride that the orders soon exceeded their wildest expectations. Alfred expressed his own satisfaction, spiced with some sarcasm, in an inauguration speech to his colleagues on the board: "Well, gentlemen, I have now given you a company that has all expectations of being successful, even with the worst mismanagement on the part of the esteemed board of directors. . . ."

George McRoberts was appointed as factory manager, and toward the end of the 1880s he was succeeded by a Swede, C. O. Lundholm. Lundholm served with such distinction that to this day the road leading up to the factory carries his name. He later became a technical advisor to the Nobel Dynamite Trust Company.

The years immediately following the founding of the Ardeer factory brought no resolution to Alfred's difficulties in the British Isles. The press's sensationalistic coverage of new accidents led to an absolute prohibition against transporting nitroglycerine products on English railroads. The law stayed on the books for two decades. During that long period, all transport had to be carried out by horse and carriage "and the man with a cart loaded with dynamite," to use Alfred's own expression, "was Ishmael on the royal highway."

Not only had the authorities adopted a hostile attitude toward his explosive products but the customers had, too: they thought his dynamite was too weak. Alfred took their criticism seriously, since he was aware that his personnel had reduced the blasting effect in order to ensure greater safety. Alfred holed up for weeks on end in his Ardeer research laboratory, which until then had been used mainly for simple quality control. Alfred had often attacked a problem with such ferocity. Once, when told that the workers in the coal mines at Kilwinning were using blasting oil in their lamps instead of ordinary rapeseed oil, Alfred became alarmed. Sequestering himself in his laboratory, he quickly designed a mine lamp that used risk-free fuel and still gave off a strong light. However, all he could do was try to discourage those who persisted in using blasting oil to grease the wheels of the coal trams.

Tragedy struck in January of 1875. John Downie was killed in an explosion. The circumstances seemed so peculiar that Alfred decided to investigate the matter himself. A load of dynamite had been returned to Ardeer with a complaint, and Downie had established that the load had been water-damaged during transport. He decided to destroy it on the spot, using the same method that Alfred often used. He started a fire and threw one cartridge after another into the flames. The process was taking a long time, so Downie grew impatient and threw a batch of cartridges into the fire. The result was a horrific explosion in which Downie was so seriously injured that he died shortly thereafter.

Alfred concluded that the dynamite had been damaged by rain during the transport and that the cartridges had begun to "bleed"; that is, the nitroglycerine had seeped out and become extremely sensitive to impact. Alfred was more convinced than ever that he must develop an explosive even safer than dynamite.

In 1875, Alfred invented blasting gelatin. With this new substance he felt he had managed to reduce the risks to a minimum. He was eager for it to be available in the marketplace but found it difficult to convince the Scottish authorities of its advantages. It would not be until 1881 that the explosive substance inspector granted permission for the manufacture of blasting gelatin at the Ardeer factory.

Chapter 30

Paris
September 2, 1878

. . . From my solitude I write a few more friendly lines, this time without preaching. Since for your sake I have shunned society life, I have never felt so alone as I do now. I keep asking myself what kind of silly little thing you are to keep torturing yourself for no reason when you could have it so good. But when it comes to feelings, however preposterous they might be, no philosophy of life can help. I have to forgive my little goose if her common sense draws the shortest straw in the feud with her emotions. . . .

I am finally rid of Liedbeck. This delights me because to yell until one's throat is bone-dry is indeed no joy. The man, whose heart is so fine and good, cannot grasp that his deafness is a great bother to others. . . .

You worry me with the tales of your gum trouble. It sounds almost as if you had a touch of my scurvy. I have warned you against using my toothbrush — which ought to be a rule everyone should follow. Some doctors insist that under no circumstances is scurvy contagious while others harbor some doubts. In any case, grape juice is said to be an effective weapon against scurvy. I drink lots of it without noticing any great improvement outside of my gums being a little healthier. Robert has just written to me that nothing is better than a grape juice treatment. He suggests that we try one together. I have written to him to say that I prefer drinking the juice at home rather than wasting my time at some health resort. . . .

Right after I got back, I was drawn into a veritable whirlpool of endless meetings. Today I have had another visit from one of my brother's relatives. He occupied all my time between eight-thirty and two in the afternoon.

If you wish to avail yourself of some good advice, make diligent use of the pills the druggist over there has

given you. For the sake of your stomach, also drink
Carlsbader or Marienbader water — that is, until you can
get Franzenquelle water. I am so overwhelmed with duties
I have not had time to write to Dr. Walter, but I will do
so tomorrow. . . .

Paris
September 16, 1878

. . . If I only sent you a telegram, it was because I have
to leave here tomorrow, and I don't know how I will
find time to finish all my work. I have a whole book of
legal papers to plow through and comment upon, and
have been working on it for two days and nights. In addition, the rheumatism has come back, causing the most
severe pain. Last night I was feeling so poorly that I had
to go to bed at eight o'clock. My assistant Fehrenbach is
unfortunately also ill, right when I need his help the
most.

In spite of all my work, I worry about your health. If
your cook is so bad, why not pay her 60 francs and let her
go? You could always eat at the hotel again. It is good of you
to try to learn a few things and thereby give me joy. Do
buy yourself a novel by Balzac called *Deux Jeunes Mariés*
[The Young Married Couple]. It is written in the form of
letters, and the language is easy to understand. . . .

Paris
September 17, 1878

. . . Why are you worrying needlessly? Have you really
not noticed how well I wish you, and that, least of all, am
I any kind of seducer? While all I want is peace and quiet,
you imagine me philandering all over the place. Can you
not, once and for all, free yourself from this mare's nest
of silly fantasies by using your common sense? . . .

I thank you warmly for the cookies, but, however well
meant, my house staff here must have made fun of someone sending something like that all the way from Franville
to Paris.

Today I am expecting Paul Barbe for dinner. So the
whole day will be wasted. . . .

I will leave tomorrow morning, if I have managed to
finish all my letters and the packing. Before my departure,
I will write you a few lines. Regarding your absurd surmise that I would be traveling with someone, it is not
worth wasting my words. And yet in some ways you are
right, because I am traveling in the company of a tortuous
rheumatic pain. . . .

Chapter 31

While the prolonged legal process over transport of nitroglycerine was going on in England, Alfred had begun to look around for other markets. In France, against his better judgment, Alfred was forced to risk his own money to get things moving. Uncertainty regarding the French patent's expiration made finding capital for his venture that much harder. The value of the capital shares in all continental dynamite enterprises, with the exception of the German company, was not more than 750,000 Swedish crowns (about $150,000 then), a sum roughly corresponding to what a middle-size Swedish mechanical shop enterprise would be worth at this time. On such financially thin ice was Alfred's dynamite empire built. Alfred had been forced to add 100,000 crowns and Barbe 170,000 crowns.

The basis for a relationship between Barbe and Alfred was also taking a lot of time. Alfred continued to demand that his partner provide bank guarantees for his undertakings, and Barbe refused, indignantly insisting that his family's factories and real estate constituted ample collateral. He also resisted Alfred's demand that someone else have the power to sign contracts on behalf of Alfred and watch over his interests. "I don't feel that I can agree to such arrangements," Barbe wrote Alfred. "What would remain of our good relations and mutual trust?" From their exchange of letters during November and December of 1869, it is clear that Alfred finally dropped his demands, eager as he was to make use of Barbe's abilities.

Alfred did not resent his partner's getting richer and richer. On the contrary, in his opinion it was necessary that the manager of an enterprise have the "desire to acquire" in order to succeed.

A trade boom was taking place in Europe in the beginning of the 1870s, and quick decisions and reflexes were demanded. The Nobel companies best able to take advantage of the good times were those in Germany and Sweden. Even in the French company profits were increasing. In June 1875, both Alfred and Barbe were elected to six-year terms on the board. Though together they controlled barely a third of the shares, they dominated it mainly by virtue of their personalities and their experience.

The board chose a gunpowder specialist named Louis Roux to

be managing director, and he turned out to be as stubborn as Barbe. During a war of wills at the shareholders' meeting in 1877, he even forced Barbe to back down. Barbe owned a company that had earned large profits by selling equipment and chemicals to the Nobel factory in Paulilles, in the south of France. The manager at Paulilles, Xavier Bender, demanded that his company no longer be forced to buy solely from Barbe's private company. Roux spoke on behalf of Bender during the meeting, and in the ensuing vote Alfred voted against Barbe.

The French parent company, bearing the high-sounding name Société Générale pour la Fabrication de la Dynamite et des Produits Chimiques, had share capital amounting to 3 million francs divided into six thousand shares of 500 francs each. In 1884 a factory was bought in Ablon in Northern France, and the share capital was increased to 4 million francs.

Stiffening competition in the explosive substance market demanded every ounce of energy Barbe and Alfred had to offer. It was becoming increasingly clear to Barbe — though Alfred resisted for a long time — that some form of regulated cooperation between the Nobel companies was necessary. Barbe thought this "perverse competition" would, one day, become devastating.

Both Alfred and Barbe had lived in Paris since 1873 and, in spite of the occasional tension in their relationship, consulted with each other on an almost daily basis. Their deliberations led to the formation of a special staff in 1875, under the guidance of Liedbeck, whose exclusive role was product development. The Syndicat des Fabriques de Dynamite would act as an advisory organ to the Nobel companies. It didn't work. Nobel, Barbe, and Liedbeck were simply too strong-willed and independent to agree on how to proceed.

Efforts to bring about market and price agreements between companies inside and outside the Nobel concern were beginning to succeed, yet there was much work to be done. In 1882, when the French dynamite patent expired, the Swiss-Italian Nobel company formed a commercial company in England. Alfred was skeptical. In a letter to Barbe dated July 5, 1879, he writes: "The idea is excellent in theory but translated into practice . . . !"

Barbe formally presented his suggestion to amalgamate all Nobel companies on the continent with Nobel's Explosives in England. "I believe that one has to follow the road I suggest or else dispose of the shares in other countries since the competition is getting to be enormous," he wrote to Alfred on July 12, 1879, "both from Opladen, other enterprises, and between the Nobel companies themselves. Let us fuse together or be prepared to leave our businesses. Our interest and our name demand fusion. . . ."

Barbe felt that significant expenses could be avoided if the continental companies were united with the English. It would also offer a better chance of keeping the prices up on the export market. Alfred pondered the proposition, but judging from his brief comments, he was not yet open to a radical change in his companies' structure.

While waiting for Alfred to change his mind about amalgamation, Barbe managed to make him agree to unite the Swiss-Italian companies under the name Dynamite Nobel. Then he wanted to unite the German-English factories with some Latin American companies. After being subjected to an extended campaign of persuasion, Alfred finally gave in to Barbe and even accepted membership on the board of directors of Nobel Dynamite Trust Company.

He gave in because more than ever he was eager to find time for research and product development. He sensed that the market would soon be sated and new inventions would be essential if they were to keep profits up. Market division and price agreements were, in his mind, only temporary solutions. Moreover, he knew being a member of the board of directors and a major shareholder put him in a delicate position. It exposed him to criticism at shareholders' meetings, where he was once openly chastised for having tried to manipulate management.

Alfred responded stoutly, but his choice of words suggests that he understood his critics to some degree. At an early stage of operations, Alfred had added some clauses about prohibiting export — Winter Bay, for instance, was not allowed to sell outside of Sweden — to countries in which he intended to start manufacturing. Yet he had tried to make Alexander Cuthbert, managing director of the British Nobel's Explosives, begin production of blasting gelatin with an eye on the attractive export market. He later wrote to the board of directors that this was because "the German Company is getting ahead of us in getting gelatin into the marketplace." The use of the word "us" is fascinating — this was not the first time he sat on two chairs without noticing.

Along with the factory in Ardeer, the model factory in Paulilles was Alfred's pride and joy. His letters are filled with praise for Liedbeck's exemplary planning. From the very beginning, the Paulilles factory could manufacture potassium nitrate and sulfuric acid. Yet another nitroglycerine factory was built in 1880, and the share capital was increased by 25 percent. Three years later, an ice factory was added, making it possible to produce explosives even during the warmest time of the year.

To Alfred's disappointment, the demand for his blasting gelatin was not what he had hoped. He was forced to continue manufacturing and selling dynamite. Dynamite production grew to such levels that the prices had to be lowered, and profits fell. The returns from the working capital in the French company are proof enough: in 1879/1880 it was 42 percent. By 1885/1886 it had dropped to 19 percent.

An especially troubled year was 1885. "I am losing money hand over fist and am trying in vain to sell my Russian shares to anyone and at any price at all," Alfred complained. The following summer he reported even greater difficulties in a letter to Sofie Hess: "Things are getting so bad in Russia and England that soon my income is going to dwindle to a pittance."

His relations to Barbe were becoming increasingly cool. Alfred was now openly criticizing him for mismanaging the cash flow in some companies. Barbe was giving them short-term loans, and they were giving long-term credit to customers. Alfred's view was that to Barbe, a chance for quick profit meant more than solvency. He was becoming increasingly worried that his companies were involved in questionable transactions that, as a responsible member of the board of directors, could threaten him personally. It turned out, of course, that he was right.

Chapter 32

Cologne
September 19, 1878

. . . I have been forced to stay here yet another day in order to visit our nitroglycerine factory, so I won't be able to write you before the train leaves. . . .

My stomach again hurts so much that it is pure torture to travel. They have provided me with fried chicken and some other stuff — this time I ordered what I wanted — but I have no appetite. I simply don't feel well when I eat. Only your cookies taste good — probably because they come from you. . . .

Tomorrow morning — I have to travel all night! — I will arrive in Hamburg. Tomorrow night I continue on to Stockholm. The trip is very uncomfortable and draining, especially since my rheumatic pains leave me no rest. . . .

The slightest effort gives me a nosebleed. Here is another drop — this time on this letter.

Stockholm,
September, 1878

. . . A whole shipload of relatives has gathered here, and they are quarreling over who gets some of my valuable time. It is absolutely impossible for me to find any free time. So you must forgive me for only sending you a few brief lines. When I am not with you, I worry increasingly about my dear little one so far away. Write me in detail and tell me how you feel. . . .

Stockholm, Hotel Rydberg
September 25, 1878

. . . It brought such great joy to my old mother to see all of us gathered here with her. Even if life has not given me the gift of such joy — but great pain! instead — I can well

imagine my mother's feelings. When life moves toward its
conclusion, and only a brief path separates us from the
grave, we do not tie any new bonds of friendship, but
value our old ones the more. I would like to stay here
with Mama — it would probably delight her — but there
are too many of us for her, and we can't discriminate.
Therefore we are all staying at the Grand Hotel Rydberg,
where the furniture is gilded but the food rotten.

On the water outside my window a boat glides past,
and I wish it would take me to you in Franville. Since
that is impossible, my thoughts alone have to make the
journey. They remain faithful to you and will be so forever. I wish you all good things and kiss you tenderly on
the pretty mouth under the blonde little head of hair. . . .

P.S. It is cold and damp here. My health is not good.

Stockholm, Hotel Rydberg
September 26, 1878

. . . It is almost time for the mail and I haven't had time
to write you a few lines about how deluged I am with
pleas for money from people I don't know. Sometimes
they disguise begging as business propositions. My
brother is even more overwhelmed by them — he has
hardly a free moment to spend with our mother.

We are now quite a group here, including two sisters-
in-law with five children. I don't yet know how many of
them are coming to Paris. In either case, my two brothers
and two of their sons will come. I hope their wives aren't
coming as well, since that would make it harder for me to
arrange my time. . . .

I would like to write you a longer letter but my nephews are running around in my room and climbing on the
desk. But my thoughts are with you and the memories
of our pleasant moments cheer the long, boring hours here.

Chapter 33

Because the patent business was of critical importance to his enterprise, for a long time Alfred handled it himself, without a secretary or an attorney. He also composed his own balance sheet four times a year in order to know exactly where he stood financially. Unlike many, Alfred never dealt with anticipated annual profits. Profits had to be on the books before he allowed them to be included in his accounts. Nor did he pay any dividends to shareholders if results did not justify it. To attract working capital, balance sheets in many other companies were often dressed up. Alfred's business ethics were more puritanical.

It would take many years for Alfred to accept the idea that sometimes business failures were inevitable, that steps forward in one market were very often followed by decline in another. Alfred learned to steel himself so that the disappointments would not depress him into inaction. He thickened his skin to the fallout from each new accident. But he was beginning to experience mental blocks as an inventor, and this, more than anything else, was at the root of his growing melancholy. He felt he was getting old before his time.

As the Nobel companies' finances improved, complaints from worried shareholders were few. Hence in only a few instances did Alfred intervene directly in the daily routine of a company — and then only if it were a question of accounting or some technical detail.

As tends to happen to anyone with growing wealth and reputation, Alfred began to be viewed less as an individual than as an institution. The general effect of this was that he relied increasingly on his own judgment. The more he felt isolated, the more his distrust of others grew. He kept an especially sharp eye on those in key positions who might be exposed to temptation, those with "fat bellies and even fatter calculations."

Fully aware that self-interest guides actions, he believed strongly that the greed for money must be contained within reasonable limits. He was filled with disgust for the lawlessness of capitalism *in extremis*. The word humbug, in the sense of bluffing and cheating, crops up with increasing frequency in Alfred's letters. "Humbug practitioners" described those who unscrupulously copied his techniques and gave their imitations names such as "Nitroleum," "Railroad-

powder," and "Vigorite." However clever these humbug practitioners were, few attempted to take Alfred on face to face.

Of course, Alfred knew lying was sometimes a necessary ingredient in business. Within certain limits, he forced himself to tol-
erate lies as a business method.

The writer Robert Musil once declared that some wealthy people
experience their fortune as an extension of themselves. Nothing could
have been more foreign to Alfred. Each new million contributed not
one inch to his mental and spiritual growth. Clichéed though it might
sound, what he was seeking could not be bought for money. The
letters he wrote late in life bear the imprint of a severely — even
clinically — depressed human being. In his solitude, he counted how
many real friends he had. Every year, their number declined in his
calculations. He felt nothing but loneliness was waiting for him at
the end of the road.

Chapter 34

Stockholm, Hotel Rydberg
September 27, 1878

. . . Dear child, you complain that my letters are too brief and reticent, but you seem not to want to understand the reason why, although it is evident: everyone and women especially are egoists who think only of themselves. Though I knew this at the beginning of our acquaintance, it is now even clearer to me that your view of life has been twisted. I am therefore forced to remain aloof to prevent your affection from becoming too deeply rooted. You may believe yourself to be fond of me. But it is merely gratitude, perhaps respect, and such feelings are not enough to fill the need for love in your young soul.

The time will come — perhaps fairly soon — when your heart will be filled with love for another man. How you will blame me then for the way I tied you down with an ardent love's inextricable bonds. I see this clearly and therefore rein in my feelings. Do not believe, however, that I really have a heart of stone, as you so often charge in your letters.

More than most, perhaps, I have lived with the pressure of desolate loneliness, and in the past have sought an intimate communion with someone. But this someone could hardly be a twenty-one-year-old with whose philosophy of life and spirituality I have little or nothing in common. Besides, your star is rising in the heaven of fate while mine is descending. Youth lends colors to your hope, while in me the bright colors are few and more reminiscent of those in a sunset. Two such essentially different people do not fit as lovers, but in spite of this can remain good friends.

I know that you are a truly kindhearted and sweet little girl. Even if you have brought and continue to bring me trouble, I am deeply fond of you and think more of your happiness than of my own. My happiness! I can hardly

keep from laughing. As if that concept could have anything to do with a nature that seems to be created purely
for suffering.

But on you, little one, life smiles. Should some little
disturbance occur, it will probably last only a moment.
Then you will be merry and cheerful again. But for true
happiness, you still lack the education that befits your position in life. Therefore you must continue to improve
yourself. Because you are still a thoughtless child and it is
good for you to have an older, thoughtful uncle to keep
watch over you. . . .

Here comes my sister-in-law with her children and I
end with a loving kiss from your old brooding one.

P.S. I will remain here until October 1. If you want to
send a telegram, the address is Grand Hotel Rydberg,
Stockholm. But include my first name since my brothers
are also staying here.

How are your finances?

Stockholm, Hotel Rydberg
September 28, 1878

. . . The food served here is very bad, and since I don't
like to eat alone, I suffer stomachaches most of the time.
Being careful doesn't seem to help. Though I neither
smoke nor drink wine, my headaches are so terrible that
life seems filled with bile. I hope you are feeling better;
judging from your letters you seem to have forgotten all
about me already. That is not nice of you, since you live
always in my thoughts and in my heart.

Chapter 35

If the correspondence between Robert, Ludvig, and Alfred gives a true picture, the brothers never touched upon their father's bankruptcy and fall from grace: from a life of plenty in St. Petersburg to a grim existence in the run-down building in the south of Stockholm, where all he and their mother had to keep the wolf from the door was Alfred's help.

When Immanuel had given his factory over to the creditors in 1860, they made the fortunate decision of electing Ludvig as the new head of Nobel & Fils. Ludvig only accepted the post after some hesitation, since Robert was the oldest of the brothers, and Ludvig did not want to hurt his feelings.

Ludvig demonstrated not only a knack for dealing with machines but with people. He had an astonishingly easy way of making others feel good, an asset that would serve him well throughout his career. It took him two years to rebuild the company. Then, in 1862, the creditors informed him that they had sold the mechanics shop to a Russian, who immediately changed the name to "Technical Engineer Golubyev's Sompsonievsky Mechanical Shop." Ludvig had managed to save 5,000 rubles from the salary the creditors had paid him, and on October 13, 1862, he was able to lease his own little shop on the so-called Viborg side of the Neva River. Under his guidance, his new company grew with remarkable speed. Besides military equipment, such as mines, guns, and cannons, he manufactured steam hammers and hydraulic presses for the civilian sector. He was helped by Robert and also by Alfred, who had rented a small apartment where he'd set up a laboratory in the kitchen for small-scale experiments.

Ludvig cultivated his strong connections with Russian military authorities to increasingly good effect. As more orders came in, he had to employ more workers, and eventually his shop produced gun carriages and pig-iron grenades, tool machinery and lathe benches. After twenty years, the turnover was eight times greater than it had been at the start.

In 1858, Ludvig married his maternal cousin, Mina Ahlsell, and on June 22, 1859, she gave birth to their first child, who was named Emanuel. Robert Nobel married Pauline Lenngren, the daughter of a wealthy Finnish businessman in Helsinki. At first they lived in St. Petersburg, but Pauline disliked it, so they moved to Helsinki, where, with financial support from his father-in-law, Robert started a brick-yard and tilery, as well as a store that sold lamps and lamp oil. With grim humor, Robert described the latter as a brilliant business in every way except financially. All his life Robert felt inferior to his brothers, mostly because he was less successful as an entrepreneur. Feelings of inferiority later turned into bitterness and sarcasm.

When Alfred established himself in Winter Bay, he offered Robert the chance to market nitroglycerine in Finland. Robert accepted, sold his business, and established a factory for explosive substances in a block of buildings on an estate outside Helsinki. He had no more than settled in when he was informed that the czar intended to prohibit all manufacture of explosives in the Grand Duchy of Finland. Robert had no choice but to close up shop.

These setbacks affected Robert's mood, and he showed tendencies toward hypochondria. Something was always causing him pain. When the managing director's position at Winter Bay became vacant, Alfred offered it to him, and for a little over three years Robert ran the company. It soon became evident that he had problems working with people, and before long he had locked himself on a collision course with the temperamental multimillionaire and co-financier Smitt, as well as Alarik Liedbeck.

In 1870, Robert turned forty-one and didn't seem sure what to do next. Ludvig suggested that he return to St. Petersburg and become a partner in Ludvig's now extremely successful mechanical business. Ludvig's wife, Mina, had died the year before after a brief illness, and he was now getting married again to a young Swedish woman named Edla Collin. They went on a honeymoon trip that lasted seven months. Before he left, Ludvig transferred the managing of his company to Robert.

In 1872, Ludvig signed an agreement with Peter Bilderling, the head of the gun factory in Issyevsk, located near the Ural Mountains. The two of them agreed on a fifty-fifty split on an investment in the manufacture of a rifle called the Berdanka, a Russian variation on the Remington.

At first Robert disdainfully called the project "the Issyevsk adventure." He soon changed his mind. After only three years, Ludvig reported triumphantly in a letter to him that he had just gone to a Sunday worship service in Issyevsk, and noticed that the workers and their families were remarkably well dressed: "What a contrast to the earlier poverty in these areas. This new sight filled me with joy!"

Despite Robert's misgivings, Ludvig gave him an assignment critical to the success of the project, which was how Robert came to play a decisive role in the birth of the Nobel oil empire in the Caucasian town of Baku. Ludvig wanted Robert to study the activities at other gun factories in Europe and to buy a large quantity of first-class walnut wood for the rifle butts. Robert saw the mission as a good excuse to leave St. Petersburg.

First he visited gun factories in Switzerland and Austria, gleaning technical information. Then he went on to Paris to inform Alfred of Ludvig's plans. Since Alfred was about to buy his building at Avenue Malakoff, they inspected his future home together. By 1873 Alfred already ran twelve dynamite factories, and in his letters to Ludvig, Robert not only reported the amazing success dynamite had brought Alfred but was effusive about Alfred's new home. He and Alfred together composed a letter to Ludvig in which they commented on methods and new machinery in European rifle manufacturing. Robert then went to Baku where, according to the experts, the best-quality walnut trees grew.

Robert arrived by river steamboat to the port Astrakan in March 1873, and from there he was taken by a smaller passenger boat to Baku, a meeting point between East and West. During his trip, Robert got to know the Dutch skipper, a man by the name of de Boer, who told Robert that he and his brother owned a couple of oil wells in Baku, where they had also established a small refinery. Robert knew something about the oil business since he had imported Russian paraffin oil for his Helsinki lamp business and now saw a chance to profit from his experience.

Robert returned to the Issyevsk rifle factory with his errand unaccomplished, but obsessed with a new idea. Roaming among the walnut trees on the Caucasian slopes, he had become contaminated by the "naphtha fever." He told Ludvig that he wanted to establish a paraffin oil (kerosene) factory near Baku. Ludvig dutifully provided his older brother with some start-up capital, though he was unconvinced it would come to anything.

Returning to Baku, Robert's first impression was substantiated: there was oil in unlimited quantities, but drilling was primitive and done on only a very small scale. He walked across the oilfields day after day, making estimates. Everything was done the old-fashioned way: extracted oil was transported in leather bags on two-wheeled carts from the fields to primitive refineries in and around Baku.

Robert concentrated first on the problem of transportation. He consulted with Alfred by letter and soon discovered that the oil could be brought from the oil villages to Baku's harbor by pipes. The cost for such a pipe structure was significant, but it was a one-time expense. There was another problem: the area had no railroad, and, while the Volga was an excellent waterway, it was frozen over for four months a year.

Robert bought de Boer's oil wells and refinery. As the new owner, he delighted in the sweetish smell of oil and was wholly convinced that immeasurable riches were hidden below ground. In letter after letter he pleaded with Ludvig to come to Baku. Ludvig wrote on October 31, 1875, to Alfred:

> Robert has returned to Baku from his journey to the eastern coast [of the Caspian Sea] and has found excellent naphtha at a depth of sixty feet on the island Tcheleken. So now he has the raw material. We shall see if he understands how to handle the development and the general marketing; his future success and fortune will depend on that. . . . I, for my part, have done what I can to aid him by giving him money and technical advice. Robert says that he has made new inventions in the distillation and refining of the oil. . . . I cannot judge their value since I am unfamiliar with the profession. . . . The main thing is that he understands how to run the business in a generally sensible way. I think that we, that is you and I, ought to go there together and see if we can help him in any way. Since we have managed to achieve economic independence, we should try to help Robert to arrive at that position, too. So think of a trip to Baku.

The brothers hesitated about making the long journey. Ludvig went first, in April 1876, accompanied by his son Emanuel. Alfred, on the other hand, could never be talked into making the trip, even though over time his financial involvement in the Baku oil project became very extensive.

During his stay in Baku, Ludvig went to see the brother of the czar, Grand Duke Mikael, who was governor in the provincial capital of Tiflis. Ludvig wanted to probe the grand duke's support for Robert's grandiose plans. Grand Duke Mikael was not difficult to convince; he was well aware of Ludvig's accomplishments both in St. Petersburg and at the rifle factory in Issyevsk.

Ludvig decided on the spot to act on the idea of a seven-mile-long pipeline from the oil wells to the refineries. The prototype was the American pipeline in Pennsylvania, which was imported from Glasgow. To Alfred he wrote:

> The factory in Baku is now finished and has begun pro-
> duction; the capacity is large, estimated to be half a mil-
> lion puds [a pud is a little over thirty–five pounds]
> annually using current techniques. With additional facili-
> ties, which would not cost much since the buildings are
> already finished, the production could be doubled, even
> quadrupled. At any point we could therefore produce an-
> other million puds annually if the transport and storage
> problems were solved. But this is where the problem
> lies. . . . So far as the quality goes, Robert has achieved
> really splendid results, for while the usual Baku manufac-
> ture yields 30 percent heavy and inferior product, he gets
> from the same naphtha 40 percent first-rate light kero-
> sene, which could measure up to the best American
> grades. . . . We can therefore start right into the market
> with a product that will give a "shining" reputation to
> the business.

"Nobelevski" — the Nobel era — in the Russian oil industry had begun.

Ludvig's frequent letters to Paris kept Alfred informed of developments in Baku. The two brothers had another interest in common as well, since Ludvig had accepted Alfred's offer to market dynamite in Russia. As the owner of the principal agency, Société Franco-Russie des Dynamites, he made important contributions to the cause. But none of them would see a dynamite factory built in Russia during their lifetime. It was feared that dynamite would be used in assassination attempts against the czar. In February 1880, a dynamite load had exploded under his dining room. No import prohibition against explosives existed. The dynamite had come from one of Alfred's European factories.

Chapter 36

Stockholm, Hotel Rydberg
September 29, 1878

. . . I have just received your delightful, dear, intimate little letter of September 24. It hurts me to not be able to respond to it immediately and on the spot with a loving kiss. That is unfortunately not possible and not even with my pen am I able to say what I actually would want to say. Because we are leaving for the factory and will spend the whole day there. In this bustle and flurry, I am constantly and nostalgically thinking of our peaceful time together in Wiesbaden.

Stockholm, Hotel Rydberg
September 30, 1878

. . . Today is Mother's birthday so you might imagine that I have no time to write many lines to you. Tomorrow I leave, and on the 4th of October I have an important meeting in Hamburg. I will be back in Paris on the 6th or 7th. Most likely it will be the 7th, since I have to visit our factory outside Hamburg. . . .

London, the Midland Grand Hotel
November 10, 1878

. . . Though I am not feeling well, I have to stay in this boring hole a while longer. I sit in conferences all day every day with lawyers, of whom one has not yet showed up but is letting us wait for him. Never have I longed for home as much as this time.

London, the Grosvenor Hotel
June 2, 1879

. . . After a rather unpleasant journey by sea — moderate winds but high waves — I arrived in London around seven o'clock at night. Of course rain was pouring down as if the sluices of heaven had been opened, and naturally the bad weather continues today. The sky is as gray as lead and the ground a mixture of puddles and mud. No wonder that May and June are celebrated in song and praised in lofty terms by the poets! . . .

How was your trip to Paris? Tell me a little about it and address it without scribbling:

> Alfred Nobel Esq
> Dynamite Works
> Stevenson
> Ashire
> SCOTLAND

Glasgow, the Queen's Hotel
June 3, 1879

. . . Years ago Brugger wrote: "Hop, hop it went in a rushing gallop." The same could be said about the express train from London to Glasgow: in ten hours more than 700 kilometers (400 miles), and we arrived half a minute early. I spent the time reading a historical novel by Victor Hugo dealing with Napoleon's coup d'état in 1852. The book is very well written. So the hours went by rather quickly, though not as fast as the locomotive. A good book will make even a stay in Scotland bearable. If you are disheartened by anxiety or any other female folly, it is only from a lack of things to do. Buy an entertaining novel and your anxiety will be transferred to some character, and you will feel good again . . . .

Nothing is as repugnant to a man as endless crying and eternal reproaches. Especially if they are served day in and day out like a repulsive dish of leftover food. Lies and betrayal are almost easier to endure, because at least they offer a little variety.

From this follows, my dear child, that despite all your good qualities, instead of bringing cheer into a man's life you could very easily make it taste worse. These are words of truth that in all probability you will not be able to understand, since it is foreign to your nature to make the slightest sacrifice for anybody else.

Now I don't have any more time to moralize — besides, the effort is wasted on you. Am sending you instead very warm greetings and wish you truly happy days until we see each other again.

Your Alfred

Chapter 37

With the help of Ludvig's loan, Robert was able to build a kerosene refinery — kerosene being the American name for naphtha — adjacent to the oil wells. At first there were only eight distillation pumps with a capacity of two thousand pounds, and the boilers worked around the clock. Robert's first deed as factory manager was to introduce smokeless combustion. He did not want to make the air of the region even sootier than it was. Robert also gained an advantage over his competitors by using special coolers for the waste. Whereas his rivals had to be content with one distillation per day, he could do ten. It would take many more years before the process could be done automatically. A Swedish chemist, Erland Théel, supervised everything.

Robert's greatest advantage was that his refined lamp oil was of such high quality that he was the only one in the Baku region who could successfully compete with the imported American oil. In October 1876, when three hundred barrels — an English barrel is 159 liters (or 42 gallons) — arrived in St. Petersburg from Baku, it was a historic event in the Russian oil industry: the beginning of the end of the hegemony of American oil. The more Robert and Ludvig's companies expanded production, the smaller the American share of the Russian market became. Finally it became so small in 1883 that American companies stopped exporting oil to Russia altogether.

When Ludvig, Robert, and the still skeptical Alfred began discussions in 1876 about the easiest way of bringing the first-class oil into the world market, there was a host of problems to be faced. Pipelines had already begun to replace the time-consuming and expensive horse-and-carriage method of bringing oil to the factory or the harbor in Baku, but the real challenge remained.

Thirty years later, the oil expert in the Russian commerce and industry ministry, Stephan Golisjambarov, during a visit to Baku, characterized the Nobel brothers' solution to the transport problems as "the most important event in the Russian oil industry's history." He even considered the innovation comparable to Alfred's discovery of dynamite.

A recapitulation of the development of Nobel activity within the Russian oil industry shows:

- In 1870, the world's consumption of lamp oil was approximately 5 million casks of 48 gallons each.
- In 1872, the Russian state monopoly was abolished. At the time there were a little more than 400 wells in Baku, which together produced 22,000 tons of oil. Less than a year later, Robert Nobel arrived in Baku.
- In 1875, in concert with Ludvig in Petersburg and Alfred in Paris, Robert expanded their oil enterprise.
- In April 1876, Robert began drilling for oil, having up to that point devoted all his time to solving problems involving the refining process.
- In 1877, there were around two hundred oil companies in Russia as a whole, producing 75,000 tons; Robert's company produced 2,500 tons.

In 1878, a European oil expert visited Baku and echoed what had been said fifteen years earlier: when you drill deeper than fifty feet, you are unlikely to find oil. According to this logic, Nobel's steam-driven drills therefore lacked practical value. Ludvig and Robert paid no attention to these "experts" — and rightly so. Before long, nearly three hundred steam-driven drills were in operation. Ludvig and Robert also introduced electrical power during oil drilling.

In 1879 Ludvig made a general estimate of all the activities in Baku. For him and Robert to challenge the competition, they needed to become major distributors of oil products. To do that, a lot of money was needed — Ludvig's estimation was 2 to 3 million rubles. He also suggested that if the share capital were set at 3 million, it could be divided into six hundred parts of 5,000 rubles each. In this way, any new shareholder would only be given the right to vote at the shareholders' meeting six months after they'd bought a share, thereby preventing shortsighted speculation. Eight percent of the profits would be set aside for dividends on the share capital. Thereafter (and here Ludvig's idea was truly radical for its time) 40 percent of the surplus ought to be divided between the management and the staff. The remaining 52 percent could be placed at the disposal of the shareholders.

Ludvig described all this in a letter to Alfred, expressing his hope that they could get together as quickly as possible. Their meeting took place in Vienna, and Alfred promised, after initial hesitation, to invest "at least a smaller sum." He set one condition: the business must be run as a joint-stock company with limited personal liability. Ludvig was opposed to having a board of directors because he feared that it would restrict his freedom of action. Robert agreed with Ludvig.

Alfred, however, was convinced that the considerable capital they required would necessitate the creation of a joint-stock company. As usual, he was right and in 1879 the Tovarishchesto Nephtanavo Proisvodtsva Bratiev Nobel (or "Naphtha Production Stock-Company Brothers Nobel") was founded. Everyone called it simply "Branobel."

The share capital of three million rubles corresponded to approximately 7.5 million Swedish crowns (about $1.5 million then) and was divided as follows:

Ludvig	1,610,000	rubles
Alfred	115,000	"
Robert	100,000	"
Peter Bilderling	930,000	"
Alexander Bilderling	50,000	"
I. J. Zabelskiv	135,000	"
Fritz Blomberg (head of fi- nances at Ludvig's company in Petersburg)	25,000	"
Mikhail Beliamin (chief engi- neer at the same company)	25,000	"
A. S. Sundgren	5,000	"
Bruno Wunderlich	5,000	"
total	3,000,000	"

Ludvig would be the principal shareholder by far. As for the second largest shareholder, Alfred limited his first investment in the company to 115,000 rubles, but over the course of the next few years, he participated in all new sales of shares and debentures. Whenever there was an acute need for money, he came to the rescue.

By 1884, the share capital in Branobel had quintupled to 15 million rubles. By the time of the Russian Revolution in 1917, it had reached 25 million rubles. Alfred had insisted early on that the nominal value of the shares be lowered to 250 rubles, so that the interest of small investors would be stimulated and the company would have greater access to risk capital.

In spite of dry spells, Branobel expanded so quickly that by the end of the century the company was handling 30 percent of the Russian export of kerosene and no less than 50 percent of the sales of lubricating oil to other countries. By then, its founder Robert Nobel had long since left the company and moved back to Sweden. One reason he did this was that he could not accept the idea that the company he had created was being run behind his back. He was also dissatisfied with the 100,000 rubles he received in free shares for his pioneer work.

One day, without warning, he failed to show up at work. A month later, he informed one of his colleagues that he had gone to a Swiss health resort to rest. Officially it was announced that he had contracted tuberculosis, a common enough illness in Baku at the time, but it was not the whole truth. Ludvig wrote to Alfred that he had received "hate-filled" and "bitter" letters from Robert, who had managed things in Baku for so long that he simply could not stomach being subordinated to a board of directors.

Faced with the choice of being a powerless local boss or returning to Ludvig's factory in St. Petersburg, Robert chose a third alternative and moved back to Sweden, where he retired prematurely at age fifty-two. First he and his family lived in a large apartment in Stockholm. In 1889 he bought a manor house in Getå outside of the city of Norrköping, where he lived until his death in 1896.

That there was scant room for sentimentality between the brothers is evident from Alfred's comment to Ludvig when Robert left his work: "At least now he can busy himself with his ailments from morning to night" (a rather remarkable thing to say given Alfred's own hypersensitive nature). A letter Alfred sent to his brother after Robert had invited him to visit operations in Baku is ample testimony that Robert and Alfred were much alike. Alfred turned the invitation down, and then used it to launch his own diatribe:

> . . . The only thing that could lure me there would be
> the company — yours and perhaps Ludvig's — but the
> waterless, dust-laden, oil-soiled desert seems to me less
> than tempting. I want to live among trees and bushes —
> silent friends who respect my nervousness — and as

soon as possible I will escape both metropolises and desolate wastelands. . . .

You allude to my many friends? Where are they? At
the cloudy bottom of fleeing illusions or attached to the
clattering sound of collected coins. Believe me — you
have many friends only in dogs you feed with meat from
others, and in worms who feed on you. Grateful stomachs and grateful hearts are twins. . . .

The house at 9 Norrlandsgatan in Stockholm, in which Alfred was born in 1833.

View of Nevsky Prospect as it would have looked when Alfred arrived in St. Petersburg at the age of nine.

Photograph of Immanuel Nobel in 1853, when he was a businessman in St. Petersburg.

Laying of Immanuel Nobel's mines in the Gulf of Finland.

Seventeen-year-old Alfred with his older brother, Ludvig.

Drawing showing the devastation of the Heleneborg accident outside Stockholm on September 3, 1864, in which Alfred's younger brother, Emil (pictured below), was killed.

Immanuel Nobel in 1870. He used a cane after suffering a stroke. Alfred is seated at far right.

Robert Nobel,
the oldest of the brothers.

Nobel's home at Avenue Malakoff in Paris. (Below) The winter garden at Avenue Malakoff.

Bertha von Suttner.

Nobel in his forties.

Copy of lease to the apartment Alfred rented for Sofie Hess on Avenue D'Eylau in Paris.

MAISON SISE A PARIS *Avenue D'Eylau N° 10*

ENTRE LES SOUSSIGNÉS :

M. AUGUSTE-IRÉNÉE DEFRÉMICOURT , propriétaire , demeurant à Paris, 19, rue d'Antin, D'UNE PART ;

Et M. *Madame Sophie HESS* D'AUTRE PART ;

IL A ÉTÉ CONVENU ET ARRÊTÉ CE QUI SUIT :

M. AUGUSTE-IRÉNÉE DEFRÉMICOURT fait bail et donne à loyer, à partir du *premier Juillet* mil huit cent *quatrevingt* à M. *Madame Sophie Hess* ce acceptant, les lieux ci-après désignés, savoir :

Un appartement situé au deuxième étage composé d'une antichambre, d'une salle à manger, d'un grand et d'un petit salons, de trois chambres à coucher et cabinet de toilette, d'une cuisine et office de lieux d'aisances à l'anglaise, de trois chambres de domestiques au cinquième N° 1, 2 et 3 et de deux caves. Plus une écurie pour deux chevaux avec une petite pièce à côté pour mettre le fourrage et une remise.

Tel au surplus que le tout se poursuit et comporte, sans plus ample description, le preneur déclarant parfaitement connaître lesdits lieux.

La durée du présent bail sera de *trois, six ou neuf* années consécutives, au choix respectif des parties, qui devront s'avertir réciproquement et par écrit six mois avant l'expiration de *Chaque* période , au cas où elles voudraient le résilier.

La susdite location est faite moyennant un loyer annuel de *Cinq mille Cinq Cents francs* que le preneur s'oblige à payer en espèces d'or ou d'argent, et non autrement, à Monsieur DEFRÉMICOURT , en sa demeure ou à son fondé de pouvoirs porteur du présent, par quarts, aux quatre termes ordinaires de l'année : pour le premier terme, montant à *treize cent soixante quinze francs* échoir le premier *Octobre* mil huit cent *quatrevingt* et ainsi de

16° De ne pas avoir de chien, de perroquet, ni d'autre animal quelconque, malpropre ou bruyant ;

17° De se faire assurer à ses frais, pour les risques locatifs, et avec condition qu'il ne pourra être exercé aucun recours contre le bailleur.

18° Dans quelque circonstance et pour quelque motif que ce soit, il ne sera pas permis de placer des clous, ni de pratiquer ou faire établir des scellements aux murs, soit intérieurs, soit extérieurs de la maison, en quelque endroit que ce puisse être.

19° Lorsque l'une des parties aura donné ou reçu congé dans les délais prescrits, le bailleur aura le droit de mettre un écriteau à l'une des fenêtres, à son choix, de la présente location ; et le preneur devr*a* souffrir que l'on visite les lieux, pendant les six derniers mois, tous les jours, de midi à cinq heures du soir, sous peine de payer une indemnité d'un terme de location, en cas de refus constaté de *la* part ;

20° La présente location n'est faite que sous la condition que le bailleur pourra, à défaut de payement d'un trimestre de loyer, faire cesser le présent bail à la fin du terme en cours par simple congé signifié six semaines seulement avant l'expiration de ce terme, le preneur renonçant à se prévaloir de tout usage contraire. En cas de résistance, l'expulsion pourra être requise et ordonnée sur simple référé.

De son côté, le bailleur s'engage à tenir les lieux clos et couverts, selon l'usage.

Et Madame *Sophie Hess* déclare accepter et prendre à bail lesdits lieux, tels qu'ils se poursuivent et comportent, et sous les conditions ci-dessus stipulées, qu'*elle* s'engage à accomplir de bonne foi.

Fait double à Paris le vingt sept avril mil huit cent quatrevingt

lu et approuvé

Deffenncourt   *Sophie Hess*

A reconstruction of Nobel's laboratory in San Remo. *K. W. Gullers* (Below) Alfred's igniter, which detonated the nitroglycerine by means of a blasting cap.

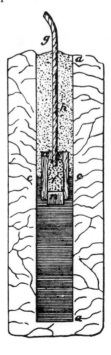

Emanuel Nobel, Ludvig's son.

Ludvig Nobel's palatial St. Petersburg home. The Branobel offices were located on
the second floor.

The last photograph taken of Alfred Nobel.

Alfred Nobel's handwritten last will and testament.

Testament

Jag undertecknad Alfred Bernhard Nobel förklarar härmed efter moget betänkande min yttersta vilja i afseende å den egendom jag vid min död kan efterlemna vara följande.

- - - - -

Öfver hela min återstående realiserbara förmögenhet förfäges på följande sätt: Kapitalet, af utredningsmännen realiseradt till säkra värdepapper, skall utgöra en fond hvars ränta årligen utdelas som prisbelöning åt dem som under det förlupne året hafva gjort menskligheten den största nytta. Räntan delas i fem lika delar som tillfalla: en del den som inom fysikens område har gjort den vigtigaste upptäckt eller uppfinning; en del den som har gjort den vigtigaste kemiska upptäckt eller förbättring; en del den som har gjort den vigtigaste upptäckt inom fysiologiens eller medicinens domän; en del den som inom literaturen har producerat det utmärktaste i idealisk rigtning; och en del åt den som har verkat mest eller bäst för folkens förbrödrande och afskaffande eller minskning af stående armeer samt bildande och spridande af fredskongresser. Priset för fysik och kemi utdelas af Svenska Vetenskapsakademien; för fysiologiska eller medicinska arbeten af Carolinska Institutet i Stockholm; för literatur af Akademien i Stockholm samt för fredsförfäktare af ett utskott af fem personer som väljas af Norska Stortinget. Det är min uttryckliga vilja att vid prisutdelningarne intet afseende fästes vid någon slags nationalitetstillhörighet sålunda att den värdigaste erhåller priset antingen han är Skandinav eller ej.

The first Nobel Prize ceremony in 1901, showing Wilhelm Roentgen, the discoverer of the X ray, receiving the prize in physics.

Chapter 38

Scotland, Ardeer
June 4, 1879

. . . Life here is not particularly pleasant. But even the bitterest of life's pills must be swallowed. There are so many matters demanding my attention that the managers must have all been paralyzed during my absence. On the other hand, if one had no work, this would be the most desolate place on earth. Our construction gives it the impression of being a small village, with most of the buildings hidden behind the dunes. A few hundred steps further lies the ocean; between us and America there is nothing but water! Sometimes the majestic waves roar and swell beautifully.

Now you have an idea of the godforsaken place where I spend my time. But the work makes me able to endure anything. Through intensive mental effort, lots of new things are created here, and because of that I can easily do without all comforts.

Vienna
August 8, 1879

. . . Your little letter has just arrived and gave me much joy. I gather from it that you understand I have to go to Stockholm. You have realized that I have no choice. It would be unseemly for me to deny my old sick mother the joy to which she has become accustomed, namely, to have her sons around her for a few days once a year. Of course I would have preferred to have you come along on this journey, but you would not have been able to stand the hardships. In a few days — probably already tomorrow or the next day — you will not be able to travel at all. And staying in Stockholm would give you rather little in the way of pleasure, since the tight time schedule would have made it impossible for just the two of us to

undertake any excursions. Our visit to Stockholm together must therefore be postponed until next year. . . .

Hamburg, Streits Hotel
August 16, 1879

. . . I feel rather depressed here among so many ordinary
people. I would rather be in Paris where I can work, or in
Ischl where affection and peace await me. . . .

Paris
[End of August 1879]

. . . Since my return, the pace has been unbelievably hectic. It has made me so nervous that I can barely hold my
pen steady in my hand. The old managing director has
left our French company and Paul Barbe has taken over
the business. Changes are taking place in such a frenzy
that our daily meetings last four, five hours. Pure torture — yet I cannot avoid them since Barbe's predecessor
created such a mess. Furthermore, a mountain of letters
has been accumulating. The suggestion to merge our
companies is also creating a lot of work. Finally, research
projects cannot advance without my direct guidance. All
this nervous tension is making me ill. . . .

In Stockholm my mother was in better health than I
had dared to hope. If she continues like this, the dear old
woman will be able to live another twenty years. I did
also meet up with my brother Robert; he was perhaps a
little more cheerful than usual but generally the same hy-
pochondriac as before. Daily and hourly he imagines himself contracting new illnesses. . . .

Your letters make me worry about your health. But
then it is complete madness, feeling as poorly as you do,
to roam around in the world like this. Indeed, it is against
all common sense. Sometimes I feel that your dog Bella
acts with better judgment than you. At times you can
bubble over with high spirits and be mischievous or
lovely, but sensible — never! What you are especially
lacking, so much the pity, is an understanding of the feel-

ings and efforts of another human being. Yet that is where
the secret of how to win someone's heart lies. It is truly
woman's greatest virtue. But it presupposes a refinement
and a culture, which you are totally lacking. I am writing
this for your own good, so that you will put your shoul-
der to the wheel and improve yourself further.

Hamburg
June 23, 1880

. . . Sitting all alone and so pained by disagreeable business that my already less-than-sturdy nerves are destroyed — I feel with redoubled force how dear you
really are to me. The hustle and bustle of the world is
less bearable to me than to others. I would be so happy if
I could settle down in a quiet corner and live there without great ambition, but also without all these worries and
torments.

When this legal business has been finally wound up, I
am firmly resolved to retire from the business side. Of
course, it cannot happen at once, but I am going to do it
as soon as it is practically possible. . . .

P.S. Always keep my letters so that no unauthorized eyes
can see them!

Hamburg
June 25, 1880

. . . You speak of love; to me this feeling could not exist
if it weren't for all those eternal sorrows and torments.
Love should be enjoyed in peaceful serenity where no
tribulations can reach one. Take some good advice — do
not waste your young life as you have done so far. Seek
the bright sunshine and not the shadow, cheerful individuals and not a sad old log like me.

To me — I've known this a long time — there is no joy
in this world. I wish you so very well, my dear child.
Take advantage of my attitude toward you and find a safe
harbor in your life. . . . Don't chain your youth to a sorrowful old man. . . .

Hamburg
July 6, 1880

. . . It makes me so happy to hear that you are feeling a
little better! I would very much like to have you with me,
but, on the other hand, you must of course not interrupt
the treatment if it makes you feel good. I have absolutely
no time to join you there. My court case is not going
well at all, and nothing but my old patent from 1864 can save
the situation. More dishonest witnesses have appeared.
You can probably imagine — you who know my nature — what a nervous strain this puts on me. My stomach is just about ruined and I can hardly eat at all.

Your Alfred

Glasgow, St. Enoch Station Hotel
December 5, 1880

. . . I should actually have continued on to London last
night, but the train that brought me here from the factory
was so late that I missed the connection. Since no trains
run on Sundays in this God-fearing country, I am sitting
here alone, imprisoned in a hotel as large as a city block.
   Nowadays, when I have to associate with people, I cannot fail to notice how enormously the lack of social inter-
course these last few years has damaged me. I feel so
stupid and awkward that I would prefer to avoid the
people I encounter. I have my despicable shyness to thank
for that. I will probably never again in my life recapture
my spiritual sprightliness.
   I am not blaming you, my dear sweet little one, for
things turning out this way. When all is said and done, it
is my own fault, and you cannot be held responsible. Our
views of life — on the need for constant mental improvement, on our duties as human beings with a higher education — are so hugely different that we should never even
attempt to understand each other in these matters. It is
with great pain that I draw the conclusion that my own
nobility of soul has withered away and, my head bowed
in shame, I am stepping out of the circle of educated
persons.

Actually, it is totally senseless for me to write this to you. You will never be able to understand me on a deeper level. You understand only what suits you. You are not capable of grasping that for many years I have sacrificed my time, my reputation, all my associations with the educated world and finally my business — all for a self-indulgent child who is not even capable of discerning the selflessness of those acts.

Today I write these bitter lines because my heart bleeds with shame at having become so spiritually inferior to other people. Do not be angry that I pour out my feelings this way. You were unconscious of the fact that by using my lenience, year after year, you were undermining my spiritual strength. It is always so in life: when one withdraws from educated society and neglects the interchange of ideas with thinking individuals, he finally becomes incapable of such interchange and loses respect for himself as well as the respect of others, which he had formerly enjoyed.

I am ending, my dear, good, tender Sofie, with the heartfelt hope that your young life will be better than mine, and that you will never be struck by the feeling of debasement that embitters my days. . . .

Chapter 39

After Robert's departure from Baku, Ludvig took over the running of Branobel. Ludvig was in constant contact with Alfred. Their letters are filled with discussions about technical problems; Ludvig considered Alfred's advice and viewpoints invaluable. From time to time he suggested that they meet, and when they did, it was either at some German spa or in Vienna. When he returned to St. Petersburg, Ludvig's briefcase was usually stuffed with suggestions for improving operations.

Ludvig became known as the uncrowned king of Russian oil and acted simultaneously as the company's manager, chairman of the board, head of production, chief engineer, head of marketing, and manager of finance. Most of all, he was a brilliant entrepreneur, virtually without peer in Russia. After the construction of the pipeline from Baku, Ludvig came up with the idea for the world's first oil tanker. Russian shipyards showed minimal interest in his plans, so he decided to contact the Swedish shipbuilder and chief engineer Sven Almquist. Construction began almost immediately, and in record-breaking time the hold of the world's first oil tanker was constructed at the shop in Motala, Sweden. It was christened *Zoroaster*, a Russian variation on one of the sage Zarathustra's many names, "The God of Fire and Light." In May 1878 it sailed into the harbor at Baku, carrying 250 tons of oil.

Before long, Ludvig ordered two more ships, the *Buddha* and the *Nordenskjöld,* whose midships consisted exclusively of an oil tank (like the modern design). Ludvig remained loyal to the Swedish shipyards. Besides the one in Motala, shipyards in Lindholmen, Bergsund, Lindberg, and Kockum all received orders for no fewer than fifty-three oil cistern steamers, for a total cargo space of 38,000 tons and a construction value of 10 million Swedish crowns. Ludvig proudly noted that he had given these Swedish shipyards six years of business. The development of the business was spectacular. By 1907, 276 such ships existed in the world, 136 of them in Russia alone.

Robert's pioneer work in Russian oil was remembered when a tanker was named for him. Alfred declined firmly when they wanted to christen another ship *Alfred Nobel*: "There are grave objections to this," he wrote Ludvig. "First of all, a ship is female, who ought to be criticized for frivolously attempting to hide her sex — and when you tell me that she is both pretty and yare, it would seem like bad luck to christen her after an old wreck."

As usual, Ludvig had plenty of irons in the fire — at times perhaps too many. His three primary responsibilities were oil production in Baku; Nobel's Machine Factory in St. Petersburg, and (with Peter Bilderling) the rifle factory in Issyevsk; and the Nobel Brothers Company's board of directors in St. Petersburg. At times he could combine businesses, for instance when the machine factory manufactured steam engines and steam boilers, vents, and so-called *farsunki* (naphtha pulverizers) for oil drilling in Baku. Normally, the factory produced various kinds of war materiel as well as wagon wheels and axles.

During the summer of 1882 Ludvig wrote to a Russian business acquaintance that progress in Baku "fills my soul with joy." He could note with satisfaction that his new distillation method made it possible to obtain 35 percent kerosene from the raw oil; the competitors barely extracted 20 percent. The pipeline system had the capacity to transport four million barrels per year. Furthermore, Branobel owned forty wells on the oil fields of Balakhani where the refineries covered an area of an English square mile. The company maintained a fleet of twenty oil tankers on the Caspian Sea (and twelve that sailed on the Volga); 1,500 tank cars for railroad freight; and employed between 5,000 and 10,000 persons, depending on the time of year and the economic conditions. Work in the drilling fields and in the distillation factories in Baku went on year-round, though shipping from the Black Sea harbor was impossible during the six winter months.

As managing director, Ludvig took great pride in providing his employees with as good a work environment as possible. Besides being the first employer in Russia to include his personnel in discussions about subjects as radical as profit sharing — loud protests came from the Russian industrial establishment, but Ludvig stood his ground — he guaranteed salaries that were considerably higher than average and saw to it that his employees were paid punctually, which was atypical in Russia. Ludvig also built housing for his workers and financed the establishment of schools and libraries, hospitals, and recreational facilities. The first telephone was installed in Baku in 1880, making direct contact between the harbor and the oil fields possible. All the workers who lived in Villa Petrolea, the company housing project, soon had access to this newfangled invention.

All of this meant that Ludvig acquired a national reputation as an exemplary employer. Former serfs flocked to the Nobel factories seeking employment. Ludvig refused to employ minors in production and under no conditions hired children under the age of twelve. The work hours at his companies in St. Petersburg, Baku, and Issvejk were cut from twelve to fourteen hours to 10.5 hours, a move that was all the more controversial later when Russia's finance minister was removed from his position for trying to push through a law calling for shorter workdays.

Employees were proud to be known as "Nobelites." About a visit to Villa Petrolea, Ragnar Sohlman recalled:

> Having stayed in Baku for a while, I took a trip on my own and went on a rather extensive walking tour in Caucasus. So as not to arouse undue attention, I had dressed myself in Georgian costume with "kin shawl" and all. I encountered constant difficulties in responding to the constant inquiries as to where I came from since the concept of "schwed" [Swede] was unknown to the country people. I tried to clarify my nationality through explaining that I came from the same country as Nobel and always got the reply: "Ah, you're Nobelsky." For the sake of simplicity I adopted this and always answered when asked: Yes, Nobelsky.

Needless to say, Ludvig's ideas were looked upon with great disfavor by his competitors. M. Charles Marvin observed: "That he never became discouraged by the resistance he met with every step he took is an exceptional witness to the imperturbable steadfastness which was typical for Ludvig Nobel." Indeed, Ludvig seemed to enjoy it when there were challenging problems. Unlike Alfred, he preferred being surrounded by co-workers, and was forever involved in discussions with engineers, foremen, and workers about timely matters. He raised his many children in the same spirit of tolerance and involvement. "My childhood did not spoil me with quick success," he wrote Ludvig in 1884. "I know on the other hand that integrity and perseverance will always win in the end."

During the 1880s, it was said that among the two hundred "oil princes," there were at the most ten who were honest: "Ludvig Nobel, one Armenian and eight Muhammedans." Ludvig, in response to an interviewer from a Russian newspaper, said on the subject: "If you can find a single man in Baku who can prove that we have acted dishonestly or sought to cheat, we are willing to undergo cross-examination in your presence and, if found guilty, pay a severe fine."

Karl Hagelin, the technical manager and later local managing director in Baku, wrote: "We had in our service men of different nationalities, but whatever country they belonged to, they were first and foremost Nobelites. The company was our company, its improvements ours, and all failures were felt by us as if we had suffered them personally."

Chapter 40

Stockholm
June 9, 1881

. . . Thanks to a work of philosophy I had brought along, my journey went rather well. You will never guess whom I ran into in Cologne — on his way in the opposite direction, but also staying at Hotel du Nord.

First thing the next morning I saw him again, from the back and this time recognized him immediately — it was my brother Ludvig! Man plans but fate rules. He said that he would like to talk to you and was wondering if it would be possible to arrange a meeting in Paris. Naturally you could arrange it best. . . .

Stockholm
June 10, 1881

. . . My mother seems immensely happy to have me here, and she actually looks ten years younger. Since Ludvig is expected to arrive tonight, yet another happy surprise awaits her. I am more fond of Ludvig than of his mother-in-law — but the latter will perhaps mellow with time.

Although it is summer, it is awfully cold here. The climate does not at all suit my health. You should be glad, child of my heart, that you have warm weather in Paris and won't get chilblains. There is actually the risk of that here. No snow has yet fallen this week in June, but who knows if tomorrow the ground won't be fit for sleighing. Anyhow, your boy is freezing terribly and will be glad to turn his back on the North before long.

Yesterday I spent almost all day out at the nitroglycerine factory and was with Nordenskiöld until late at night. Palander, on the other hand, is out of the country along with the king.[1] So now you know more or less what's

[1] Between 1878 and 1880, Adolf Erik Nordenskiöld led an Antarctic expedition, after which he was knighted. Louis Palander was commander of the steamship *Vega* during the same expedition.

going on here. From my hotel window I can see the steamer *Gauthiod* sailing in with my brother Robert aboard. I will go to meet him and my nephews. . . .

Paris

August 17, 1881

. . . As soon as I arrived here, the business carousel began turning again, and soon I think I will have to barricade my doors. Today the never-ending stream of visitors began at eight-thirty and continued without interruption until one o'clock. Tomorrow I must have dinner at Bilderling's. Yesterday I visited Sevran and have to go there today again. We are involved in extremely important experiments there, so you see how many demands there are on my time.

The new laboratory is far from ready yet, but it already looks to be exceptionally efficient. I feel more lonely than ever, especially as I cannot use the laboratory either in Sevran or here. . . .

Paris

August 19, 1881

. . . The Arab Ali has just showered and massaged me. After such treatment, I am free from various pains, at least for a few moments.

I am presently spending most of my time in Sevran, where everything demands my presence. In spite of this I still find the time to write to you, while you have left me totally without news. . . .

Paris

August 21, 1881

. . . Let me know in good time when you need more money. Why, by the way, are there so few nice people visiting the health resort this year? Could all the fine ladies have possibly become healthy so suddenly that they no longer need any water cures? Or have they simply arrived at the conclusion that these cures are not much use?

Except for the dinner at Bilderling's, I have not visited anyone and am generally not invited anywhere. People are probably not even aware that I am here. It is difficult for anyone to catch a glimpse of me since I spend most of my time in Sevran. . . .

Paris
August 22, 1881

. . . I write these lines late at night, and it is almost completely empty here. I hope the move to Sevran will be completed soon so that I can start my research work in earnest. . . .

Take good care of your health, because nothing in the world has any value if one is ill. Even poverty can look rosy as long as it is accompanied by robust health. Think of that, my dear child, and don't let yourself be led astray by stupid low spirits.

Your Alfred

Chapter 41

Before adversities began to beset him, Ludvig had achieved remarkable success as an industrialist.

Alfred noted in hindsight that he had severely underestimated the importance of the oil products. He knew kerosene lamps were becoming an increasingly common source of home lighting, but, unlike Ludvig and Robert, had never imagined the success that the company would have marketing kerosene in Russia and abroad. He had invested mainly to show solidarity with his brothers, and he was amazed by the financial returns. At the beginning of the 1880s, the Baku works seemed to be a horn of plenty pouring out wealth. Yet it was precisely then that Alfred began to sense something was not quite right about Ludvig's financial situation. The risks of over-extension were becoming clear, and oil prices were fluctuating so wildly that it was impossible to make realistic calculations. In his own field, Alfred could adjust his dynamite prices to the needs of the marketplace — by and large, he decided what the market price should be.

At this point, Alfred was moving in the finance world's most influential circles. With a minute-long conversation he could arrange million-dollar credits, while at the same time buy and sell securities on the stock market. He not only put his financial know-how at Ludvig's disposal but his credit.

However, his brother's rapidly growing need for capital was beginning to create problems for Alfred. In increasingly blunt language he began warning Ludvig about this. Alfred believed they had to guard their liquidity, or the company could end up in a serious economic crisis. He accused Ludvig of faulty planning. "A serious problem is that you build first and then look around for the necessary money," he wrote him.

Another cause for concern arose in 1881. Alfred had just loaned Ludvig 656,000 rubles to cover an advance remittance to the Motala shipyard, where Ludvig had contracted for a new tanker. Alfred had hardly approved the payment when he received word that the *Nordenskjöld* had exploded and the *Buddha* had been seriously damaged during a storm on the Caspian Sea. After the loss of the *Nordenskjöld,* Alfred wondered if Ludvig was right about transporting flammable kerosene in tankers. Soon word came that an extensive fire had broken out in Ludvig's machine factory in St. Petersburg. A miscommunication led the international press to believe that it was the Nobel refineries in Baku that were being consumed by flames. The resulting front page headlines created severe anxiety in the financial world before Ludvig had a chance to correct the mistake. Alfred believed now more than ever that a devastating fire could occur at the Nobel oil works in Baku.

But Ludvig managed to ride out the storm. His reputation as an honest entrepreneur helped him once again defeat the intrigue going on in the wings. A wave of xenophobia was sweeping across Russia, and jealous competitors printed pamphlets and used other methods to plead with those considering giving Ludvig credit not to assist "a foreigner who allowed himself to play a much too significant role."

Ludvig's factories had long been known for their punctual and first-class deliveries to the Russian government. In 1875 he had been awarded the St. Anne Order, Second Class. A few years later he received, as had his father Immanuel, the Imperial Golden Eagle. In 1882, he was awarded the Imperial gold medal for the second time, which was rare for a foreigner. The official notification accompanying the latter lauds him having accomplished a "first-class production of axles and wheel pairs made of Russian iron, which has made further import from other countries unnecessary." St. Petersburg's Imperial Technological Institute bestowed upon him an honorary degree in engineering.

But Alfred continued to criticize his brother for how he was handling Branobel's financial matters, all the while assuring him that while he took no pleasure in acting as a Cassandra prophesying doom, his warnings were well founded.

Ludvig was too busy with his own problems, however, to pay enough attention to what Alfred was trying to tell him. He had launched the world's first diesel-driven tugboats and was waging a battle on several fronts with giants such as Standard Oil and Royal Dutch Shell. At stake was nothing less than control over the world's oil markets. He was simultaneously involved in extremely delicate negotiations with the Rothschilds, who had their tentacles deep inside Baku. When oil prices suddenly plunged, Ludvig had to continue selling oil, losing considerable sums of money, until the prices began rising again. Often the violent fluctuations were artificial, brought about by competitors in an ongoing petroleum war that would last for so long that it went down in industrial history as Europe's second Thirty Years' War.

With each new year-end account from St. Petersburg, Alfred's concerns mounted. He could see that a new era was beginning. He could also see that Ludvig seemed unconscious of how rapidly his burden of debt was increasing. Branobel was having trouble getting credit extensions. Even Ludvig was beginning to realize the gravity of the situation. He made heroic efforts to reply to Alfred's letters in detail.

Between critical comments, Alfred was careful to show his respect for Ludvig's and his staff's technical knowledge. The problem, he thought, was that the company's finance departments were not as competent. Alfred summed up his views in a memorandum of twenty-eight pages that has been preserved. In it he analyzed the problems that had brought on the present crisis and suggested solutions. He thought it would be advisable to include him in the decision process. His conclusion was that, despite generally good profits, the company was being held back by a lack of working capital. On that matter, for once, Alfred and Ludvig were of one mind.

By 1883 the Baku works had become one of the world's largest oil companies, and a new head of production needed to be selected. Alfred declared that he knew of only one person with the ability to manage such a gigantic business, and that was his own partner, Paul Barbe.

Alarming rumors were circulating about Branobel's financial condition after its rapid expansion. While it was never clear who started the rumors, it was exactly at this point that Standard Oil suddenly and drastically lowered its oil price. Through Standard Oil, the Rockefeller family controlled nine-tenths of the American oil export and had a leading position in every oil-producing country — except Russia. Branobel's export successes had become a thorn in the flesh of the Standard Oil management. Its countermove was an abrupt price dip and, in all probability, the organized spread of rumors. Profits decreased and loan interest increased.

Until March 1883, Alfred had never accepted the invitations to visit Baku and St. Petersburg that Robert and Ludvig had extended from time to time. Now, sensing the severity of the crisis threatening Branobel, he felt he had no choice. Though the youngest, his experience made him the respected figure of the three brothers, and certainly the one best equipped to clear up the situation.

His health, he maintained, was poorer than usual, and his company still involved in a complicated adjustment process, but Alfred went to St. Petersburg to see what he could do. Little of what he found was to his satisfaction. Alfred had written that he had watched with admiration Ludvig's "exceptional personal accomplishment of rapidly creating such a large-scale organization," but insisted that his brother had lost control of things because he had not followed the maxim, "Never do yourself what others could do better or equally well." Anyone who tried to do everything himself would become "worn out body and soul and probably ruined to boot." During the deliberations in St. Petersburg of that week in March 1883, Alfred branded the actions of one Branobel executive as unprofessional. The man had "been gallivanting and bustling around Europe" and his improper attempts to obtain loans had destroyed their credit at the large establishments in Paris and London. In a letter to Ludvig Alfred called the man "a real ass."

Not even the profitable oil drilling in Baku escaped Alfred's sharp tongue: was it worth his while to invest in "a business that during seven months out of the year only means expenses and nothing taken in?" He was convinced that his involvement in this adventure would one day cause the family terrible losses. (Of Alfred's net assets at the time of his death, nearly one quarter would be from Baku's oil wells.)

His stay at Ludvig's home in St. Petersburg was short, but after a few days Alfred had worked out a plan of action. First, he granted Branobel a loan against a promissory note of 4 million francs with low interest. Second, he committed himself to contributing considerable sums of money when new shares and bonds were issued in the future. Third, he suggested that the share dividends be decreased from 20 and 25 percent to only 2 percent. Fourth, he was willing to put up his own Russian government bonds as security to guarantee available means for paying the required excise tax. Fifth and finally, he promised to pledge, along with Ludvig, his total share holding in the company as security for a loan of one million rubles Branobel would get from the Russian national bank.

Alfred still feared, however, that Branobel would have difficulties regaining its economic health so long as they were competing with such powerful companies as Rockefeller's Standard Oil and the Rothschild-financed Bnito. Ludvig was convinced that, with Alfred's help, the company would not only ride out the present crisis but come out stronger than ever.

At the annual board meeting a couple of weeks following his departure, Alfred was elected, in accordance with his wishes, into both management and Branobel's board of directors. In a letter of April 3, 1883, Ludvig expresses sincere gratitude: "The help you now give us is of truly great value, and I hope that when your election as manager is announced officially, everyone will stop insisting, as they do now, that the Nobel Brothers Company is Ludvig Nobel."

Chapter 42

Paris
August 26, 1881

. . . Thank you for the small article about the projected Panama Canal. I had already heard about it. It is a grand scheme with an aura of American boldness surrounding it. But Ferdinand de Lesseps's canal construction supposedly is wrestling with great difficulties. The workers are dropping like flies and the finance marauders are being permitted to create havoc in the most upsetting ways.

In Sevran, things are progressing in earnest, and the construction will expedite things enormously. I now have to spend almost all my time there, which means I cannot take care of my health as I ought to do. My new doctor's method has otherwise been working well, so far as I can judge. My gums are actually a little less sore and the lesion in my mouth has at least not worsened. Least said soonest mended, however — perhaps the improvement is only illusory. The reason could very well be that, due to the favorable weather, I have not caught a cold. My eyes are not good at all. I can read and write only with effort.

On the whole, it is probably preciously dull and uninteresting to you if your old grumbling bear sees, lives or doesn't live, if he has rheumatism or not — no rooster will crow about it. Nobody would actually miss him if he were suddenly to move beneath the earth instead of living on top of it. . . .

Enclosed you will find a little purse fortification: 1,000 francs, which according to the Vienna exchange will translate into 467 gulden. The exchange right now is around 214.

Today I have been busy without stopping with our French company. Things got a bit heated since important decisions had to be made. . . .

Paris
September 1, 1881

. . . You complain that I don't use words of love in my
letters. Yet for years I have been pointing out that nobody
can command anyone's emotions. You are kind and lovely
but also pushy, and it is part of my freedom-loving nature
that I could not live day in and day out with such a person. Even less so if that same person were mistrustful,
jealous, and childish. I admit that at least things seem to
have improved somewhat. But even if that really is the
case, solitude is preferable.

I have myself become a stranger to society and hardly
see anyone. For me, a trusting relationship with someone
who understands me — man or woman — seems like
something truly worthy of being coveted. But you do not
understand me. You cannot grasp that the free spirit does
not want to know any chains or bonds. He could only put
up with them if he were not allowed to feel them.

I feel pity for you, all the more so the better I get to
know you. Perhaps you would have been able to bind me
to you if from the beginning you had made life pleasant
for me instead of unpleasant. But at that time you did
everything to push even someone with the best intentions
away from you. Now your young, weak soul is thirsty
for a reciprocated affection that you rightfully find to be
feeble.

Enough of preaching! . . .

P.S. Do you still have some Tokay wine left? Otherwise
perhaps you could order a few bottles.

Paris
September 4, 1881

. . . Since my return here, I have not been to visit anyone
at all — not even Victor Hugo.

Today it is Sunday, however, and I felt so lonely that I
decided to hitch up my horses and travel to St. Germain
for breakfast. It is certainly very beautiful, but since the
weather has become so chilly, the trip there gives one
faint pleasure. . . .

London
February 1882

. . . The business here is further from being set up than I
had hoped and as they had led me to believe. The general
opinion is that if any deal will come of all this, it can only
happen in Glasgow and through the influence of acquaintances. Therefore one must make good use of the fact that
my name as a businessman is very well known in all of
Scotland.

The whole matter is particularly repulsive to me. If I
were not so deeply involved in it already, I would withdraw completely. I don't mean to say by this that I
wouldn't do anything I could for my brother Ludvig.
Only that our ways of looking at things are far apart
enough in so many respects that we should have never actually worked in the same company. Still, I am going to
introduce him to the gentlemen in Glasgow and then leave
the rest to him. Possibly I will sketch the activities in
broad outlines before I withdraw.

It pains me to have to leave you alone right now. However, if you knew how much it means to me, I am certain
you would understand. In truth, it is astonishing, when it
comes to finances, how blind in both eyes the people who
manage this gigantic enterprise can be. Through a secretary I have learned, however, that fortunately it will be
run by the company manager in Petersburg, in other
words by Ludvig. . . .

Glasgow
February 28, 1882

. . . I journeyed here from London in a large empty Pull-
man car, if you don't count one Scotsman who boarded
shortly before Glasgow. So I had plenty of time to think
without being disturbed. I also tried to read *Sohn des
Flüchtlings* but, as usual with novels that have passed
through your hands, lots of pages were missing, such as
from page 92 to page 97. You should really buy hardcover
books.

My time will now be so occupied that I will hardly find

any time in which to write; besides, one is never alone in
Glasgow. People want to entertain you and do not realize
that all they are doing is bothering you. . . .

Stevenson
March 4, 1882

. . . There is much to do here; due to my long absence,
the company is in a precarious situation from which I
have to save it. The factory cannot even deliver half of the
orders it has received — truly a wonderful consequence of
your — irresponsible child that you are — having divided
my attention for a long time. But it is no use reproaching
you — it will hardly put the past right again.

As is evident from my handwriting, all the hard work
is making me nervous, and sleep has completely deserted
me. Still, I feel much more satisfied now when I am at
least not wasting time in useless ways, but accomplishing
something. . . .

London
July 8, 1882

. . . I had hardly arrived at my hotel before two of the
gentlemen here invited me for dinner at their club — in
which, by the way, ladies are not allowed. I did not return until around two o'clock in the morning. To fall
asleep was downright impossible, so I had my second
sleepless night. This is nightmarish, and my stomach is
totally out of sorts. Today we are all eating at Dr. Dewar's club. Tomorrow — Sunday — I was forced into
promising to go visit Mr. Webb in the country and spend
the day there. So far as Monday is concerned, Professor
Abel has appropriated me for dinner at his club. So this
could go on until doomsday if I don't brusquely refuse all
invitations.

The matters regarding the company are progressing
somewhat. One has every right to expect that after having spent fifteen hours every day sitting in meetings. . . .

Paris
August 1882

. . . I spent both the day before yesterday and yesterday in
Sevran. Since I had a deluge of English letters to answer, I
could not devote much time to my chemical work. I have
been at my desk since eight o'clock this morning without
yet having removed my slippers. A propos, it would be
splendid if you could find my blue-lined boots, which
were left behind in Kaiserhaus. They are exceedingly
comfortable and suitable as evening or theater shoes. I
would find it difficult to replace them. . . .

It is very nice of Ludvig to have asked you to write to
him. Don't forget however that your handwriting leaves
much to be desired. Furthermore, make an effort to write
briefly and yet to slip in something memorable. . . .

I feel that the summer has passed terribly fast without
anything truly being accomplished. My conscience pains
me almost as much as my neuralgia. . . .

And how are things going with my little clinging vine,
who is still so lovable? . . .

Among other things, I am working on getting my
brother a loan, but it takes time that I could use more effectively in Sevran. As you can see from my handwriting,
I am again plagued by nervousness. My chores are piling
up and time is getting shorter and shorter. . . .

Chapter 43

Alfred's "Account Book 1880–
1890" reveals that in March 1883 he granted Branobel a promissory
note loan of 4 million francs, which was to be paid back before the
end of the year. At the half-year mark one year later, the same source
reveals that he had invested a total of 9.5 million francs in the company. As a point of comparison, it has been documented that Alfred's
dynamite shares at this time were estimated to be worth a little over
4 million francs, and other assets 5 million.

Apart from Branobel, both he and Ludvig made a point of
keeping their businesses apart. A small but illuminating example
involves two restaurant bills from a family dinner at the Hasselbacken
restaurant in Stockholm. Their totals are relatively modest: 455 and
106 Swedish crowns respectively. Nonetheless, the two magnates
and brothers found the time to discuss by letter how they should
divide up the total.

From Alfred's letters in the fall of 1883, it is evident that he
harbored few hopes that the St. Petersburg crowd would keep his
warnings and advice in mind and move cautiously. These letters
seldom touch on the Russian oil business, and when they do it is
never in glowing terms.

Alfred was deluged with work in Paris, and his health was a
source of mounting worry. In his letters, he maintains that he had
contracted scurvy, convinced that he suffered from its most debili-
tating symptoms: an increasingly pale complexion and a paralyzing
fatigue. Fashionable doctors at health resorts such as Voslau in Austria
(where he would see Robert, who frequented the spa) told him to
eat radishes and drink grape juice. Alfred could not stand too many
days of inaction, however, and seldom stayed for the prescribed
amount of time. While building his dynamite empire, he had driven
himself so hard that after 1883 he often writes of wanting to be free
from the "slavery to which I have been subjected for years."

Ludvig was keeping to his old ways, apparently still wanting to
decide everything himself. Alfred felt it was as if he had learned
nothing, and in protest he relinquished his post on the board of
directors. In a letter to Robert on July 7, 1883, Alfred expressed his
anxiety: "Ludvig does not intend to give up the smallest bit of his

authority and will hold on to a method that is a burden to his health and drains his strength. None of us actually has the constitution to manage a gigantic mechanism such as Baku. We must be satisfied with our mental activity and leave all the mechanical work to others."

At the end of 1883, Ludvig noted that the oil drilling in Baku had been more successful than ever, but when the solvency of the company was again threatened, the antagonism between the brothers intensified. The situation is clear in a letter Ludvig sent to Robert, when the latter had informed him that he wanted his money plus interest returned without delay:

Dear Brother Robert,

In your letter to Nobel Brothers Company, you ask that your outstanding accounts plus interest, which probably corresponds to 68,000 rubles, should be transmitted to you by the end of the year, and that all losses due to exchange differences will be compensated.

You have not chosen the best moment to make your demand.

In order to cover the expenses for the years 1882 and 1883 that are due by urgent, unrelinquishable demand, the decision has been made to offer new shares amounting to five million rubles and 6 percent bonds (the former issuance of two million rubles, 5 percent bonds, is withdrawn). The government has authorized it, and the papers are therefore ready.

I have just returned from abroad, where I have worked for two months to prepare the market for our bonds, which should be issued in London in February.

The shares should be placed, for the major part, among the old shareholders, who instead of profit dividends take shares; first refusal for the rest shall be given with a premium of 20 percent to buyers of our bonds in England.

By doing this, we hope that when there has been time to arrange this and that when the income from the sold kerosene comes in, we shall be unencumbered (not counting the bonds) and provided with enough working capital so as not to have to resort to credit.

But until then, I don't feel that any of us three brothers ought to take our money out of the company nor speak of exchange differences. If you did it, why shouldn't I? The company owes you 68,000, but it owes me 2.5 million.

If you stand fast on the exchange question, I will deal with it personally, because to bring it up at the annual board meeting would be unseemly. This is a question of principle, and it must not be brought up because all the company's creditors could make similar demands.

When you consider this question more closely, I hope you will find it totally in accordance with our dignity to allow your outstanding accounts, at least for the most part, to be left in the business until the company has been able to finish the operations alluded to above.

At the upcoming board meeting I shall seek to clearly present the reasons the company has acted the way it has and how I hope the future will take shape.

With the New Year, which has already begun where you are, you and your family are wished all earthly happiness and comfort from

> Your affectionate friend and brother
> Ludvig

The solvency crisis of 1883 over, Ludvig once again felt the need to expand operations. Alfred warned him about new loans, but Ludvig refused to change his mind. Alfred, not able to stand by passively when the company was again close to breaking down, reiterated that he could have expanded his dynamite operations at least as much as Ludvig planned to expand oil production, but that he always made sure that he had the means at his disposal before he undertook an action.

Although Alfred had resigned from Branobel's board of directors, in his own way he remained loyal. He didn't sell his shares and he continued to support the company financially. He even made an effort, in a letter written sometime in 1884, to adopt a more conciliatory attitude toward Ludvig:

. . . Your warm friendly letter from Vienna delighted me more than you could know. We are both standing on the tilting plane of life and when evening is already pushing toward night, any inclination toward pettiness does not rise, an inclination that is almost always the foundation of

any kind of disagreement. Your thoughts and feelings are
too lofty for it, and as for me, I actually live in peace
with everything and everyone except with my own inner
being and those spirits from Niflheim. Least of all do I
want to fight with you, and if there has been any shadow
between us, it has long since fled, driven off by the light
of the heart.

The creditors had again begun to put the thumbscrews on Ludvig, who was increasing the size of his tanker fleet and number of
railroad cars. The tankers were now his weapon in the ongoing oil
war with the Rothschilds and Standard Oil. The sanguine Ludvig
waved off the Branobel board of directors' mounting concerns. He
maintained that in order to uphold company interests against the
stiffening competition, storage facilities were critical, and that meant
new tank structures and reloading harbors plus more depots located
not only in Russia but England and the rest of Europe.

Adding to Branobel's financial woes was that the Rothschilds,
with their seemingly infinite resources, continued to infiltrate Ludvig's Russian domestic market. They financed the building of the
railroad between Baku and Batum, and when it was finished they
let their French bank establish Société Commercial et Industrielle de
Naphte Caspienne et de la Mer Noire (soon abbreviated to "Bnito,"
after the Russian initials). Confronted with this financial giant, and
aware that Standard Oil could bring duty-free oil into Russia, Ludvig
demonstrated his great strategic skill by quietly probing the possibility of coming to an agreement with the Rothschilds.

Later Alfred would write to Robert about the Russian oil business: "The Americans are themselves beginning to find it necessary
to stop the deadly export competition. . . . They are already being
pressured to consider negotiating with Baku — a sign of the hoisting
of the peace flag. I wanted you to know about this somewhat calming
and comforting prospect."

Chapter 44

. . . To my telegraphed inquiry as to where the tortoise combs should be sent, you have given me no response. It is probably too late to send them to Ludvig since he will only stay in Marienbad until the 26th. He writes that he intends to visit you before he leaves.

I was ready to write to you earlier this morning, when Mr. Barbe's visit was announced. You cannot imagine how he has changed, and it must be due to his first losing his mother and then his father. To be honest, the latter was not at all a particularly affable individual, but he was still someone close with whom Paul Barbe could consult. Now being without parents, the spleen has him in its grip, to quote him. . . .

Other than that I have little news to report. Day before yesterday I had to accept an invitation to dinner at Victor Hugo's since it was the old gentleman's name-day party. Only the regulars were there — with the exception of a captain who talked about a daring project to create an ocean inside Africa. He has found support for his grandiose plans from the same man whose initiative started the Panama Canal, de Lesseps. Since the captain made a modest impression, he was a pleasant acquaintance. . . .

Stockholm
August 29, 1882

. . . My mother will turn seventy-nine in a few weeks, but she is as healthy and vital as one can be under the circumstances. The old lady was so happy to see me again that her eyes were shining. . . .

Stockholm
September 1882

. . . I have been forced to spend so many hours writing
letters that I have not really been able to give Mother the
attention I would have wanted. She is actually like you:
when she is happy, she can stand anything but otherwise
the slightest thing upsets her. . . .

I hope you have better weather than we have in Stockholm. Wind or rain — those are the only variations. It is
certainly not warm, and I am wearing my winter coat. I
have not yet had time to look up Nordenskiöld and Palander. There has not been enough time since Mama doesn't
live in the city during the summer but in a house in the
country. . . .

Brussels
September 11, 1882

. . . I will consult Metzger about my migraine. Perhaps
something can be done. As you have probably already figured out, I shall make use of the baths in Aachen. This is
how I see it: The Aachen water is — like the water in
Aix-les-Bains — sulfuric although much stronger. I figured I would avoid a lengthy detour if I could finish my
treatment in Aachen. But my calculations did not hold
water. I took only three showers in Aachen, and they gave
me such a headache that it has not gone away yet. . . .

Aix-les-Bains
September 21, 1882

. . . You wonder why I don't want you to come here.
The reason is very simple: Mr. Shaw and a few other
gentlemen from Glasgow are here and, as you know, all
Scotsmen are Puritans. . . . I have not forgotten what
scandalous rumors were spread about poor Downie, and I
don't want to be the subject of similar slander. A human
being can acquire ever so many costly things, but each of
us has only one name, and it is our duty to keep it as
immaculate as possible. . . .

I paid your insurance premium in Paris. It was due July 2nd. . . .

I went to Amsterdam to consult with Dr. Metzger. He told me: "You have chronic muscle inflammation but not locally; all your muscles are affected. Even though it happens to be my specialty, I cannot help you, because in your case you were born with it. My treatment methods would not lead to any lasting cure." What do you say to that? . . .

London, Army and Navy Hotel
May 22, 1883

. . . It is terribly difficult to find a roof over one's head here. I went to twenty-three hotels before I finally found accommodations in a hotel that opened its doors only yesterday. . . .

Marienbad
August 18, 1883

. . . I suppose that it is not particularly good for my health to live as lonely a life as I do. Since I came here, I have not spoken a word to a living soul. This means that I am brooding worse than ever. Of course I'm deluged with work since there are piles of letters. I have sent off eighteen today! Yours is the nineteenth. This is of course interfering with my treatment. But what to do? I cannot leave important business letters unanswered, and a secretary to help me with my correspondence is not easy to find. To write technically sophisticated and other letters in five languages is no easy matter. . . .

Dresden
September 4, 1883

. . . During the train journey I had an occasion to see how easily appearances can fool us. At first, my fellow travelers' faces seemed totally uninteresting. For several hours I had no desire to say even one word to any of them. Then, suddenly, I noticed a shy smile on the face of a young man, which gave a hint of education. I began a conversation with him, and it was not long before we were involved in an exchange of scientific ideas. He turned out to be a Dr. Thomson from London. He knew several of my acquaintances there and was himself a truly interesting person. The trip went by so fast that when we arrived in Dresden, I was surprised to learn that the train was late. Your telegram was waiting for me, by the way, along with one from Ludvig, in which he informed me that he will be arriving here tonight. . . .

The sudden request for more capital in Scotland comes at a bad time. I may have to ask for payment in cash from Russia instead of in shares, in spite of the favorable prospects there. . . .

Ostende
September 9, 1883

. . . There is a wonderful beach here. I am convinced that spending the summer here would have been better for you than Ischl and Karlsbad combined. But the child has a will of her own. . . . I am aware that people with nervous dispositions can easily develop neuralgia from the sea air, but this would disappear after a little while. Some cannot take swimming in the open sea, but one doesn't necessarily have to do it to invigorate oneself. . . .

Paris
September 21, 1883

. . . For years I have been telling you to get a female companion. Almost everything you have suffered and all the unendurable things I have been forced to go through have resulted from your disobedience about this. Can you not understand what an enormous burden it must be for a hurried man to have a fellow-traveler who knows absolutely nobody, and who as a result makes unreasonable demands on his time? This utterly draining situation, in just a few years, has aged me twenty. . . .

Isn't it a little ridiculous for you to keep an apartment here? You spend the summers away, and now you don't

want to be here in the winter either. But you are probably
right: you are not for Paris and Paris is not for you. You
ought to choose a place, however, where you really will
settle down. It could be Montreux or any place of your
choice. Anything to stop scurrying around the way you
do now. . . .

In Petersburg, it seems, a hair-raising chaos reigns.
They have not honored two of their bills of exchange.
Not from lack of money, but because the payment had
been sent to the wrong bank. What do you think of that!
Don't discuss this with anyone, and burn this letter with-
out delay!

Ludvig's address is simply: Mr. Ludvig Nobel, St. Petersburg. Write "For his own hands" on the envelope,
otherwise the letter will be opened in the office. . . .

Chapter 45

Ludvig had made a peace offering to the Rothschilds in Paris and it had been met with a favorable response. Because Alfred had so strongly advised Ludvig against competing with the Rothschilds, he noted with satisfaction in May of 1884 that Ludvig had sent two representatives — Mikhail Beliamin and the financial executive manager Ivar Lagerwall — to Rue Lafitte in Paris to begin negotiations with the Rothschilds.

The Rothschild dynasty traced its origins to Frankfurt and was known for its far-reaching connections. The family had gained political clout acting as an intermediary for state loans during the eighteenth and nineteenth centuries and maintained ties with the governments of several countries. Indeed, the Rothschilds were frequently accused of supporting reactionary regimes. But it was profit, not political goals, that guided the dynasty's actions.

When Ludvig contacted the Rothschilds' Paris office, it was headed by Alphonse Rothschild, who had been given credit for France's ability to repay, quickly, the compensation claim of 5 billion francs following the Franco-Prussian War. Alphonse did not participate personally in the negotiations with Branobel, but was represented by their Russian expert Jules Aron, who, under an oath of secrecy, informed Beliamin and Lagerwall that the Rothschilds had made a decision in principle regarding Russia: they did not intend to extend competition with Branobel any further nor enter into collusion with Branobel's rivals. Aron was willing to commit Rothschild to an agreement with Branobel, even to offer some sort of merger. This first meeting was the start of what would turn into a long series of discussions about whether or not it were possible to divvy up the world market for refined oils between them — and between them and the hard-dealing John D. Rockefeller.

Ludvig, after consulting with Alfred, gave Beliamin and Lagerwall instructions to offer the Rothschilds one-fourth of Branobel's shares, although not until the share capital had been increased from 15 to 20 million rubles. The value of those shares, Ludvig suggested, should be determined by impartial auditors. He estimated that over the next few years the company would need to raise 5 million rubles, mainly to improve its plants in Baku. Ludvig felt that his and Alfred's proposal was substantial and that it ought to interest the Rothschilds, given that they would get unlimited access to the Russian oil market at a fairly good price.

Three weeks later, Ludvig's representatives returned to Paris and were greeted by the news that they could not meet with Jules Aron, due to a family illness. The representatives who spoke on his behalf curtly refused Ludvig's offer, stating that out of principle the Rothschilds never invested in a business unless they were given majority control. They also warned Ludvig, courteously but firmly, of the Rothschilds' very considerable financial power. Ludvig's representatives responded as curtly. There could be no question of their relinquishing control over Branobel, and with an average production of thirty-two tons of oil per day they had little reason to fear the Rothschilds' financial power.

Beliamin and Lagerwall returned to St. Petersburg, and Ludvig decided to seek the loans from Berliner Disconto Bank. Jules Aron sent a telegram suggesting a new meeting in September. The meeting took place but never led to an agreement. Still, a sign that the Rothschilds remained interested in a deal seemed clear when Aron let slip that "Baron Alphonse himself" had been reading all the documents pertaining to the matter. Ludvig was invited to Paris, but this time he was the one who pleaded ill health as his excuse for declining.

Following the breakdown of negotiations in Paris with Jules Aron in 1885, Ludvig was forced to accept diminishing returns. That year, Branobel paid out only 3 percent in dividends to the shareholders and, since they planned to cancel the dividends for 1886, whispering began anew in the corridors of the European finance establishments.

The need for capital had become so great that Alfred was beginning to hesitate about offering more. Selling Branobel was hardly a realistic alternative, since the Russian government in all probability would not give permission. Realizing this, Standard Oil had begun to buy shares on the open market in order to win control over Branobel.

The tremendous pressure under which Ludvig had lived during these two years had seriously affected his health. Alfred noticed for the first time that his brother seemed vacant and dispirited. Alfred himself was close to exhaustion. The only thing that could still fill him with enthusiasm was his laboratory work. In 1885 he wrote to Alarik Liedbeck: "After the improvements with which I am involved have been completed, I intend to retire from all business life and live like an old spinster on my dividends. I will therefore eventually sell my various shares in my dynamite and other businesses. When I say that I want to live like an old spinster on my interest income, I do not mean I am going to be idle, but shall just choose a scientific rather than industrial sphere for my work."

Possibly Alfred did honestly wish to retire from the business end of things when he wrote the letter, but he was nonetheless continuing to oversee his companies. He was familiar with what was going on in Baku, and even though he was convinced that, in the end, he would lose significant sums, he had amiable discussions with Ludvig about pipelines, drill towers, and refining capacities.

Alfred's eyes and ears in Branobel was Ivar Lagerwall. Through him Alfred received confirmation of what he had suspected: the dividends to the shareholders had been too high during certain years, deviations from the budget had been too great, and last but not least overproduction had produced a drop in prices. Alfred shared Lagerwall's opinion that things had to change radically to avoid bankruptcy.

There was other news from Russia. Alfred's total dynamite income from the whole of Russia during the period 1880–1885 was only 750,000 marks, which corresponded to only a fraction of what he got from England and France. He expresses his displeasure in several letters to Ludvig.

While Ludvig's health problems — heart disease and chronic bronchitis — worsened, Branobel became even more the object of intensive interest on the part of the Rothschilds and the Rockefellers. In June 1886, Jules Aron made the lengthy journey from Paris to Baku, where he inspected the Nobel works and even drew up plans for the modernization of a refinery that Bnito had purchased. In September, it was Standard Oil's turn. They sent William Herbert Libby, fully equipped with power of attorney, to see Ludvig in St. Petersburg. Conversations between them led to nothing, though "the oil king of Baku" felt flattered by the visit. Libby's interest cooled rapidly when he realized that Branobel did not have total control over the Russian oil export. Libby had nourished the idea of dividing the export with an eye toward stabilizing the price of oil. Again, the experts at Rockefeller headquarters felt that for the foreseeable future they had no reason to fear Nobel's presence on the world oil market.

In 1886, things got worse for Branobel and Ludvig. Overproduction increased and the value of the Russian ruble sank. Acquiring the necessary credit was becoming more and more difficult, and even the most patient shareholders were beginning to sell off their holdings. Ludvig tried to keep his spirits up and wrote to Alfred that fall: "It is not worth bowing one's head because one meets with adversity; it will not last forever." Since it was turning out to be impossible to obtain credit under any conditions, he was beginning to feel defiant despair: "Even if the public — thoughtless as ever — denies me credit, I say to them: I CAN MAKE IT ANYHOW, maybe with less profit, but I CAN MAKE IT!"

In the beginning of 1887 it was discovered that Ludvig's bronchial trouble was caused by tuberculosis. The course of his illness was slow, but Ludvig decided to retire (exactly eight years after Robert's early retirement). He handed over the management of Branobel to his twenty-nine-year-old son, Emanuel.

For two months, Ludvig remained bedridden in St. Petersburg, then, with his wife and some of their children, he went to Cannes. It was too late to do him much good, however. French physicians diagnosed advanced angina with arteriosclerosis in the arteries surrounding his heart. He died on April 12, 1888, at the age of fifty-seven. According to his death certificate the cause of death was a heart attack. Ludvig's body was brought back to St. Petersburg.

One French newspaper thought it was Alfred, not Ludvig, who had died. Knowing that the inventor of dynamite had also been somehow involved in the weapons industry and had invented a new gunpowder for cannons, the obituary characterized Alfred as a "merchant of death" who had built a fortune by discovering new ways to "mutilate and kill." Alfred was in his laboratory in Sevran when he read this, and it pained him so much he never forgot it. Indeed, he became so obsessed with his posthumous reputation that he rewrote his last will, bequeathing most of his fortune to a cause upon which no future obituary writer would be able to cast aspersions.

Ludvig's funeral was on April 28, 1888, in Holy Katarina's Swedish Church. Both Robert and Alfred had been advised, for health reasons, not to make the long journey to St. Petersburg. The German-language newspaper St. Petersburg Zeitung wrote that the burial ceremony was carried out "unter grossen Beteiligung der ganzen Residenzbevolkerung" [with the participation of the whole local population]. More than two thousand people joined the funeral procession from the church to the Evangelical Lutheran Smolensky graveyard at Vasiljevsky Ostrov. "Mounted policemen had been ordered to keep order," continued the account.

Chapter 46

Aix-les-Bains
June 17, 1884

. . . Ever since I came here to rest, I have been up to my
ears in work. The Glasgow crowd leaves me not even one
moment of peace. Writing like this all day long means
that no treatment in the world could improve my health.
Just today I have had to write a 17–page letter to Glasgow
and feel absolutely dizzy. But the people over there have
made such a mess that fairly soon no one will be able to
clear it up. . . .

I spent most of the journey here reading the Turgenev
novel [*Fathers and Sons*] I had brought along. It is indeed
very moving. I shall send it to you. . . .

Aix-les-Bains
June 19, 1884

. . . When I say that I am staying at a hotel, that is not
accurate. I feel as if I had been committed to a hospital,
where those who are least ill have suffered at least three
strokes. If anyone manages to walk faster than one step
per minute, that person is a comparatively healthy speci-
men. That's not even the worst: everywhere I look, I see
nothing but ringworm, abscesses, and other skin problems in the faces of strangers. These ghastly visions make
me nauseous and so I wear dark glasses. A line from
Schiller keeps echoing in my mind: "The earth is a vale of
tears." To recuperate from all this misery, I had the idea
of going to the theater. They were putting on *La Baule* —
a rather humorous little farce piece [named after a famous
resort town in northwest France]. But when the actors
laughed, their teeth were so rotten that a stench of death
spread throughout the theater. The faces of the actors
made me think so much of an anatomical mausoleum that
after my return to the hotel I almost felt pleasure seeing
the slightly-less-rotting half-corpses there.

A fifty-year-old, half-paralyzed, hunchbacked, tooth-
less, pimply-faced, red-nosed, moustache-adorned, pock-
marked, stammering, filthy, flat-footed, red-eyed beauty
with sweaty feet and filthy nails, dressed in German
clothes and snuffing tobacco, has gotten it into her head
that I am totally in love with her. Yet she looks as un-
appetizing as those actresses I saw if one sits too close to
the stage where the illumination is not as merciful. . . .

I groan under the burden of so many complaints —
most of them from England — so that for a few moments
I must be allowed to joke.

Whatever else one says, the scenery here is very beautiful, the facilities excellent, the food tasty and not expensive, and for a person losing a million francs a month
right now that's not something to sneeze at. . . .

I wanted to make you laugh but don't know if I have
succeeded. In any case I seal the jokes with a heartfelt
kiss.

                                                    Alfred

                                                Hamburg
                                            July 7, 1884

. . . You continue to seek peace and rest in the most faraway countries, to which I neither can nor want to accompany you. This is how it has been for almost seven
whole years now — in the most thoughtless way, with no
advantage to you and with such great sacrifices on my
part that they have devastated my life. My only wish is to
devote myself to my profession, to science. I look upon
all women — young and old — as disturbing invaders
who steal my time. I have been pointing this out for
seven years, and you have been unable or unwilling to understand. Instead of completing my laboratory work, I
have been forced to become a nanny to a grown spoiled
child, who believes that she can indulge in any whims
whatsoever. Had you been content with a permanent residence in the country where I live, your existence could
have been so pleasant. That way, you also would not have
complicated my life in such an inconsiderate way and
to such a degree that I have become an object of ridicule to

my acquaintances. Between us exists a past filled with bitterness for me; I would be willing to forget it, however, if
lost time could somehow be made up.

But let us forget the past. I am cautioning you only in
order to make you open your eyes. How do we arrange
things in the near future? You want a small villa in Ischl?
Fine, we'll buy it. But what then? I am as likely to make a
pilgrimage to Ischl as I am to make one to hell. . . .

Paris
August 9, 1884

. . . It doesn't take much imagination to tell you that this
supposed nobleman is an idiot who is making a play for
you. Let him run, because people who grab hold that way
are not worthy of one's company.

From a real Excellency I received an exceptionally
friendly letter yesterday. The courteous tone could hardly
be topped. During my stay in London, the Finance Minister of France sent me an official decree, signed by the
President, announcing I had been appointed to a higher
rank in the Legion of Honor. About the honor itself I
could not care less, but the manner in which it was com-
municated to me has made a very strong impression. I am
beginning to see that the French can be quite delightful.

I have paid your rent and enclose the receipt. Do not
lose it. . . .

I need to explain my reason for being in Paris today.
There have been two explosion accidents — one in Paulilles and one in Portugal. They want to close our French
factory and naturally we are protesting strongly and
firmly. A meeting has been announced for Friday and of
course I have to be present. . . .

Vienna
August 19, 1884

. . . I almost admire the ridiculous things a little woman
can manage to cook up in her pretty head. No idea is too
insane. In other words, you would drive from Ischl to Vienna and back again in order to spend a few hours with

your unpleasant old Grumble Bear. Into the bargain, your journey would be utterly risky since, according to the calendar, you might be indisposed during the trip.

Paris
August 29, 1884

. . . The past few days the weather has been chilly and more like autumn. It is probably also getting colder in Vienna, so that you hardly need to seek to refresh yourself at Sennerling. In fact, you must take care not to catch a cold, so put on your woolen underwear.

Write me diligently and tell me how you are, do not spoil coachman # 665, who has already been too spoiled by me with tips, do not cry when there is thunder, do not shiver before the devil, honor the emperor and admire the empress, say hello to little Olga [Olga Boettger, Sofie's sister], even if she is of less noble family, throw pebbles at Bella [Sofie's pet dog], and be warmly embraced by

Your
Alfred

[n.d., 1884]

. . . The first page of your letter makes it obvious that you are having a very good time without me. You even suggest that I should not pain myself by making unnecessary trips, from which I conclude that you would rather not be bothered by me. You can be sure of it; I am indeed not going to disturb you. You also don't have to write such long letters. Your handwriting makes it all too clear that only a sense of duty forces you to darken that many pages. But that's how it is: when young ladies need money from old gentlemen, they feel forced to formulate wordy compliments and curtsy with their pen. In fact, their thoughts are with someone else and they think one too stupid to figure that out. Yet, I could become reconciled to this if at least you did not use my name everywhere so that people wouldn't be secretly laughing at me. . . .

I am living nearly full-time in Sevran and in one week

have accomplished more in my laboratory than during the three months you were here.

Never before have I seen Paris so empty of people. Everyone able to go away has gone, and there are no tourists here at all. The fear of cholera is the reason. All the restaurants and hotels have hardly any guests. Day before yesterday I ate at the Grand Hotel — there were eight other people!!! Normally, several hundred would be dining there at this time of the year. . . .

My coachman has given notice. He did not like it when I criticized his being late half an hour when he had to harness the horses — which I had ordered him to do at a definite time. So now I have to go to the trouble of finding a new coachman and can't leave here before I have hired someone.

I understand that you are having a pleasant time. As with all fun things, it is indeed not inexpensive. What is truly costly is that as a consequence my name is being slandered. You lack the delicacy necessary in such a situation to preserve other people's reputation and good name. I am your friend, but I would like you more if you married a fine, honest young man and became a good wife. Your frequent association with beaus will only lead you astray — and is compromising me. . . .

Paris
September 20, 1884

. . . I have carried out the tasks you gave me, so far as possible. Your scribbles made it next to impossible to form any idea of what you actually wanted. "Pieds" for instance means just "feet" and since feet are hardly for sale at the Louvre,[1] it was not possible to purchase any. Amputated human feet are generally not goods offered for sale in civilized countries. Anyhow, the dress has been ordered at Moret. At the Louvre I bought gloves, ruche, veils, and scarves in great numbers and had everything sent to Meissl's Hotel in Vienna; it ought to be there Wednesday. I could not buy any hats at Reboux since I

[1] A store, near the museum of the same name.

did not know where I should have them sent. . . . Your
errands are becoming difficult to carry out to the letter,
since I have to leave on a trip and cannot postpone it for
your silly clothes.

Here I am all alone in the big metropolis, so isolated
from all humanity that my life feels more deserted and
empty than ever. At my age, one needs to have someone
around, someone to live for and to love. You could have
been that person, but you have done everything imaginable to make it impossible. From the very first day I
begged you to educate yourself, since it is impossible to
love someone of whose lack of delicacy one feels ashamed
every day, every hour.

You must not have been aware of my embarrassment,
because otherwise you might have made an effort long
ago to acquire at least some little cultivation. Even if I
were head over heels in love with you, your latest letter
would have been like an icy shower. It is impossible to ignore the disgrace caused by someone writing — or rather
scribbling — in this wretched manner, all the more so
when she uses an honest man's name when she sends her
wretched epistles out into the world.

It happens to be so, my dear little child, that if you pay
no attention whatsoever to your education, you will have
to be satisfied with an inferior position in society.

You are always saying that I am incapable of loving
anyone. This is completely wrong; I could even hold you
dear if it were not that your lack of education pains me
and brings me humiliations. But what use are all my ex-
planations? You can't even grasp that a man could attach
such significance to concepts such as respect and self-
esteem. If we had only been of the same mind on that
point, things would not be as they are today. . . .

Paris
October 11, 1884

. . . To judge from the way you bade me farewell, you
seem to think I ought to feel fortunate to be your cash
steward and obedient servant, the one toward whom you
don't need to go to any effort. . . .

Paris
October 15, 1884

. . . It is becoming highly objectionable to me that you are introducing yourself to people using a borrowed name. If you cannot understand that, things are not well in your head. . . .

My nephew is here in Paris and staying with me. In addition, I have more than enough work and endless conferences. . . .

In the past whenever I left, you always accompanied me to the station. And you wrote to me every day — now things are different. I am not complaining, just establishing that this is how things are now. At the same time that you seem to want to get away from me, you make more and more claims on me, and avail yourself of my name more and more frequently. If you have the capacity to put yourself at all in my position, you must realize what injustices you are committing against me. . . .

Paris
October 26, 1884

. . . I am worn out and deathly tired of all the meetings here. They begin at nine o'clock and last until the wee hours of the morning. Even today — Sunday — will be the same. I have to sneak out in order to quickly jot down these few words to you. The whole process is horribly strenuous and I don't feel that I can see the end of it all yet. But I hope that this time we will achieve something so that all our efforts have not been in vain. . . .

Chapter 47

After Ludvig's death, the responsibility that fell upon the shoulders of his son was heavy indeed. Not only did Emanuel take his father's place as head of the oil company, he became the guardian for his seven younger siblings. His brother Carl, who was twenty-six at the time of their father's death, became manager of the machine factory in St. Petersburg.

To Alfred, Ludvig's death was an expected but nonetheless painful experience. They had never agreed on Branobel's invest-ment program but that didn't prevent their relationship from being marked by brotherly affection. Whatever their differences, Alfred had invested more than a quarter of his fortune in Branobel.

To Alfred's delight, Emanuel had shown a definite propensity for business early on. Alfred had therefore been systematically introducing him to the twists and turns of the international finance maze. When Emanuel turned twenty-two, in 1881, Ludvig nom-inated him as Branobel's finance manager — possibly because of pressure from Alfred, who was critical of how the company's accounting was being done.

When Emanuel took over the business, he soon got his bap-tism by fire. For the company to survive, a bank loan of 4 million rubles was critical; with discreet assistance from Alfred, Emanuel managed to obtain the loan. He put up future deliveries of kerosene as security, and this was accepted. Alfred touches on the affair in some letters to Robert:

Semmering
August 30, 1889

Dearest Brother Robert,

Letter-writing neglect burdens my conscience, but if you knew to what degree I have been overloaded with work, you would find it totally natural that letters to which there is no chance of responding immediately are daily put on my list and marked with XX (i.e., must not be postponed) — and then still go unanswered for months.

I am too much of a philosopher to think of anything as truly all-important, but you enter the ring, and if you have even a trace of that perverse quality called a sense of duty, you slave until you drop.

Thank you for Hjalmar's photograph. The sun does not flatter him. His own appearance, as I remember it, is a good degree more attractive and pleasant. Besides, of all the Nobels, I believe him to be the only one who is truly happy — in my eyes, the greatest of all virtues, although it often leads to mischievousness. But that is also a virtue and — like a seed — is at the root of all virtues as well.

You ask if I am going to Petersburg. I would gladly do so, for several good reasons, but of late I have been immensely tired and far from in satisfactory health. I have even begun to take medicines that I detest and to which I do not resort unless I absolutely have to. If I felt well enough, of course I would go there.

The point of my going would be to help make the Baku shares marketable, which actually ought not to be a superhuman feat.

Have for some time been negotiating on Emanuel's behalf with Disconto Gets in Berlin, but they are overly cautious, and I have to believe that we should not make ourselves dependent on them. The largest market for these shares will surely be in Russia, but the capitalizing will scarcely rise above an 8 percent dividend. . . .

With Alfred behind him in the shadows, Emanuel was able to survive his first big confrontation. Three years later, Alfred had become worried about Emanuel's closest colleague. He makes no attempt to hide his concern from Robert:

San Remo
September 13, 1892

. . . I have long thought there to be "something rotten in Denmark," as Hamlet expresses it. Replace "Denmark" with "Branobel" or the Nobel Bros. However, the cure is often more dangerous than the disease. You cannot remove even a good-for-nothing without being certain of his successor. Beliamin is no wastrel, although he does lack all leadership abilities. . . . Replacing him will mean finding someone who in a short amount of time can get

a clear general picture and who has the ability to
lead. . . .

It would be better to look among Finns or foreigners,
such as Scotsmen who speak Russian and who have managed some large works or some large business in which
they have demonstrated considerable administrative talent.
It is not necessary for them to be currently unemployed
because they should be offered such advantages that they'd
be more than willing to leave their present position.

Emanuel insists that such a person will not be found in
Russia. All that proves is Emanuel's inability to find him.

You find suitable candidates in two ways. One is by acquaintances recommending somebody who might fit the
description, and then carefully inquiring into such person's capability and moral character. The second is
through advertising. But the ad must be intelligently done
and clear in style so that you get a limited number of responses and aren't bothered by eternal inquiries. I have always had success with the advertising method.

When you find a person who inspires total confidence,
he should be employed in management, and then asked to
recommend another extremely capable person whom he
knows. Present employees should not be considered. If
the management is constructed this way, Beliamin's capacity for causing further confusion will be immediately paralyzed. As soon as the new man has had time to take
stock of things — for which studying all contracts and
settlements is necessary — and some of the correspondence, then B. could be dropped. Before then, it would
be a dangerous thing to do.

That would be my program. . . .

*Emanuel's negotiating manner resembled Alfred's, according
to accounts by witnesses. He was courteous and flexible, and Uncle
Alfred gladly assisted his nephew during the negotiations with the
Rothschilds and Rockefellers. With Alfred's approval, Emanuel
was hoping for either an arrangement or a sensible division of the
market. He was a brilliant negotiator but lacked Alfred's ability
to surround himself with competent workers, a problem of which
Alfred takes note:*

Paris
September 23, 1892

. . . I would be very glad to accept your extremely kind
invitation if I were only even halfway "cut from the
same cloth" as most normal people. But I have been a
frozen wretch my whole life, hardly able to stand a whiff
of wind or rain, and at night, when Getå began to get
little calls from the North Pole, I felt hoar-frost in my
veins.

It is miserable to be so constituted, and even more miserable that such a monstrosity wasn't immediately
drowned in Lethe's deep and spacious river.[1] My sensitivity to cold, and nothing else, has driven me to the shores
of the Mediterranean Sea, where people are not at all as
educated or trustworthy as in the North, and where the
ocean surf is the only washerwoman and flushes away im-
purity from the shore.

But the summers are so warm that even my paws
thaw, and all the mosquito bites are proof that these little
jolly but bloodthirsty creatures accept me as a host.

I have written to Emanuel about the importance of
employing one or two energetic and skilled co-managers of
more independent mind than those presently employed,
who would be able to make use of Beliamin without
being his subordinates, as is the case with the present
ones.

It is an immense mistake to try to force the Americans
out of the European market in order to guarantee the sales
to India and Australia. The Rothschilds have in this respect been much wiser.

If I remember correctly, the sales to India amount to
220,000 tons and about 14,000,000 pounds, of which a
large amount goes through the Rothschilds, and the prices
there are considerably higher than in Europe.

I wrote to Emanuel that bringing in fresh, competent
management is of greater importance than he believes,
since otherwise the large shareholders, who from a distance cannot keep track of the details of the business,

---

[1] According to Greek mythology, Lethe is the river of forgetfulness in the
underworld.

might gain a pessimistic view of things — which easily could lead them to quick sales of shares, i.e., disposing of them *à tout prix*. That would be irreparably damaging to the Company's credit, as well as to Emanuel's and the Company's position. . . .

San Remo
September 16, 1893

. . . But now a few words about Baku. I am aware that Emanuel is quite indecisive, but so are all the Nobels, you less than the rest of us, but even you have inherited a little of it. This would in itself not be so dangerous if he only understood how to choose his people. Ludvig XIII [Louis XIII, king of France, 1610–1643], that miserable beggar, was the most indecisive of human beings but at his side he had a Richelieu, who understood in a way seldom seen how to handle an enormous administration.

If I knew of some truly suitable person, I would force him to join the company as managing director. Emanuel could reign — pro forma preside — but the reins must be put into the hands of someone with true leadership ability. As long as this is not the case, the Baku shares are somewhat shaky.

Regarding Standard, I do not completely share your opinion. They could ruin a Russian company here and there, perhaps many of them. But they cannot block Russia from competing on the world market. They will soon enough realize this and come to a sensible agreement. . . .

Mailand
March 14, 1884

. . . I met with Emanuel in Berlin. Even though he only "sings songs of hints," I believe the situation in Russia to be very serious. How could it be otherwise? Beliamin is old and worn out and is supposedly unable to involve himself in the business for weeks on end. Emanuel has absolutely no leadership ability, at least that is the general consensus in Petersburg. Everything drifts aimlessly. Now a cartel has come to life that seems to puzzle Emanuel to no end. . . .

I consider it extremely urgent that the Company get a director — but, having never had anything to do with the people in Russia, I am not competent to judge who within the Company would be suitable for that position. However, it is my opinion that if no competent head is appointed, the Company is going to meet with a not-too-distant ruin. Perhaps I am exaggerating the blackness of the picture, but as you well remember, Lagerwall has prophesied something along those lines for quite some time, and even if his pessimism sometimes leads him astray, it is not completely without foundation. . . .

Chapter 48

Next to Beliamin, the other key member of Emanuel's management group was Karl Hagelin, who played roughly the same role for Ludvig and Emanuel that Alarik Liedbeck did for Alfred. No fewer than two hundred Swedish engineers and other specialists had sought work in faraway Baku, but Emanuel's closest advisor became Hagelin, whose father, Wilhelm Hagelin, had been employed by Ludvig as manager of the St. Petersburg factory. "I am diligent because I am actually lazy," wrote the younger Hagelin in his memoirs. "I want to get my work done and over with so I can laze about, but my work has always grown faster than I could finish it."

The "lazy" Hagelin had realized at a tender age that Branobel could give him a place in the sun if he had the right knowledge and skills. He had therefore saved his money for years to go back to school, and he attended Stockholm's Technical University from 1883 to 1885. Hagelin's diligence as a student brought him recognition: under Ludvig's personal guidance he was invited to carry out experiments in the St. Petersburg laboratory to find a better method of extracting kerosene from oil, which would improve the profits in Baku. What was involved was breaking down the internal carbon bonds to obtain lighter hydrocarbons.

The challenge suited Hagelin. After a year of experiments, he came up with a process that improved the yield. Following suggestions from both Ludvig and Alfred, Hagelin's method for transferring the oil's heavier hydrocarbons to lighter hydrocarbons would in time be of decisive importance to the world's automobile industry. It opened the door for American researchers, who two decades later extracted gasoline from oil using essentially the same method.

With typical modesty, Hagelin reports in his memoirs that "the Americans got into the act at least fifteen years after Ludvig Nobel had posed the problem and I, by degrees, had solved it our way, a way the Americans had not used. . . . In this experiment in the field of the naphtha industry, Ludvig had shown his great foresight and vision. And I had the privilege to work with him and perhaps even show that I was good for something."

Hagelin had won his stripes, and he was transferred to Baku, where he became technical chief of Branobel.

In 1893, Emanuel's younger brother Carl died suddenly at the Bellevue Hotel in Zurich as a consequence of his severe diabetes. He was never replaced as head of the machine works in St. Petersburg; Emanuel took over his responsibility. Despite Alfred's skepticism about his nephew's leadership qualities, Emanuel had been showing proof of both presence of mind and an ability to act, once he was out of the shadow of his dominating father.

Unlike his father and grandfather, Emanuel felt no connection to his Swedish roots. He was and remained a Russian gentleman with almost princely habits. At his banquets the ladies might find a diamond brooch under the artfully folded napkin. The nurse Maja Huss provides the following snapshot: "We received flowers and gifts yesterday, just as if it were Christmas Eve. Mr. Nobel gives me so much that Mrs. Nobel is really upset and just told me that he spoils everyone in the house, and I feel unhappy — a beautiful gold chain with an egg of Siberian stone and a diamond pin. He is so terribly kind, and he can afford it, too."

As the head of one of Russia's largest businesses, Emanuel received plenty of recognition. As his grandfather and father did, he received the highest Imperial honor, and in 1896 Czar Alexander III traveled to Baku to visit the Nobels. The czar in fact stayed with Emanuel for so long that he had no time left to visit the competition, which his host did not mind at all. Acting upon a direct suggestion from the czar, Emanuel became the first and only Nobel to apply for and receive Russian citizenship.

Less than six months after this royal visit, Branobel faced a new crisis that threatened not only the family's good name but the very existence of the company. Alfred's death on December 10, 1896, caused the company stock to take a dramatic dive on the world's financial markets. Rumors spread in European financial circles that Alfred's will requested that a large amount of his shares in the Nobel businesses must be sold without delay to finance his new foundation. In a panic, Emanuel's friends and advisors pleaded with him to contest the legality of Alfred's will.

Yet up until his death, Alfred had discreetly but effectively supported Emanuel in the latter's attempts to reach an agreement that would end the thirty-year oil war. On March 14, 1895, a preliminary agreement regarding raw oil and refined products was reached between Emanuel, the Rothschilds' Jules Aron, and Standard Oil's

William H. Libby. Standard Oil received 75 percent of the world market, and Emanuel, the Rothschilds, and the Russians 25 percent. Thereby the lengthy oil war was ended, and three men — Emanuel Nobel, Aron, and Libby — had divided the world between themselves.

In 1899, Karl Hagelin was called back to St. Petersburg, where at Emanuel's suggestion he had been appointed to succeed the retiring Beliamin. Hagelin, Emanuel's closest technical advisor, had become one of the five managing directors who, under his guidance, ran Branobel's day-to-day operations. When Branobel celebrated its twenty-fifth anniversary in 1904, the following figures were recorded:

    12,000 employees
    13,000,000 Swedish crowns in annual salaries
    5 refineries
    7 factories for spare parts and repair
    150 depots
    1,500 tank cars
    12 large tankers and innumerable barges
    30,000,000 Swedish crowns in annual transport
        costs

By then Nobel oil production in Baku topped the American and was the second largest in the world. One hundred and forty wells pumped 15 million tons of oil annually, which meant that Russia accounted for more than half of the world's oil production. Had Alfred lived to see this development, he would have been the first to admit that he had misjudged oil's ability to generate fabulous profits and underestimated Emanuel's performance.

The first major strike in Russia's history broke out in 1904, and, by the end of that year, a general strike was called by the oil workers as well. Lenin called the disturbances in Baku "the large rehearsal." In 1901, the police had opened fire on a crowd of people in Tiflis, and Lenin had characterized the incident as "the beginning of an open revolutionary movement in Caucasia."

Nobel's competitors were by and large profiteers and lacked Ludvig's and Emanuel's sense of responsibility toward their employees. The result was that revolutionaries like Stalin found fertile ground in Baku. Stalin would later declare in a newspaper interview that it was there he received his "revolutionary christening in combat" and "learned what it means to lead great numbers of workers through the storm of conflicts between workers and employer."

In 1905, Emanuel managed to get a twenty-year loan of 34.4 million Swedish crowns from the Berliner Disconto Gesellschaft at 5 percent interest. The strikes in Russia were viewed as a temporary phenomenon.

As a consequence of management's generous personnel policies, Nobel's employees were content with establishing permanent committees in order to avoid "misunderstandings between management and workers." For his part, Emanuel was prepared to accept many of his workers' demands, except the right to have a voice in decisions directly affecting the production. Having Russian citizenship was now an advantage to Emanuel (he kept it until 1923). In 1906, there were demands to weed out the nation's capitalists and Jews, as well as to confiscate all assets of foreigners.

In 1911, Branobel's annual profits were the highest in the company's history. Emanuel had built himself a new office, located near the Jekaterinensky canal, which was so impressive it looked like a palace. In 1912, Ludvig Nobel's Machine Factory was transformed into a joint-stock company with 4 million rubles in share capital. During the first year of the World War I, 25 percent of the shares in Branobel were paid in dividends. The following year, in 1915, the dividends rose to 30 percent.

By 1916, the third year of the war, 40 percent of the shares in Branobel were paid in dividends. That year Branobel controlled businesses, either directly or indirectly, employing more than fifty thousand workers. In Baku, the "Nobelites" produced one third of all Russian oil, 40 percent of all fuel oil, and more than 50 percent of all lubricating oil. Even given the ravages of wartime inflation, the year's profits exceeded 75 million rubles. Alfred died leaving assets worth more than 33 million Swedish crowns; there is no exact figure of Emanuel's fortune at this time, but it was probably several times that. By 1917, dissatisfaction among the starving populace of St. Petersburg, now called Petrograd, found violent expression. Karl Hagelin wrote in his diary: "Thursday, March 8. The streetcars in Nevsky have stopped. Strikes in several factories. The police are clearing the streets of people yelling 'Bread!' "

Under the leadership of Lenin, Trotsky, Zinovyev, and others, the October Revolution succeeded, and the Bolsheviks took over the government. The following year, the Bolshevik party would change its name to the Communist Party. The assets of the Nobel enterprises were seized, and the companies were nationalized. Two members of the Nobel family were thrown into jail.

A quarter of a century earlier Alfred had written to his brother Robert: "A new reign of terror, arising from deep within society, is working its way out of the darkness, and one can almost already hear its hollow grumble from far away."

Emanuel and his family sought refuge at the health resort Jessentuki in Caucasia. Disguised as a farmer and using a false passport, he brought his family out of Russia. They arrived in Stockholm in December 1918. Emanuel was so exhausted by the ordeal that he had to be carried on a stretcher. By 1919, economic chaos and starvation dominated large parts of Russia. The oil industry in Baku, which might have provided the new regime with export income, was paralyzed. Karl Hagelin would later receive an inquiry asking if he were interested in acting as a "technical advisor" and organizing a reconstruction of the Russian oil industry. He chose instead to accept the post as Swedish consul general in Petrograd.

On July 30, 1920, Emanuel's son Gösta Nobel signed an agreement with Standard Oil in Paris, thereby assuring financial security for the Nobel family members. Through the Standard Oil's holding company in Switzerland, $6,560,000 would be paid for 13,000 shares of Branobel, and another $4,932,000 against 5,000 more shares when the Nobels had regained their property.

The Americans were not the only ones acquiring nonexisting Russian enterprises. Paris cafés were becoming veritable broker offices where shares, jewelry, paintings, icons, and other valuable items were sold for close to nothing by desperate refugees, the White Russians who had lost everything they owned.

After a stay at the Hotel Meurice in Paris, Emanuel decided to move to Sweden permanently. Branobel thereby acquired a legal home in Sweden, from where the Nobel family's non-Russian assets were administered, out of reach of the new Russian power structure.

Emanuel regained his Swedish citizenship in 1923. He lived with his sister Marta and her family on the fourth floor of an apartment building in Stockholm, facing life's adversities with a stoic attitude. The only touch of bitterness anyone ever heard from him was when

he said that "nationalization is a beautiful word for a very ugly thing."
He suffered a stroke on March 6, 1931, and died on May 31, 1932.

Branobel was dissolved in 1964, its eighty-fifth year.

In 1971, Ingrid Agrell, the daughter of the Nobel nurse Maja
Huss, visited Leningrad, as St. Petersburg was then called. She went
to the place where the Nobel family's princely palace once stood.
The house was still standing, its facade covered with posters providing information about the activities it now housed: study circles,
theater, concerts, different kinds of courses. When she returned again
in 1984, she found the building bolted and barred, the windows
nailed closed; all activities had ceased. An elderly female guard refused her entry. In 1991, the new government decided to establish
a Nobel Museum, as well as erect a monument to honor Alfred
Nobel. This could be seen both as a celebration of the world-
renowned benefactor, who had spent his entire youth in St. Petersburg, and as a sign of the new appreciation for capitalists like the
family Nobel, who played a decisive role in Russia's emergence as
an industrial nation.

Chapter 49

Berlin
January 5, 1887

My dear little Sofie!

I am leaving for Paris tonight and write these lines surrounded by piles of luggage. . . .

One's whole life is a fight to reach new goals, but if everyone who has the ability to do so didn't make his contribution, nothing would be achieved. Human beings would live like wild animals in the forest. In your family, however, the contributions don't even add up to zero; on the other hand, much is spent. If everyone did that, it would be terrible. . . .

[n.d., 1887]

. . . My dear weak child — you are afraid of loneliness. Yet you refuse to understand that the main reason that I cannot stand being with you is the total lack of intellectual stimulation. You believe that I am so restless I can't stand to be with anyone anywhere. That isn't so — nobody is less flighty than I. But I do not wish to deteriorate. Neither do I want to associate with someone who cannot grasp that one has certain social duties, and that these have to be fulfilled if one does not wish to hurt others' feelings, or make oneself into a figure of ridicule. All this is of course Greek to you. It is a pity. . . .

Paris
October 1887

. . . For nine days I have been sick in bed. I have nobody around except for a paid servant. Nobody inquires after me. All my acquaintances avoid me because of all the malevolent gossip that was further fueled by your behavior in Vienna, when you used my name, which you have no right to do. For you then to calmly ask me for money, I consider a bit too thick. . . .

It is possible that I am more seriously ill than my doctor thinks. The pain will not go away. My heart is as heavy as lead. . . .

Paris
October 31, 1887

. . . I thank you for your kind offer to come here, but I know exactly what your visit would entail. I would have to run around with my sick lung to find an apartment for you. Then I would have to listen to your eternal complaints about it not being good enough. After that you would hurl unjust accusations against my relatives that would border on pure slander. Added to this would be your limitless pretensions.

In spite of all this, I cannot forget that once you were fond of me. Of this not even a glimmering remains, and hasn't for some time. Even a woman's common habit of sending birthday greetings didn't happen this year. . . .

Paris
November 13, 1887

. . . By and by things will go downhill for you. Soon — possibly even very soon — when I am resting in my grave, who then will be left to show you generosity? Everyone is withdrawing from you. Actually, you have a good heart, but your egotism and thoughtlessness irritate others and create loneliness around you. . . .

[n.d., 1887]

. . . My hair has turned gray but not as gray as my soul by a long shot. It feels strange when someone at my age — with the tomb as my closest neighbor — is alone because there is nobody who cares. In addition, I have my fifteen-hour-long workdays, filled to the brim with worries and difficulties of various kinds plus a nearly total collapse of health.

If only I had someone around who truly understood me and who had not set out to rob me of honor and respectability. To find such a person would probably be possible — since age and sex do not matter — but it takes time and of that I have less than ever. . . .

You and I have never understood each other. As a blind person cannot grasp what colors truly are, you have not the slightest inkling of what concepts such as consideration and tactfulness mean. . . .

Paris

December 1, 1887

. . . My hearing is beginning to go, I am depressed, and my digestion has never been worse. I feel that the old machinery will not work much longer; therefore I work like a horse in order to get everything done. It does not go as fast as I would wish, and since I have more severe headaches than ever, even my thinking activities take longer. . . .

Paris

December 24, 1887

. . . I would gladly have gone to Vienna during the Christmas holidays if the following reasons had not presented obstacles. First, I would not have been able to stay at Meisel's, and I would have wanted to save you any trouble by going to another hotel. Secondly, spending Christmas Eve with your family would have been unavoidable, something that, as things stand presently, would only have been unpleasant. Thirdly, I no longer have the strength to make long-distance trips without rest. I feel that I have aged, and that my future is more uncertain than ever.

Alfred

Chapter 50

It is your wounded honor that puts a fever into your blood.

Nemesis, Act III, scene i

Alfred's headaches were sometimes so severe that he had to remain in bed for days on end. After such an ordeal, he would sometimes travel to the health resort at Trouville-sur-Mer in Normandy, world-famous for its invigorating ocean baths. During his brief stay there in September 1878, he wrote a few lines to Sofie that, bearing in mind that he was then no more than forty-five years old when he wrote them, are remarkable: "An ashen veil has settled over Paris, and a lemming procession of vehicles and human beings moves along its boulevards. Such racket after the calm of the country! How a person can change! Only a few years ago, I longed for the big city with its hectic life. Today I long to go away from here to enjoy a period of earthly calm in a serene place to prepare for the everlasting peace."

Apart from fulfilling his duties, Alfred isolated himself more than ever before. One Friday night in the late 1870s, however, his partner Paul Barbe managed to induce him to come along to the salon of the patriotically-minded Madame Juliette Adam at Rue Poissonière in the center of Paris. This lady was celebrated for her ability to bring together eminent figures in the arts, literature, science, and, not least, politics. For many years she was the editor of the well-known periodical *La Revue nouvelle*. She was also a passionate admirer of the successful politician Leon Gambetta, who, by assuming almost dictatorial power, had organized the French defense against the German invasion in 1870. After the humiliating peace treaty was signed, Madame Adam was consumed by a desire for revenge, and had adopted Gambetta's words as her own: "Never speak of it, always think of it!"

When Alfred first came into contact with this purposeful lady, he assumed a wait-and-see policy. He could not identify with her passion for revenge, although even he was concerned about Bismarck's dream to complete Germany's unification under the leadership of Prussia. He did not hate Germany, nor was he an uncritical admirer of the country. On the other hand, he was a pronounced friend of France — so far. Although Alfred had little interest in Madame Adam's political opinions, he continued to visit her salon periodically for twelve years.

After becoming a widow in May 1867, at the age of forty-one, Juliette had remarried the wealthy founder of the bank Comptoir d'Escompte, Edmond Adam. Until his death, they maintained two "salons" — a winter salon on Rue Poissonière, and a summer salon at their country home. Following Adam's death, Gambetta became an increasingly frequent guest in Juliette's home, even acting as host at some of the parties. In Juliette Adam's eyes, he was a statesman of incomparable talent. "He is a lion!" she told her friends.

Bertha von Suttner's memoirs provide a portrait of Madame Adam: "She was wearing a dark red velvet gown that emphasized her shapely figure. She had a diamond pinned to her chest and another in her graying hair, in spite of which her facial features were still youthful."

Bertha also describes how Madame Adam received her and her husband: " 'Oh, my dear Baron,' she said to my husband with an amiable smile, 'I am so charmed. You spoke so stirringly and animatedly of the almost barbaric milieu in Caucasia that I was fascinated.' " Bertha continues: "It is well known that anything Russian stimulated Madame Adam's lively imagination. I thought to myself: How can a woman spend so much energy on politics — it is, after all, a venture that without exception exposes one to unpleasant experiences, if one is not outright ridiculed."

Alfred noted with satisfaction that the discussions in Madame Adam's salons would inevitably move from the political to the literary arena, since he harbored an intense dislike for political bickering. To him, Madame Adam's salon became an observation post where he could indulge in a little chat with the creator of the Suez Canal, Ferdinand de Lesseps, or with such literary giants as George Sand, Gustave Flaubert, and, most especially, Victor Hugo, in whose home Alfred became a welcome guest.

War ministries' demands for improved military explosives in nearly every European country were greater than ever before, and Alfred's plan was to to create an effective alternative to gunpowder for use in weapon ammunition. It was clear a cannon could not be loaded with dynamite; were it possible, both the distance a shell could travel and the effect it would have when it hit would have been far greater.

In a lecture at the Academy of Science in London, Alfred said of gunpowder: "This old powder possesses really an admirable elasticity, which makes it possible to use it for the most diverse purposes. Thus, in mines one wants it to blast without driving and in a gun to drive without blasting. In a grenade the two purposes are served simultaneously; in a fuse it burns as in fireworks, slowly without exploding." Modern science, he went on to say, with its improved technology, was conquering new territory. The audience was composed of military people, and, though a friend of peace, Alfred was the technician who, without emotional involvement, could discuss how devastation could be increased.

In order to improve the effectivity of ammunition, Alfred needed to effectuate a "phlegmatizing"; that is, a slower combustion of the gunpowder. His detailed journals show eight years of laboratory experiments to produce a stronger and less smoky blasting powder. He and his assistant, Georges Fehrenbach, were traveling in uncharted territory, and for a long time their efforts led nowhere.

Efforts to transform high-explosive blasting substances into a stronger, smokeless gunpowder finally succeeded in 1884, but, for various reasons, Alfred would wait three years before seeking a French patent. He had managed to create a gunpowder that produced only steam when it burned and was consequently generally smokeless. He gave it the name *ballistite*. In Sweden it was called Nobel-powder and among specialists it was referred to as C-89. The slow-burning ballistite consisted of a combination of nitroglycerine, nitrocellulose, and camphor.

Ballistite revolutionized the munitions industry, especially with respect to artillery pieces and shells. Some have characterized ballistite as Alfred's most disturbing invention. For his part, he was conscious of its devastating power; his hope was that the deterrent aspect of it would prevent future wars.

Since Alfred had been able to use the French firing ranges for his experiments, he offered the rights to his invention, in accordance with primary patent number 181179 of November 28, 1887, to the French government. The French declined, however, because they felt they already had the same product. The chemistry professor P. M. E. Vieille had managed to produce an almost smokeless gunpowder to which he had given the name Sarrau-Vieille, Poudre B. He had contacts among influential politicians, and the powder was already coming into use by the French military. Alfred's comment on the matter was ". . . to all governments, weak powder with strong outside pressure is obviously better than strong powder without this necessary complement."

On August 1, 1889, he signed a contract with the Italian government for the delivery of three hundred tons of ballistite; a large factory in Avigliana was equipped for the manufacture of it. Alfred received his compensation in the form of licensing fees. Against a royalty of 1.45 francs per kilo, Alfred signed over his Italian patent on September 16, 1889.

A problem arose in France. The French gunpowder monopoly, the Administration des Poudres et Salpêtres, asserted that Alfred had inappropriately exploited the privilege accorded by the French government to let him use their shooting ranges. The patriotic press jumped on the assertion and accused Alfred of espionage and treason. Alfred was banned from the shooting ranges and forbidden to manufacture ballistite at his dynamite factory in Honfleur. Furthermore, his laboratory was searched by the police, and the sample stock was confiscated.

Nothing was harder on Alfred than to have doubts cast upon his integrity and honor. When the French authorities, through various means, had let him understand that he no longer was persona grata, Alfred realized how he could be a helpless victim in the face of malevolence and slander. The unfavorable climate of public opinion was immediately exploited by his competitors — and Alfred could not do much about that either.

Paul Barbe, who had carved out a political career and had served for a while as France's minister of agriculture, tried to use his connections, but even he could do little. All the many influential and well-informed persons who were fully aware of Alfred's great services to France didn't lift a finger in his defense. An unofficial letter from the Swedish-Norwegian legation was ignored by the Minister of War.

Alfred was doubly pained that the country he had valued so highly, which had extended him such hospitality, had suddenly designated him a traitor. When the French police broke into his laboratory, he experienced a psychic shock — it hit a nerve. Even his normal way of escaping the pressure, by seeking refuge in his laboratory, had now been taken from him. When he learned that the media campaign against him had been sanctioned at the highest levels, he left France.

San Remo became the site of Alfred's voluntary exile in 1890. The Mediterranean climate was beneficial to his health and, since he had entered an agreement with Italy regarding ballistite, it made sense to open up shop there. He was able to install a new laboratory in San Remo rather quickly, since the French authorities had not confiscated his equipment in Sevran. The palm trees and the flower arrangements outside his Italian villa seemed to fit the name the former owner had given the place: *Mio Nido* — "My Nest." When Gustaf Aufschlager jokingly pointed out that a nest ought to have two birds, the hypersensitive Alfred immediately changed the name to Villa Nobel.

In San Remo, Alfred's every third thought was of his death. Beginning in 1887, his heart condition had become so severe he often had to take to his bed. Several friends, among them Victor Hugo, had passed away, and his mind was filled with dark forebodings. He wrote to Sofie in 1888: "When at the age of fifty-four, one is left all alone in the world, and a salaried servant is the only person to show any friendliness, dark thoughts come, darker than anyone can imagine. I see in my servant's eyes that he feels sorry for me, but of course I cannot let him notice this."

In letter after letter, Alfred expressed his anxiety about things going downhill. As is the case with most people in the last third of their life, his thoughts were more and more preoccupied by death and the transience of all things. His acquaintances report he had already acquired the look of an old man, and his eyes were often red from lack of sleep.

In letters to Robert he explained that he did not want to be buried "according to the sacramental so-called Christian manner that we have inherited from the Jews. Even cremation seems to me to be too slow." Instead, he provided gruesomely detailed instructions regarding the chemical annihilation of his corpse: "I want to be dipped in hot sulfuric acid. That way the whole thing is done in one minute and nothing is lost to agriculture because one neutralizes the acid with limestone, and limestone combined with sulfuric acid happens to be a fertilizer. It seems to me, since I have struggled so hard, that one could afford to use the necessary quantity of sulfuric acid which for me would be around 30 kilos — if it is strong and warm — otherwise, 50 kilos."

Worse than any fear of death to Alfred was the fear of being buried alive — an anxiety he shared with his father — and, although he was a man who believed in rationality, he viewed "apparent death" as a real threat. It is in the context of that fear that his wish to have his main artery cut after death and to be cremated becomes understandable. The fear of suspended animation being interpreted as death was widespread during the 1800s. Alfred's case was complicated by his claustrophobia. On January 4, 1881, he paid 100 francs to become a member of the Sociéte pour la Propagation de la Crémation in Paris.

When Alfred and Robert weren't writing to each other about death and decomposition, they wrote about their health. Robert's letters sometimes read like a hospital journal. Since Baku, he had become depressed and negative, and when not lamenting perceived injustices, he worried about his own and his children's health. His daughter Ingeborg, he felt, was in particular need of a change of climate.

Alfred got the message and suggested that the children should come and visit him in San Remo. They arrived in the spring of 1891, and Alfred immediately sought out a prominent physician for the sickly Ingeborg. After a while he could report to Robert that Ingeborg's frailty would put a strain on a family "but to a bachelor as utterly busy as I am, it was a gigantic task. . . . Whether your little daughter will be able to recover her health completely, I am not prepared to say, because even to a physician that question would be hard to answer. In either case, she is immeasurably healthier than when she arrived from Sweden. The dark bags around her eyes are practically gone, and the dark thoughts that like Niflheim spirits were following her everywhere have nearly disappeared."

Chapter 51

Paris

January 15, 1888

My dear Sofie!

. . . The night journey on the Orient Express was sleepless, and since we parted in Vienna, I have not slept a
wink. Partly this is due to some unpleasant incidents involving a couple of employees at my house. Upon my
return I gave them half an hour to clear out. It did not
serve their case that they squabbled about it; I was firm in
my decision. That does not prevent me from feeling sorry
for the old woman because how will she now find any
good employment? . . .

Paris

January 18, 1888

. . . To be absolutely honest, you were a hundred times
nicer in Brunn than in Vienna. Is this due to big city air
or some other influence? In Brunn you were quite sweet
for two whole days, and I was even beginning to believe
that I could be with you without getting grumbly.

However, it was too good to be true. In Vienna, not
only your mood but even your facial features underwent a
visible change. They became hard and non-beautiful. I am
certainly no professional psychologist and will not try to
discover the reasons. I only record the facts. . . .

Paris

[n.d., 1888]

. . . I am so isolated in the twilight of my life that a kind
person's company would be most welcome, yes, eagerly
longed for. Now I know that for several reasons you can
never fill that place. . . . For some years now, you have
most contemptibly played a part when you were with me

and kept all kinds of things secret. For almost three years, at my expense, you have been running around with your ill-bred suitor and thereby brought ridicule to me. Although you're well aware of what enormous sums of money I have lost these last few years, you have not decreased your excessive waste. You seem also to believe that you can continue to make use of my tolerance to the same extent. . . .

You want me to trust you, but after all your deceit and lack of considerateness, that is not possible. You said once that I am insolent. But which one of us has acted with insolence? I leave it to your conscience to answer that question, and send you many greetings from your old, sad, and woeful

Alfred

P.S. Almost everyone is unfaithful to me; I can therefore only trust those few my common sense tells me deserve it.

Paris
April 8, 1888

. . . I have just returned from Cannes and am so exhausted that I am barely able to hold the pen. . . .

My brother Ludvig is bedridden with severe heart trouble and will probably never be well again. The doctors think it a mystery that he is still alive at all.

I am myself in such a bad way that I probably won't last much longer. It is very difficult for me — I am especially pained by being conscious of the fact that nobody will grieve for me. Least of all those in whom I had placed so much hope. . . .

Paris
April 13, 1888

. . . My poor brother passed away quietly in his sleep yesterday, most probably without pain and after long and hard suffering.

Since the funeral will take place in Petersburg, I am not

returning to Cannes. But Ludvig's family will stay with
me for a couple of days as they are passing through. . . .

Paris

April 18, 1888

. . . Lately I am so tired that when I return from Sevran
in the evening, I go to bed around eight-thirty. That
means that even more work piles up. This makes me so
nervous that it keeps me from working as intensely as I
need to do. . . .

Paris

[n.d., 1888]

. . . Between us exists now not just one chasm but a
thousand. You write that I am turning to other people.
That is absolutely incorrect. I associate with no one and
have become so lonely that I never eat out nowadays. . . .

People of low character do not interest me. I don't actually know why — but I harbor an intuitive dislike for
them. You ought to have realized that a long time ago.
That is, if you had understood that it is possible to help
another human being without wanting something in return. Among the Hebrews only one discovered this
idea — Christ — but then because he did he was called
the Son of God. . . .

Why you are going to Paris, I do not understand at all.
You probably see it as a fine chance to spend even more
money. But be aware that the supply is running out. In
either case you will not see me, because I now live in
Sevran and, besides that, I am soon going on a long,
very long, journey. . . .

Vienna

July 1888

. . . How lamentable it is not to have someone around
whose kind hand would one day close one's eyes, having
whispered a few true words of solace. I must find such a
person, and if there is no other way, I will move in with

my old mother in Stockholm. In her at least I have one human being who has never tried to use me. And who never would bring whims and tantrums into a sickroom.

Around two o'clock in the morning I suddenly became so sick that I had neither the strength to call anyone nor open the door. I was forced to spend several hours completely alone without knowing if they were my final ones. Probably it was angina, which I have been so involved with, but only in chemical laboratories. In any case, I felt so utterly depressed afterward, and my heart is probably — like this piece of stationery — surrounded by a black border.

In the most resolute fashion can I now give you the advice to find yourself a permanent place to live once and for all. This ceaseless gadding about must come to an end. It cannot be in your interest either to compromise me in the most atrocious manner. You must finally realize that I will not allow you to use my name without my permission. . . . Either I am married, in which case I have no reason to refuse the use of my name, or else I am not, in which case it is shameful for any woman anywhere to use my name. . . .

Chapter 52

As long as his mother was alive, Alfred's devotion to her was uninterrupted and extraordinarily generous. He literally showered her, as well as her relatives and friends, with Christmas presents and birthday surprises: shares, bonds, cash, and bric-a-brac. Alfred had the habit of sending her a sum of money every time he made a profit or earned some royalties. Her bank account kept growing. In February 1888 she wrote: "Through Öberg I have received another 3,000 crowns from my sweet boy. Thank you, thank you, my beloved Alfred, for all your great gifts! Through your goodness I can even give a widow's mite to those who have nothing and cannot afford the daily necessities. Therefore I have not put what you have sent most lately into the bank."

Around Christmas of the same year she wrote:

> Words cannot describe the joy I felt when I first received
> your telegram and then your dear, so longed-for letter.
> Because it came from my beloved son, whose tireless
> goodness never forgets to multiply the delights of young
> and old at any holiday. . . . I have received everything
> through my Alfred's hardworking efforts. I own so
> much and can fulfill any of my wishes — except for two
> that cannot be bought for money: excellent health and to
> see my Paris darling as often as I would want. But if that
> would be possible, I am afraid you would tire of this old
> lady, although I am your oldest friend.

Her sons had talked Andriette into moving from her house at 32A Götgatan Street, with its many tiresome stairs, to one in a nicer neighborhood. Alfred knew how lonely widowhood must be. "Little mommy gets so much joy from my presence that it really breaks my heart to leave the old lady alone most of the year," he wrote Sofie Hess. "Lately, when my brother Ludvig had to leave, she was so affected by his departure that she fell ill and only recovered her health slowly. At age seventy-nine, she no longer has a constitution of iron, and it does not take much to break down her body. When she is happy and content, she can stand anything; when the opposite emotions are at work, she is hurt by the smallest thing. Yesterday we went to Djurgården and had dinner. The food did not agree with me — I was sick all night from it — my mother on the other hand felt fine."

Alfred's letters might mirror his growing disgust with people, but this never extended to his relationship to his mother, which remained warm and intimate until her death. It pained him deeply that he was not able to reach her before she died in 1889, at eighty-four.

Alfred had never been swayed by family bonds, but his mother's death affected him deeply. His sense of loss was so great that he developed heart pains after the funeral and returned to Paris in poor condition. From there he later wrote to the executor of her will: "As I already mentioned in Stockholm, for myself I only wish to keep my mother's portrait and a few small things that she liked and that significantly remind me of her. I do, however, reserve the right to dispose over the third that would be my share. I want a certain sum to be put aside for a beautiful but not pretentious nor ostentatious memorial. Another part I want to donate to a charity fund in her name; for that, I consider 100,000 crowns to be a suitable sum. I do not mind advancing a considerable part of this sum against comparable deductions when the amount comes in."

Her home changed little after Immanuel's death, although she had become a rich woman and left an estate of more than 840,000 Swedish crowns ($168,000, then). Alfred decided to give his portion of the estate to the Karolinska Institute, creating the Caroline Andriette Nobel Fund for Experimental Medical Research "within all branches of medical science, that this research can be used both for education and for literature."

He also donated money in his mother's name to the New Children's Hospital and the Gymnastic Central Hospital, and he gave 17,000 Swedish crowns to a charity run by the Swedish Colony in Paris. About 24,000 crowns were left, and he wrote to Sofie: "It seems as if the whole of the kingdom of Sweden wants me; every day brings a huge pile of letters from my native land with the craziest suggestions for donations. Yesterday a man wrote that he needed just 30,000 crowns in order to buy a stone quarry that he had had his eye on for some time, and he felt that I ought to give him this small amount."

Regarding his mother's tombstone, Alfred wrote three letters to Robert:

Paris
February 6, 1890

Dearest brother Robert,

I am thinking of a small tombstone and feel that it ought to be done for both our parents together.

What do you think of a rather large granite block with a marble bas-relief of our parents? I would make it very simple but surrounded by a beautiful lattice.

Write me a few lines about the matter and give me some good news about you and yours.

Paris
February 12, 1890

. . . A letter from Adolf informs me that it is a family plot.

I had no knowledge of this, nor did I know that no suitable gravestone had been created for either our father or Emil.

This can only be explained by the fact that at the time I was not only very ill but also fighting what seemed like hopeless financial troubles.

Now, I have suggested in writing to Adolf that a profile relief of our parents and of Emil be done in marble and that it be fastened to a suitable, beautiful but not ostentatious tombstone, perhaps made from polished granite, and that a place at the side also be reserved for the next guest, meaning myself.

Paris
August 3, 1890

. . . My sight is also getting worse but although I slave every hour in order to free myself from pressing tasks, benefiting neither my health nor my mood, this seems not to be accomplished in a hurry. If someone were to judge these conditions superficially, he would think that anyone who has enough money to live on can take off from work at any time he wishes.

Unfortunately, I see all too clearly that such is not the case, because even when I am sick in bed I am forced to work to hold to certain agreements to which I am bound by contract.

It is leavened dough left over from the old days, when I used to assume any kind of obligations to get people to invest money in our business.

It would be my pleasure to order the medallions on the tombstone from Adlersparre, but it would also be desirable for them to resemble those they are supposed to represent, and if this is difficult for Adlersparre to accomplish, it might be better to turn to someone else.

Your heartily affectionate
Alfred

Chapter 53

Paris
[n.d., 1888]

Dear Sofie!

. . . I have just arrived, totally worn out. A telegram was awaiting me, in which Robert and my nephew plead with me to come to Petersburg. I have a feeling that I might prevent something foolish from being done there. On the other hand, I am so deluged with work that I have no desire to make the long, strenuous trip. . . .

Berlin
August 1888

. . . It looks as if I have succeeded in making Robert change his mind. At least for the time being, he is going to refrain from removing the whole board of directors [of Branobel, after Ludvig's death] and replacing them with his own people. . . .

If you really want me to come, I will do what I can to arrange it. However, I have to get to Stockholm before late fall. My mother is now at an age where I cannot postpone the joy I have already promised her. Besides, nobody knows when I myself might cause her the greatest grief of all. Lately at night I have been experiencing such a strange feeling in the area of my heart. . . .

Paris
August 8, 1888

. . . Your little letters — which were waiting for me here when I arrived — made me glad. Stylistically they might not compare with the writings of our greatest poets, but there is a warmth of feeling and a joy in them. What do you say to such praise for what your pen has achieved? . . .

I have lost my desire to travel alone. Therefore I have tried to find a solution to the problems in Petersburg without going there personally. It seems as if I have succeeded, to some extent at least, because a telegraphic message just arrived saying that they no longer considered it necessary to talk me into coming. . . .

The construction has begun here. My people seem trustworthy, and all ought to go well. With Sevran and Paul Barbe, however, I have problems. . . .

Paris

October 15, 1888

. . . You have a small and yet substantial enemy by the name of Sofie who does you more harm than you think. Instead of sending me proper statements of account, which would reinstate my faith in you, you are once again trying to throw dust into my eyes. In sober earnestness, you are attempting to contend that a small single female like you, who spends 100 florins a day, if not more, is starving to such an extent that one can hear all the way from there how her bones rattle. Once upon a time, when your little stomach was even emptier than today, you managed on one florin a day. Yet you were rather rosy of cheek and did not look particularly emaciated then. Consequently I find, my dear child, that the holes into which you tuck the money are unnaturally large, and I have no desire to fill these oceanlike vacuums with my savings.

Paris

October 25, 1888

. . . You cannot imagine the agitation that reigns here. Four weeks now it says on my agenda that I am supposed to go to the dentist — it is absolutely necessary — and yet I have not had a free moment to do it. Paris is now a total inferno. People are arriving from every direction. Since they have apprised me of their arrival in writing, I cannot refuse to see them. In addition there are ongoing experiments, the more-extensive-than-ever correspondence, the

bookkeeping, and the constructions underway. It is so
hectic that it could drive one insane. You should be glad
that you are just a silly little thing and don't have my
troubles. . . .

Paris
November 1888

. . . For some time I have been sick and depressed. This is
what happens each time I overexert myself. But what can
I do? The work has to be done. Letters have to be answered, people received, my books kept in order, and at
the same time I have to be in Sevran from morning to
night. I am asking myself how long it can go on like this.
If I were to employ a secretary, it would perhaps get a
little easier in six months, but until then I would probably
have more work rather than less. Can you imagine, I was
recently recommended a private secretary who had been
an ambassador. Now the only thing missing is for me to
be offered a full-blooded prince for the same pay. . . .

Paris
November 22, 1888

. . . When will my suffering end? It only gets worse with
each day. I am almost beginning to curse this earthly life.

Your Grumble Bear

[n.d., 1888]

Dear Sofie,

Sometimes I have a feeling that your family believes that
my generosity and tolerance stem from pure stupidity.
This surmise is of course faulty but understandable: how
can one comprehend qualities in other people that one is
absolutely lacking in oneself. . . . They look out only for
themselves — everyone else exists only in order to be
used. Perhaps they are right, but then they ought not to
be surprised if they themselves get treated in a similar
manner.

Imagine if I were poor and your family rich. Do you believe they would lend me a single kreuzer without interest or interest on interest? If you believe they would, you do not know them as well as I do. . . .

Paris
March 3, 1889

. . . I have unbelievably much to do and am interrupted, disturbed, and harassed in various ways. Everything feels so unpleasant and sad that I don't know which way to turn. My health is worse than ever: I have cramps in my heart almost every other day. . . .

Paris
May 14, 1889

. . . Now they are showering me with telegraphic pleas to come to London, Scotland, Hamburg, Italy, etc. What a life! Other than that, it is completely green and very beautiful here. However, I have no time for anything. . . .

Paris
[n.d., 1889]

. . . How do you actually imagine these house purchases? Do you perchance believe that the present owners would be only too happy to present you their properties as a gift? Not even Rothschild can buy everything he sees. And after the copper crash, even he is supposed to be conscious of the value of money.

Try to understand, dear little child, that if you really had such a palatial home, everything else would have to be adapted to it. Otherwise, as a consequence of your family's weak financial situation — but even for other reasons that I want to pass over in silence — an unpleasant situation could easily occur. Believe me, if you aren't happy in simple surroundings, you won't be happy in ostentatious, elegant surroundings either.

Switzerland, Engadin, Hotel du Lac
September 1, 1889

. . . You have wired me that you want to come to Zurich.
Frankly speaking, I have had enough of all the disgrace I
have been forced to suffer. For the short time I have left, I
want peace and quiet around me. Also, I do not believe at
all that you would want to come to this hotel where eight
persons are bedridden with fatally contagious illnesses. I
was aware of this. Still and all, I came here, since I no
longer care very much about my old body. . . .

Switzerland, St. Moritz
September 4, 1889

. . . Of course I believe that you have anxieties. But they
are only worries about your own self and none about
what you might have caused others. Just the fact that time
after time you compare me to other men, with whom
you have perhaps begun a relationship, bears witness of a
base character. And yet it was you who once reproached
me for being mean. Look into the mirror and you will be
able to see in your own features how tactlessly you have
behaved toward me. My meanness seems to consist in
helping people who do not deserve it. . . .

Lucerne
September 20, 1889

. . . Shattered by illness, I am passing through here on my
way from Turin to Stockholm. This time I had to do it,
but it is probably the last time I will make that trip. . . .
    Again I have suffered severe losses and don't know
what the future holds. Anyhow, that is a matter of total
indifference to me. What could happen to me now that
would be worse than what has already happened? . . .

[n.d., 1889]

. . . And yet, I can't help but feel sorry for you. Now

you are isolated, without friends and soon without youth,
which hides and beautifies. Why did you choose the bas-
est of lies instead of telling me everything openly, I who
only wish you well? . . .

Paris
November 1889

. . . It's absolutely horrifying: since June 1st, in other
words, in less than half a year, you have squandered
48,267 francs! How unwise and what a pity! . . .

Chapter 54

Alfred once wrote Sofie that he had started to play the stock market "in order to drive off my dark thoughts, and I have suffered enormous losses." During one of Branobel's solvency crises, Alfred had even suggested to Ludvig that he might improve things by speculating on the stock exchange. His brother responded that he knew nothing about gambling on the stock exchange and preferred to put his trust in his work, for "through it I see the only chance to put our enterprise back on its feet."

The brothers' positions on the matter could not have been further apart. Not even in 1886 when their Russian company had been refused credit on acceptable conditions did Ludvig think stock exchange speculation constituted a viable alternative. In that respect, Ludvig was puritanical: every form of gambling was an insult to honest working people. He advised Alfred to refrain from speculating, since "that is a bad occupation and should be left to those who are incapable of useful work." In Alfred's opinion, an efficient stock exchange would be advantageous to the business community, supplying enterprises with working capital. The circulation of money was analogous to a pump through which the general public's savings were infused into companies, increasing their possibilities to expand, employ more people, and thereby reduce unemployment. Alfred continued to invest in shares, even if his investments, in relation to his wealth, were limited. A contradiction is at work here, since he destested losing money but still took risks with it.

His strength as an investor was his ability to discern both weaknesses and strengths in the balance sheets. He was especially skillful at discovering whether the assets of a business were arbitrarily defined or if they represented actual values. Another advantage he had that many stock market speculators lacked was that he never bought stock with borrowed money. After being in business only four years, Nobel's Explosives yielded over two million Swedish crowns in annual profits, and considerable income was also generated from his other dynamite companies. In addition, he had royalty income from the patent rights he had not relinquished in exchange for shares. Nearly all the wealth Alfred left behind consisted of shares in the Nobel explosive companies and Branobel, plus interest-bearing government bonds. But he had stock in two dozen or so other companies.

At the end of the 1880s, two markets were available to those who were active on the Paris stock exchange. Cash business was done in *Le Parquet* and term business in *La Coulisse,* which was mostly for speculation purposes. In *Money,* published in 1891, Zola gives a realistic picture of the world that so enticed Alfred. Men gathered under the trees on Rue de la Banque, near "the little stockmarket," where bargains were struck on securities whose prices were no longer considered worthy of an official quotation. It is not known if Alfred actually visited the Paris stock exchange or if he were content to buy and sell through agents. His correspondence seems to suggest that he was intimately familiar with the milieu. He noted how thinly civilization lay on such a place, and wondered if there had ever before been a time as marked by greed. The nouveaux riches, lacking education and refinement, were distasteful to him.

Even before the attack from the French press over ballistite, and his subsequent exile from Paris, Alfred was beginning to plan his retirement from business life, but fate was decreeing otherwise. On April 21, 1889, the *New York Times* reported: "It is now positively certain that the Panama Canal will never be completed by M. de Lesseps and the French Company." So began the so-called Panama scandal. Paul Barbe, who the preceding year had served as the French minister of agriculture, had in various ways taken an interest in the Panama project — which some experienced financiers had called the surest way toward ruin. During a routine visit to Hamburg in August 1890, Alfred received the news that Barbe had taken his own life. It would soon be evident to Alfred that he had left behind financial chaos.

Alfred at first felt deep sorrow for his partner. To help Barbe's survivors, he kindheartedly bought Barbe's Nobel shares for an inflated price. When the truth about Barbe's involvement in the Panama swindle came to light in succeeding years, Alfred discontinued his assistance.

Barbe and some of his confederates in the French companies La Société Générale pour la Fabrication de la Dynamite and Société Centrale de Dynamite had been involved in outright illegal speculation activities. Alfred had always appreciated his partner's ability to work but realized early that he had "a conscience more elastic than

rubber elasticum." Yet, never for a moment did he imagine that
Barbe was actually gambling away his life.

Barbe was also implicated in an unethical lottery and bribery
system. As a member of the Assemblée Nationale's committee for
concessions covering lottery loans, he had argued strongly against
approval of a 600 million–franc loan for de Lesseps's Panama Canal
company. Barbe's reason was that the canal company had turned
down his offer to use dynamite and imported explosives from the
United States instead. When an arrangement to Barbe's advantage
did get made, and he himself received a personal loan from Lesseps's
partner, Baron de Reichnach, for 550,000 francs, he paid back only
220,000; the rest was paid by securing a 600 million–franc loan for
canal construction through bribes. Rumors of corruption soon arose.
In 1892, a suit was brought against Ferdinand de Lesseps and Jacques
de Reichnach; the latter died just before he was to have been arrested.

Alfred learned the details of Barbe's activities during the 1892–
1893 Panama trial, which brought to light specific information about
his former partner's methods. At Barbe's initiative a syndicate for
technical cooperation between all the Nobel companies had been
formed to coordinate purchases of raw material for the dynamite
factories. When the syndicate petered out, Barbe had continued to
make increasingly risky speculations in glycerine — without informing Alfred.

The first few days after Barbe's suicide, Alfred was dispirited
and apathetic. He even asked the manager of his German company
to reserve a position for him as a lowly chemist. The man must have
thought his boss was having a nervous breakdown. Alfred dragged
himself back to Paris to find the financial circles buzzing with rumors
that his money supply was drying up, that it was only a question of
time before his business came to a dead stop.

Gradually, Alfred realized this wasn't going to happen. The
situation was serious but not desperate. His collective assets over the
years had become enormous. Fatigue, headaches, and melancholy all
disappeared, and with newborn determination Alfred took over the
position as the Nobel enterprises' chairman. He went on the offensive
and completely reorganized the business in a period of weeks. Losses
from Barbe's calamitous glycerine speculations were offset by a rather
large debenture loan that he himself covered to a considerable degree — to reestablish confidence. The entire board of directors was
let go, and a new managing director was chosen, the highly respected
Paul Du Buit. By the time Alfred wrote to his nephew Emanuel in

St. Petersburg on October 10, 1892, the situation was tense but under control:

> My position here nowadays is not what it used to be. I
> am at loggerheads with all the managers that I have had
> to get rid of. A consequence of this is that I have had to
> acquire and maintain a majority interest, which means
> 20,000 shares at 450 to 500 francs each. Even if a few
> friends support me, it is still an immense burden that I
> must count on carrying. If I wasn't majority shareholder,
> both I and my co-directors would end up in a terrible
> fix, since we would have to deal with a collection of
> blood-sucking attorneys. Nothing in the world is more
> dangerous than being part of a board of directors in a
> French company.

Soon criminal action was brought against members of the So-ciété Générale. Former senator Le Guay and Barbe's closest assistant, Arton, were later convicted of forgery and other crimes. On November 1, 1892, Alfred wrote to a British business acquaintance:

> A couple of days ago, I was asked to pay the tidy little
> sum of 4,600,000 francs for my alleged responsibility in
> connection with the Arton–Le Guay embezzlements.
> French law is indeed strange: members of a board of di-
> rectors who have acted in good faith can be held respon-
> sible if something goes out of their control. The
> members of the board and their attorneys do not think
> such has been the case, but when it comes to court ac-
> tion, even wisdom turns blind. Constipation or its oppo-
> site may often influence a judge's opinion of right and
> wrong. . . .

Alfred had finally had enough of trouble and adversities. In a letter to Robert that dates from this period he writes:

> I am totally sick and tired of the explosive-substance
> field, in which one is forever stumbling around in acci-
> dents, preventive clauses, red tape, acts of villainy, and
> other unpleasantness. I long for peace and quiet and want
> to devote my time to scientific experiments, which is not

possible when every day brings new problems. . . . I
wholeheartedly wish to retire from the business, and any
kind of business. . . .

When the Barbe scandal began winding down, Alfred started
turning down director duties in his dynamite companies to spend
more time in his San Remo villa and his laboratory. Dream though
he might of days far from the stress of the financial world, Alfred
discovered that he could not let the Nobel companies drift aimlessly.
He continued to put his personal stamp on them until the very last
day of his life.

Chapter 55

Paris
February 27, 1890

Dear Sofie,

. . . Acute obligations add up to me being stuck here as if glued, and every day brings something new for me to act on. If I had known what pain these businesses would cause me, I would certainly never have entered into them.

Paris
March 1890

. . . Upon my arrival in Vienna, it is absolutely necessary for me to have a suite in my hotel in which I can receive business contacts. This is simply a formal matter, but it is necessary. I receive more visits now than before, and you must certainly understand that I cannot expose any weak spot. . . .

Paris
April 1890

. . . I have to say, in all honesty, that I had hardly returned here, before I was already wishing myself away. I have work up to my ears. The help I get is far too minimal, otherwise things would go faster. . . .

There was nobody to talk to aboard the Orient Express. Generally speaking, travelers nowadays seem to regard each other as wild animals with whom it is dangerous to come into contact. Luckily, I had brought along a book which helped to pass the time: *Lay Down Arms!* . . .

Paris
May 1890

. . . The newspapers here keep pouring out vile stuff
about me. You cannot imagine the harassment to which I
am subjected. I hope to be able to leave soon, and this
time I turn my back on Paris with joy. . . .

Berlin
June 20, 1890

. . . I have asked my relatives if they would like to come
to Hamburg to see me. Traveling is so depressing that I
would like to have the young ones along when I visit the
factories. . . .

Perhaps I will go back to Hamburg day after tomorrow
along with my business acquaintances. I am not totally
clear as to what they want. Both of them had telegraphed
and called, assuring me that they wished to talk about
matters of great importance. . . .

June 1890

. . . Truly bad things are happening to me now. This
morning, as I was paying my hotel bill and getting ready
to leave for Stockholm, I received a registered letter from
London, and the contents are forcing me to go there
without delay. It regards an unbelievably insolent piece of
villainy that is going to cause me a lot of misery. I suppose I will not get any peace until I am in my grave. Perhaps not even then — I have a premonition that I will be
buried alive. . . .

July 7, 1890

. . . All these new hardships have sapped my strength.
There I was on my way to Stockholm to see Liedbeck regarding important matters. I had hardly arrived in Berlin
before the circus in Hamburg started. When that was finally cleared up, I received the telegram from London,
which rendered my journey to Sweden impossible, and

instead I had to travel to London, but by way of Paris to pick up important documents there. This is only the beginning of a horrid legal process that is certain to cause me limitless expenses and unpleasantness. . . .

Hamburg
August 7, 1890

. . . Barbe's death in Paris has turned all my plans topsy-turvy, and I really have ended up in a difficult and perilous situation. I had no plans to go to Paris, but, as a consequence of Barbe's death, such huge problems have been created that I absolutely must go there. I had hoped to be allowed to enjoy a little calm and get some peace of mind as a balance to this miserable business. But fate is stronger than our will. So it continues without interruptions until one day the business — as in Barbe's case — abruptly does itself in. . . .

Paris
August 1890

. . . They continue to persecute me here due to the success of my smokeless powder in Italy. It is now clear that I have to move my laboratory to another country. A confusing piece of news, right? Certainly they led me to understand some time ago that I might be forced to move, but I dismissed the idea as improbable. Now it has come to that, since I am subjected to threats on a daily basis. . . .

P.S. I am not even sure I will be able to keep my freedom. But please do not tell this to anyone — not even your relatives!

Paris
August 1890

. . . It seems that bad luck haunts me this year. Barbe's death will give rise to complex problems and an immense amount of work. Who knows what further complications might yet crop up. . . .

Paris

August 1890

. . . Barbe's suicide has resulted in even greater calamities than I could ever have imagined. Now it is a question of my very existence. . . .

Paris

October 21, 1890

. . . Today is my birthday. I am so besieged by business-people that I cannot get a moment to myself either at breakfast or at dinner. Since Barbe's death, everything has gone from bad to worse. I had hoped that the whole matter would finally be over and done with, but indeed, that has not been the case. It is all just becoming more and more complicated until one day I will probably decide to disappear without a trace, and without leaving a forwarding address. . . .

Chapter 56

Toward the end of 1890, Sofie Hess began to realize that she had lost her protector's favor. Alfred had learned that she was pregnant and, after admonishing her for lying, announced that their relations were at an end. Those letters of Sofie's to Alfred that have survived therefore involve her attempt to repair the damage and win him back.

[n.d., 1891]

My dear Alfred, if I may still call you that, because in spite of the terrible shame I have to suffer you are not yet erased from my heart. You should know that there is no foundation for all the accusations against me. They have been conspiring and plotting against me here, but that everything of which I am accused you take as truth makes me more than unhappy.

Never had I believed that you of all people would act like that toward me who loves you and respects you. By God, I don't deserve to be treated in such a way. I have not a human soul to confide in and am more alone and abandoned than ever. Don't know what I will do without you.

You were everything to me in this world, and then they just tore you away from me for nothing, without any reason. You know best the love I felt for you and how highly I valued you. I have lived so simply and hidden myself away. Lived only for you and then I have to endure such shame. Oh my God — I can't live without you, I am so weak that you would hardly recognize me. I am going half mad. Oh, what will I do —

I have moved into another house and will earn my living but not in the way you find it so easy to accuse me of — Even if you think me all kinds of things, I give you my holiest word that I am of a good family and therefore am feeling all the more unhappy.

Even if you leave me here, you have certain obligations. Even though I know I have done you wrong and now have to pay for it, don't let me become pitiful. When I

part from you, I don't expect any more than the allow-
ance you have given me until now. I am not talking about
a pension. I don't want any charity, for what I have done
for you I haven't done with a scheming mind, God knows
that. I will return your gifts as well as everything else that
now makes me feel so miserable.

What am I to do? Come, just for a moment. How hard
would I not embrace you and press your hand against my
lips. I would like to tell you so much. Perhaps then you
would believe my innocence and come.

Sofie

February 7, 1891

My dear Bubi!

. . . I promise you solemnly that I will not borrow a
single kreuzer. That you don't have to worry about. . . .

I am still upset. Because of all the reproaches and all the
shame, my strong desire to have a child has made me desperate. In the end, it will perhaps result not in a happy
baby but a poor sickly thing who will look just like you,
Bubi. . . .

I have no joy left in life, dear Alfred, and your harsh-
ness added to it is making me quite ill.

Sofie

This time Alfred wrote back:

February 10, 1891

. . . What have you and your family done now to throw
even more dirt upon my name? It must be something
horrendous because this year not even my acquaintances
have answered my New Year's cards. . . .

The enclosed money is Italian.

Alfred

Sofie hurried to send her reply:

February 11, 1891

My dear Alfred!

Your little letter yesterday depressed me a lot. Even if
your reproaches are fair, it hurts me terribly that you are
so hard on me. I don't deserve it. If you only knew how
things are with me, you would judge me differently and
act more gently toward me.

I, my dear, reproach myself bitterly and regret everything you blame me for, even if it is too late, as you yourself say. . . .

Warm thanks for the 4 Italian and today for the 4 Hungarian bills. In other words, I received 4,000 schillings and
say a thousand thanks. . . .

You are often so demanding and immediately believe
the worst. You can rest easy, nothing is happening that
could harm you, dear Alfred.

And now I ask you again: how are things with you?
What are you doing? Oh, if only my pregnancy were not
so far gone, I would leave for Vienna because I feel so
lonely and unhappy. . . It will be a beautiful child. With
so much problems and gloominess during my whole time
of waiting, it has to be!

Thousands of kisses and greetings and again a warm
thank you.

Your Sofie

With no immediate reaction from Alfred, Sofie took pen in hand again:

. . . No response to my two letters today either. I long
for such because I don't know what to do. I will follow
your advice and am sorry that I didn't do so earlier. If I
had, everything would be so different today, and I
wouldn't have such problems. To have a child in my circumstances is hard and bitter, I can assure you. I
wouldn't wish it on my mortal enemy because what I
have to endure is horrible. You wouldn't believe it possible, but all men are not as tender and good as you, dear
Alfred.

Your Sofie

Finally Sofie received a few lines from Alfred:

[n.d., 1891]

Dear Sofie,

As is evident from your letters, poor little one, you have suffered much and have had to atone too harshly for many of your earlier mistakes. . . .

There is only one thing I will never forgive — when someone tries to make me look ridiculous.

I have warned you about this for many years, but as the saying goes: against stupidity even the gods fight in vain!

Alfred

Sofie answered, almost by return mail:

Dear Alfred!

. . . Yes, against stupidity the gods do fight in vain, that's true. Unfortunately I've realized this too late and must now pay for it. Who knows for how long — that's still uncertain. Especially when one doesn't have a real mother. The mother is most important and I have none. A lot of other things make me unhappy, being neither married nor unmarried. In short, everything mortifies me.

The only one who is good and compassionate is you. But for some time everything has changed so much. You no longer care for me and I don't belong with anyone else but stand totally alone. . . .

Sofie

When Sofie received a brief note from Alfred with some money, she replied immediately.

June 1891

My very dearest Alfred!

Thank you so much for your lines and the 2,000 francs I received yesterday. I was totally broke for a couple of days and had not a cent.

There are probably few women as poor as I, without
either savings or cash. When I think of my future, I get
into the blackest of moods. What will become of me?

At night I can't sleep because of my thoughts and often
cry for hours. The child will enter the world in bitterness.
Some say that children one is anxious about turn out to be
skinny and ugly. How long are you staying in Paris and
where will you go? I have to stay here in this heat since I
will soon deliver here.

With many kisses your
Sofie

This letter was followed by yet another, dated Mitdorf, July 8, 1891:

My dear Alfred!

Without waiting for an answer to my last letter, I send
these lines to you because it could begin soon, and then
nobody knows when I will feel well again.

I am totally run-down and that makes me even more
anxious because I need my strength for this but I have lost
all I had. It's possible that I am myself the cause of my
problems. Your "silly little thing" has a bad conscience
and that's more horrible than anything else.

If I were with you, dear Alfred, I'd feel much better.
Of course you're often very strict but you can also be
mild and good. Everyone else I know is mean and egotis-
tical. I've gotten to know people for the first time and
will not forget it in a hurry. Perhaps it's been necessary,
for otherwise I'd probably stayed a stupid goose my
whole life.

Your Sofie

*Alfred was traveling when he received this letter and replied from
Gmunden, an Austrian health resort near Traunsee.*

July 17, 1891

. . . It is possible that I may be in Gmunden for a few
days, but first I have to go on a tiresome business trip.

Nowadays these are no pleasure to me since I feel ill after even the shortest of trips. . . .

Sofie had not yet had her child when she wrote the following:

[n.d., 1891]

My dear Alfred!

That I haven't thanked you for your letter and the enclosed 2,000 schillings before today is because I have had so much to take care of. More than ever I'm in a period of waiting. . . .

You are so good to me, my dear Bubs, and yet I feel only too well that you no longer interest yourself in what's happening to me. Of course everything is my fault. Because I have been so stupid, I'm now in a pickle and don't know what to do.

I went back to Vienna to find somewhere cheap to live. But everything is so expensive. Almost all the apartments have to be refurnished and I have no money. Nothing can be had under 2,000 schillings. Besides, the third floor is too high up for me, since I with my big stomach can't climb all those stairs.

Your Sofie

Chapter 57

Bertha von Suttner, the 1905 recipient of the Nobel Peace Prize, states in her memoirs that it was Alfred, and not she, who brought the conversation around to peace questions when she and her husband visited Paris in 1887. It was during that conversation that Alfred uttered his chilling premonition about a topic that was to preoccupy the next century: "I should like to be able to create a substance or a machine with such a horrific capacity for mass annihilation that wars would become impossible forever."

It was not principally Bertha who awakened Alfred's interest in peace, but her passionate appeals over the years certainly stimulated it (though perhaps not to the degree that she asserts in her memoirs). As early as April 1885 — in other words, two years before Bertha and her husband's visit to Alfred's home in Paris — he wrote to a peace worker in Belgium: "I am becoming more and more philosophical. My vision for the future is not all that different from the Diocletianii cabbage field, watered with Lethe's water.[1] The more I hear the cannons dispute, the more blood I see flow, looting legalized, and the handgun sanctioned, the more distinct and vivid this vision becomes." War, he wrote Bertha, is "the horror of all horrors and the greatest of all crimes."

The question of responsibility on the part of researchers and inventors was brought to a focus half a century later, appropriately enough by Albert Einstein, who received the 1921 Nobel Prize in Physics for his work in theoretical physics, notably on the photoelectric effect. Like other Nobelists, such as Bertha von Suttner, Mahatma Gandhi, Martin Luther King, Jr., and Bertrand Russell, Einstein was a champion of peace. During a Nobel Prize dinner in 1945, only a few months after the bombs had been dropped over Hiroshima and Nagasaki, Einstein argued that scientists were finding themselves in the same predicament that Alfred Nobel had, following his discovery of dynamite. About Nobel he said: "He invented an explosive that was stronger than any known before — an exceedingly

[1] The Roman emperor and autocrat Caius Aurelius Valerius Diocletianus (245–313) left his office in 305 A.D. after a grave illness to grow cabbages in Salona in Dalmatia.

efficient means of destruction. In order to calm his conscience, he created his Nobel Prizes."

Alfred frequently made it clear that he did not want to justify his inventions for posterity. His explosive substances were critical to mining operations and communication systems. That was justification enough. He was also all too aware, as he wrote to von Suttner, that "there is nothing in our world that cannot be misused." Researchers and inventors could not be held responsible for what politicians and generals did with their products. When Alfred began to prioritize the weapons technical development in Bofors in 1894, he still seems not to have felt any moral compunction, to judge from his letters. He was an inventor, after all, and acted from "the purest technical and not commercial and financial motives" — in contrast to those who fabricated weapons solely for profit, whom he labeled "damage-makers."

During a discussion with a weapons manufacturer in Paris, Alfred said "War must be made as deadly to the civilian populations back home as it is for the troops on the front lines. Let the sword of Damocles hang over every head, gentlemen, and you will witness a miracle — all wars will be stopped instantly if the weapon is called bacteriology." As he had in *Nemesis,* Alfred invoked the sword of Damocles, which, since the fifth century B.C., had been the symbol for the uncertainty of existence.

"On the day when two armies will be able to annihilate each other in one second," Alfred wrote in 1890, "all civilized nations will recoil from war in horror and disband their forces."

Bertha sent Alfred a Swedish translation of her book *Lay Down Arms!* which had met with worldwide success, and his reply was heartfelt:

April 1890

Dear Baroness, Dear Friend!

I have just finished reading your masterpiece. It is said that there are two thousand languages — which is 1999 too many — but surely your remarkable work must be translated into all of them. It ought to be read and reflected upon by each and everyone. How long did it take you to compose this marvel? You will have to answer that question when next I have the honor and the pleasure to

press your hand in mine — the hand of an amazon who
so valiantly wages war against war. . . .

Their continued exchange of letters reveals that Bertha had not
succeeded in convincing Alfred that her peace strategy was the best.
Yet, she could feel a certain satisfaction in being able to register the
famed dynamite king as a member of her peace association. At the
time of the 1892 Peace Congress in Bern, Alfred made a declaration
of principle, having sent Bertha a relatively small sum of money to
help defray the costs:

I do not believe that it is first and foremost the money
that is lacking, but a real program. Good intentions alone
will not assure peace, nor, one might say, will great banquets and long speeches. You must have an acceptable
plan to lay before the governments. To demand disarmament is ridiculous and will gain nothing. By calling for
the immediate establishment of a court of arbitration,
you hurl yourself against a thousand prejudices. To succeed, you have to proceed, as they do in England, with
legislative bills you cannot be certain will be accepted.

Although Alfred did not believe Bertha von Suttner's peace
movement proposed a realistic program for action, he still attended,
incognito, her Peace Congress. We know from Bertha's memoirs
that Alfred invited the von Suttners on a boat trip. The craft was a
forty-foot-long motorboat built entirely of silvery aluminum — the
world's first, and Alfred's pride and joy. He had christened the boat
the *Mignon,* and it had room for up to thirty passengers. A relaxed
Alfred sat at the rudder, using a small hand lever to feed fuel to the
engine. The idea for his light-metal pleasure boat was born in letters
between Alfred and his nephew, the twenty-five-year-old Ludvig,
Robert's second son and an engineer.

Bertha had taken time off from the ongoing Peace Congress
for the outing, during which Alfred had told her, as they were
admiring some of the large villas on the shore of the lake, that the
money behind them "was spun by many little silkworms." Her
sharp retort was that "dynamite factories were surely more profitable
than silk mills but definitely less innocent." "Perhaps my factories

will end war quicker than your congresses," was Alfred's instant reply.

Alfred may have disagreed with some of the details, but he sympathized with the central message of *Lay Down Arms!* He believed, with Bertha, that one ought to fight poverty, religious prejudice, and any form of injustice. Moreover, the Peace Congress in Berne made an impact on Alfred. After it was over, he sought to find someone qualified to keep him up to date on the peace work being done all over the world. By coincidence, a retired Turkish diplomat by the name of Aristarchi Bey happened to be applying for a position with him at this time. They came to an arrangement, but it did not work out to Alfred's satisfaction; he found the former diplomat's reports too wordy and superficial.

During their brief collaboration, Alfred wrote Aristarchi Bey a letter that says a great deal about his principles:

> I am astonished at how fast the number of competent and serious-minded congress participants is growing, but also at the absurd proposals that other windbags offer and which are likely to cause even the best intentions to fail. Without exception, all governments have a common interest in avoiding wars that are time after time incited by industrial robber barons of the Boulanger type.[2] If one could find a way to diminish their numbers, most governments would probably seize it with gratitude. I find myself asking why the rules governing a duel between individuals should not be applied to a duel between nations. Before a duel, witnesses are appointed to establish if sufficiently serious grounds exist to justify it. Such a pre-investigation would certainly not prevent nations from warring with each other, but under such circumstances, who would risk universal animosity or the danger of everybody uniting against them? As witnesses, either neutral governments or a tribunal along the lines of the House of Lords might be appointed. I would be exceedingly happy if I could assist in carrying the work of the Peace Congress forward, even if it were but a small

---

[2] Georges Ernest Boulanger, 1837–1891, French general and reactionary politician who saw himself as a future dictator.

step, and in that respect I would not shy away from expenses. This suggestion should not be dismissed as utopian; Henry IV's government was already seriously
engaged in endeavoring to solve the problem until, un-
happily, Ravaillac cut his efforts short by murdering
him.[3] Moreover, since 1816, no fewer than sixty-two
cases have been solved through arbitration between governments, which goes to show that even if the people are
totally oppressed, the governments are only half so.

In another letter, in November 1892, Alfred wrote: "All neutral
countries should give a guarantee to an arbitrating court regarding the execution of its judgment — even including, if necessary,
the use of force. Let us admit that anything at all is better than
war. All borders would remain untouched, and a declaration should
be made that any and every aggressor would have all of Europe
against him."

Alfred's idea was that through formal treaties governments
would be duty-bound to defend collectively any attacked country,
whereupon partial disarmament would take place. He was not recommending the dismantling of all armies, "since there has to be an
armed force to maintain order."

On January 20, 1897, six weeks after Alfred's death, Bertha von
Suttner elegized him in *Neue Freie Press*. She wrote, in part: "Alfred
worked indefatigably on perfecting cannons and projectiles. He believed a weapon technique's increasing efficacy would prove more
and more the absurdity and the impossibility of future wars and in
that way contribute to their abolishment." She also notes that Alfred
"regularly sent monetary contributions to the Austrian peace association, which fact has led some detractors to point to a supposedly
inherent contradiction in the inventor of dynamite and the smokeless
gunpowder daydreaming of world peace. No, Nobel was not daydreaming; he was acting in clear consciousness of his goal."

Alfred's critics have long tried to insist that his involvement
in the peace movement was merely a way to put his investments in
the arms industry in a more favorable light. His occasional inconsis-

---

[3] Henry IV of Navarre ruled France 1589–1610 and the country prospered; then
Ravaillac, a Catholic fanatic, assassinated him.

tency did not always help his cause. According to E. Schneider, the head of the French war materiel company Schneider & Cie, Alfred said to him in Paris in 1890 that "an intensification of the war tools' death-bringing precision will not by itself bring us any peace."

Alfred's extensive financial involvement in munitions, and the fact that he stood on both sides of the line, has meant that much of what he said and did was misunderstood. Yet, with dynamite factories over all of Europe, Alfred depended upon peaceful trades.

Bertha von Suttner and others believed that his interest in peace was so genuine that he would in all probability have given generous contributions to the work for peace, regardless of its relation to free trade.

On January 7, 1893, Alfred had written a letter to Bertha von Suttner that she reproduced in its entirety in the *Neue Freie Press* elegy:

Dear Friend,

I wish Happy New Year to you personally and to the noble campaign you are pursuing so courageously against ignorance and stupidity!

I would like to bequeath part of my fortune for the establishment of peace prizes to be awarded every fifth year (let us say six times, for if at the end of thirty years we have not succeeded in reforming society, we shall inevitably revert to barbarism) to the man or woman who has contributed most effectively to the realization of peace in Europe. I do not refer to disarmament, which is an ideal we can only reach slowly and with caution, nor to compulsory arbitration. But we can and ought soon be able to go at least so far as to have all states, among themselves, pledge to intervene against anyone who breaks the peace.

This would be one means to make war impossible, and to force even the least reasonable and most brutal power either to make use of arbitration or keep still. If the triple alliance enveloped all states instead of just three, peace would be ensured for centuries.

I send the warmest greetings to you and your husband.

Your most affectionate
A. Nobel

As usual, Bertha had her own point of view and felt that thirty years was too long a time-period, certain as she was that the peace efforts would be crowned with success before the year 1900. Her principal objection to Alfred's proposal, however, was in another area: those who worked for peace didn't need a prize but money, in order to further their cause.

In the will that Alfred had drawn up on March 14, 1893, he stipulated that one percent of his fortune would go to the Austrian peace association and that the peace prize should go to someone who had made pioneering contributions in "the wide field of knowledge and progress." In an addendum, he specified that candidates who had been "successful in combating prejudices on the part of people and governments toward the establishment of a European peace tribunal" would be given most serious consideration.

On December 7, 1895, Alfred asked his nephew Hjalmar (Robert's son) to investigate the possibility of buying the Swedish newspaper *Aftonbladet*. The young man assumed that his uncle felt such an acquisition would further his business interests, but that was not the case, as we see in a letter to Hjalmar, written November 27, 1895.

> You believe that my intention is to influence business matters. . . . One of my peculiarities is that my own business interests are never my primary consideration. My position as newspaper owner would be as follows: to oppose armaments and other holdovers from the Middle Ages, but with the recommendation, if they are to be built anyhow, that the manufacture be done within the borders of the country, for if there is one national industry that ought to remain independent of other countries, it is the defense branch. And since weapon factories already exist in Sweden, it is both a shame and ridiculous not to maintain them. My reason for wanting to own a newspaper is simply that I want to stuff a truly progressive point of view down the throats of the editorial staff.

Ten days before Alfred wrote this letter, he had signed his third and final last will and testament. The new version received Bertha's hearty commendation, since it emphasized both disarmament and peace congresses. Alfred had dedicated part of his fortune to a prize to that person who had "done the most or best work for the brotherhood of nations and the abolishment or reduction of standing armies, as well as for the establishment and spread of peace congresses."

That Alfred had Bertha in mind when he composed this is evident from the fact that he immediately informed her of his final version. She was overjoyed: "Whether or not I am still alive by then does not matter; what you and I have given will live on."

Chapter 58

After Sofie had given birth to her child, fathered by a young Austrian cavalry officer, Kapy von Kapivar, Alfred continued to send her friendly but impersonal letters. He saw to it that she was assured of 6,000 florins in private income per year, a good annuity at the time — but for a young woman who had grown used to luxuries, the sum did not go very far.

Sofie wrote to Alfred on January 16, 1892, to ask for more money:

My dear Alfred!

I haven't heard from you for so long. I'm very concerned because my health is poor and I have no peace. I think of you all the time and would like to know how you are feeling and what you are doing.

You write so seldom and when you do, I hear only reproaches and mean things that I don't deserve since I have never before lived so quietly and economically. But I'd like to pay the debts from before that are still in the name of Nobel, because it looks so bad if I don't. I promise you never again to get into debt. . . .

I have no money to live on and today must pawn my last brooch. It's never been as hard as this. I'm quite desperate. It was not this miserable even at home. And the poor child — what will its fate be?

Greeting you and kissing you warmly is your
Sofie

Two days later she wrote:

Dear Alfred,

For three weeks you haven't written me even a line. I don't know the reason. It's not like you not to answer at all and leave me with anxiety. I sent three letters to Paris since I didn't know that you are in San Remo and have finished your villa. People in Vienna talk about the splendor and elegance of your home.

I wish you much happiness in your new dwelling but
it's humiliating to me that you never gave me your address and that I had to get it from strangers.

How is your health? Good, I hope. The fine air will do
you good. From what I've heard, you have an active social life. The Viennese on the other hand are quite something. Sweet to one's face and nothing but falsity behind
one's back!

I would like to ask you, Alfred, to send me a little cash.
I am totally without money for fourteen days now and
have to pawn my last ring to eat, that's how far it has
gone with me. A propos — did you receive the little business card folder? I'd think you would have mentioned
something about it. . . .

A few weeks later came a reply from Alfred:

Genoa
February 1892

Dear Sofie!

. . . Most of all, you must send me, addressed to Paris, a
detailed summary of your debts. Then we will see if I
decide to help you out of the stupid situation in which
you have placed yourself. It sounds almost unbelievable
that you have managed to waste so much money and still
acquired new debts. . . .

Sofie replied immediately:

My dear Alfred,

Many and warm thanks for your dear lines and the 2,000
schillings plus telegram. You cannot imagine my happiness when I received it. I had such anxiety, was brooding
the whole night through over my fate, reproached myself
and got sick from it. . . .

The piece of jewelry I pawned gave me more than
1,000 schillings. I had to do it since I didn't have one cent
in the house. My illness and the washing cost very much.
And I've always immediately paid off the bills for the

usual goods and then again have nothing for my daily
needs. Finally I have to pawn something else. I used to
know nothing of such things. I've brought everything
upon myself by my stupidity and now I have to suffer and
pay for it. My poor child is most to be pitied. I will not
grieve on my behalf, I have made the soup and have to
swallow it. I got your lines from the day before yesterday
and there wasn't much in it that was flattering to me. It's
humiliating to receive such reproaches again and again. . . .

After having received two more letters from Alfred with money enclosed,
Sofie wrote:

[n.d., 1892]

. . . You are so good and have a heart that's rare in this
world. How often don't I think back on how well you
treated me, on your warmth, your goodness, and your
nobility. In short, on everything I received when I was
with you and yours. It's all been over for a year, and what
gives me joy in life now is my child whom I adore and
love so much that I could eat her up.

You write, dear Alfred, nothing at all about getting together, only that I should look for someone else but I am
begging you and would be so happy, dear Bubi, to see
you. You wouldn't recognize me, that's how much I have
changed in every way, being content and simple and with
no thought of anything garish. If I were with you, my
good humor and everything else would return.

You, too, wish to talk to me about so much. I believe it
would be better to meet in person than through strangers.
Don't you agree?

I have so much to tell you and want to ask your advice,
but it can't be done at a distance. I could pack quickly and
come, even to the end of the world.

Of course I am anxious about little Gretl who stretches
her small arms toward me and says mommy. She is so
smart. That she didn't get from me, only her liveliness
and friendliness. She looks as if she were a year old, that's
how big she is. She has wonderful blue eyes and a beautiful little mouth with six teeth, unusual at eight months. If

you'd see my little one, you'd like her a lot. Yes, she is all
I have now and if I also could have you, dear Alfred, then
I would embrace the whole world! But you think differently and are still angry. Yet I've promised you never
again to get into debt! . . .

February 14, 1892

Dear Sofie,

. . . Now you have a little daughter who gives you great
joy. . . .

I wrote to you some time ago that I suffered great
losses last year. It ought to have opened your eyes and
prevented you from your excessive way of living. . . .

March 16, 1892

. . . I am sending you enclosed two Hungarian bills for
you to pay your debt to K. Trensch. It corresponds to
about 2,200 florins. . . .

You must go there without delay and pay in the presence of a witness. Ask for a signed promissory note as a
receipt and send it to me immediately in a registered
letter. . . .

May 18, 1892

. . . It is said that Christ was a very good and tolerant
person. He had a dear daddy who rewarded him richly for
this and since then he is supposed to live in heaven. But
I, who do not have such highly placed relatives, cannot understand why I should be more good and more tolerant
than the Son of God. In addition, he is vastly superior
when it comes to multiplication. As soon as somebody
shows me how you from three skinny fish can manage to
create 2,000 fat ones — without any hocus pocus — I will
go and buy 3,000 fish. From those 3,000 I will then make
two million, which is going to give me a lot of money.
With my wealth, I would be more generous than the cru-
cified one. Perhaps God will be angry with me since I
have already outshone his firstborn when it comes to

charity. Until then, however, I want to tell you and your family one thing: though I have a generous nature, I have no desire to be used. Be good and observe this little word! . . .

November 13, 1892

. . . My left lung is again causing me misery. They console me by saying that everyone who has unusually long nails, as I do, is predestined to contract consumption. . . .

The various obligations I have undertaken are weighing me down like lead. When you rebuild businesses, there is nothing more difficult than to anticipate when you will be through with it. It looks at first as if one might reach the desired result any day at all. You don't know why week after week and month after month must pass before everything gets resolved. . . .

Meanwhile, Sofie writes to Alfred:

[n. d.]

My dear Alfred!

I can't find an apartment because they are too expensive. Also, I have great difficulties because I am not married. The asses here have such prejudices and the Jewish landlords are, as you know, real blackguards. I'm desperate. It's depressing to spend the winter with a small child in a cold hotel room and eat terrible food. It's as if everything is against me these days. I have never felt really happy since I left you. It's so lonely and I feel so low that often I think it would be better if I took my own life. . . .

You can't imagine what you have to endure in Austria when you are not married. Kapy wants to marry me and I might do it for the sake of the child. She's so pretty and you can't imagine how grown-up she speaks — but she has to have a last name. What am I going to do about that? Do you give your permission to use yours? Since you are everything in the world to me.

Now you get warm kisses
from your eternally loving
Sofie

Paris

December 1892

Dear Sofie!

. . . However much I slave, I cannot seem to finish my
work, and it is beginning to wear down my nerves. No
human being in this city of 2.4 million inhabitants could
suffer and be tortured more than I. . . .

On December 21, 1892, Sofie writes from Vienna:

My dear Alfred!

What most saddened me is the news that you are not as
well as I thought. When I saw you last time you looked
rejuvenated and no one would believe you to be older
than 45. I think it comes from your goodness, dear
Alfred, no one else on earth is as good as you. I also wish
you everything good, much happiness and first and foremost pleasant holidays. I would have liked so much to
come to you so that you could have seen my little Gretl.
You'd be delighted by her prattle and she's laughing all
the time. My little one has such a pretty mouth, small
hands and feet as the photo shows which I was able to
have taken, thanks to you. The photographer said he had
seldom had such a nice child in his shop. When he pulled
the black cloth over his head, she cried out "play kiss"
and ran to him. She is free and easy and nice to
everyone. . . .

What is missing in my bliss of motherhood is you, dear
Alfred, and you I have lost through my own doing. . . .

Nice

December 23, 1892

Dear Sofie!

. . . I have a difficult time with my heart trouble and am
spending Christmas here in utmost seclusion and solitude. I don't know a soul and make no effort to see if
there are any names I might know in the hotel register.

Alfred

Merano
March 22, 1893

Dear Alfred!

. . . I understand that you have no objection if the Captain Kapy von Kapivar marries me. I take this step for the
sake of the child whom I love more than everything. I
want to give her a name so that later on she doesn't have
to be ashamed and have people point a finger at her because the poor thing whose mother has erred is born out
of wedlock. Why should the wretched little one have to
suffer for that her whole life? . . .

I felt very depressed when I heard that with regard to
the child you had not done what you promised in the
matter of inheritance. You promised that if it were a girl,
you would take care of her and at least not feel any
grudge against her. A child born out of wedlock would
legally not concern you and my annuity would be value-
less, meaning that the poor little one would receive nothing after my death.

No, you couldn't be so merciless, dear Alfred, isn't that so?
You have to take care of the annuity so that my poor child
will get money after my death — She is yet so small and your
heirs will certainly not be dependent on that money. . . .

[n. d., 1884]

Sofie!

. . . What kind of fairy tales are you trying to tell me? An
attorney is no greenhorn who doesn't know what his
client must do. In July of 1892, Mr. B himself sent a bill
to you that is hardly in agreement with what you are now
declaring. In other words, your story cannot be correct.
Since God, the pope, and lawyers are infallible, I can
only draw the conclusion that you have distorted the
whole thing on purpose. . . .

August 11, 1894

Dear Alfred!

. . . From your letter I have understood that you believe
that sum was a deception, but dear Alfred, I can assure
you that I haven't received the money from him, but that
it was interest. I am not lying and implore you to speak
to him yourself if you do not believe me. . . .

I don't want to be disgraced and stand there like a beggar. Every night I dream of nothing but executions and
once even that they violated my little child! Oh, such
worry is something terrible. I would not have believed
that I would come to experience it. I have fallen from
heaven to hell and all because of pure stupidity!

Sofie

July 10, 1894

Dear Alfred!

In spite of being forced to get news about you through a
third party, I can't resist telling you that I have embraced
your religion and become a Protestant. This also goes of
course for my child. It brings us closer than before. . . .

Even if love wears off with time, our warm friendship
has to remain all the way to the grave. I also beg you to
remain a good friend to my child, who's so dear to me.
Because I feel the end is approaching. . . .

It's a bitter thing to need to speak about money but I
am begging you once and for all to give me 200,000 florins. Then you will know that my child and I are supported and can live without worries. You could deposit
the money in a bank so that I will receive the
interest. . . .

Aix-les-Bains
September 12, 1894

Dear Sofie!

I found you in better health than ever and cannot understand why you feel so sorry for yourself. Of course you

lack a good number of things, and your environment is neither the best nor the most pleasant. But all in all, you are not among those most unfortunate, though you have done everything you could to end up among them. You have had rather enormous good luck, as everyone who knows your circumstances must feel, because any other man in my position would have calmly left you to the misery you were so busy creating.

Your child is truly sweet and must now have a good education. I don't know anything about your relation to the child's father and thus cannot judge which of you is right or wrong. Moreover, it is none of my business.

Warm greetings from A.N.

Alfred sent his last letter to Sofie, whose child was now almost four, on March 7, 1895, when he learned that nearly three years after it first came up as a possibility, she and Kapy von Kapivar are to be married:

Paris
March 7, 1895

. . . Is it true that your cavalry captain wants to marry you? If so, he is acting not only correctly but wisely as well. Then you will have to renounce your vanity and stop all your caprices. When all is said and done, you are an emotional little creature and, after all, that is worth something. I believe that even you do not totally lack a conscience provided that Praterstrasse [a reference to Sofie's family] stays a hundred miles away.

Warm greetings from A.N.

Ragnar Sohlman provides some details about Sofie's marriage. During a visit to Vienna in the spring of 1919, a Swedish physical therapist who knew the father of Sofie's child told him that after his marriage to Sofie Hess, von Kapivar was forced to retire from active military service and worked as an agent for a champagne company. About the nuptials, Sohlman reports: "Von Kapivar picked up his bride at her home and brought her to the church in an elegant hired fiacre that was left waiting outside while the ceremony took place. After he had escorted his bride to the carriage,

*he chivalrously kissed her hand and bade her farewell — à jamais!
[forever]."*

It was, in other words, a marriage in name only, but it gave Sofie her
last name and the title she had desired. Yet it did not prevent her from feeling
jilted by Alfred, to whom she wrote a new letter:

Vienna, Saturday

Dear Alfred!

. . . I need to have surgery by Dr. Breus, who delivered
my child. I have gone through so much and look like a
corpse. I can't take good care of myself because I have no
money. Professor Breus pities me and is being very compassionate about my fate. . . .

Tell me, dear Alfred, don't you feel any kind of remorse? Generally you are so good to everyone. I don't
think you can imagine how difficult things are for me.
Otherwise, I'm convinced you'd behave much differently
toward me. . . .

One day the world will know about me. Life is not so
important to me. I have had enough of living like a dog. I
am exposed to scandals, as for instance here at the hotel.
The headwaiter created such a scene when I did not pay
immediately that a gentleman at the hotel took pity on me
and could not understand how my life could be so miserable. You happen to know this person. He is French.
Since then I have become so nervous that I'm frightened
by any sound. You would not recognize me the way I
look and since the doctors absolutely want me to undergo
surgery, they have suggested that I go to stay at a sanato-
rium for eight days since I have no home. Thus I stand
alone, dear Alfred, deserted by the whole world for having a child without being married. You know the Austri-
ans, this stupid people. When you don't have proof of
marriage, they think you earn your living on the street.
But those who are married let themselves be bought for a
hat or a dress by the first man who comes along, and they
are unfaithful to their husbands despite being married by
a priest or a minister. . . .

I have made the firm decision to give my poor child a

name by marrying her father. After that sacrifice, perhaps
I won't be as happy as I deserve, but I must say, without
bragging, that I'm a very good mother and prepared to
sacrifice everything for my child, God knows that. Had I
not been who I am, it would have been different, and I
would not be forced to ask for alms. You are the first one
for me, dear Alfred. If sometime you would think of how
I spent my youth, without all those occasions to rejoice
that other girls have, you'd feel more compassion. Dear
Alfred, I beg you to free me from this miserable existence
which I can't stand any longer — I beg you to arrange
that I get money each month and no longer need be dependent on a certain gentleman's mercy.

Your Sofie

*Sohlman also reports that Kapy von Kapivar even appealed to Alfred
for support for his wife over and above the annuity she was already receiving.
Alfred left their letters unanswered.*

*When the content of Alfred's will became known at the beginning of
1897, it proved a bitter disappointment to Sofie, who was left only a small
sum. She turned to a lawyer in Vienna, who in turn contacted the executor
Ragnar Sohlman to ask for more money, pleas that soon devolved into threats.
If she did not get more money, she would publish the more than two hundred
letters that Alfred had written to her.*

*Sohlman made the (probably) correct judgment that, given the opinion
climate of the time, the letters would have made his assignment to execute
Alfred's will far more difficult. Scandal would give the general public a
misleading and detrimental picture, not only of Alfred Nobel the private man
but of his life's work.*

*After distasteful negotiations, Sohlman reached an agreement by which
he would buy back the letters. Sofie Hess received a one-time compensation
above her life annuity. She had to pledge never to comment publicly on her
relationship with Alfred Nobel. Were she to break this agreement, her annuity would be cut off.*

*Those negotiations are the final vignette to the story of the eighteen-
year relationship between the empire builder Alfred Nobel and the flower
girl from Vienna, Sofie Hess.*

Chapter 59

Over the course of his visits with Robert in Getå, Alfred became more and more attached to his brother's children — his sons Hjalmar and Ludvig, and his daughters Tyra and Ingeborg. The younger Nobels had spent some time with him in San Remo during the spring of 1891, and on January 8 of the following year he wrote to their father:

Dear Brother Robert,

I ought long ago to have answered your letter of 12/8, but first an eye injury prevented me and then everything has been delayed due to business trouble and building trouble. One gets older and hardly finds time to manage, yes, hardly finds time to *mismanage,* everything that rests on one's time-broken shoulders.

For your children I have done what I can, and hope that they have benefited. . . .

All of them, but especially Ludvig, have an unpretentiousness about them that is delightful and which excuses what you call their "emotional namby-pambiness." Partly because all my life I have myself struggled with an exaggerated sensitivity, partly because I tell myself that thought and feeling are equally valuable expressions of the human nervous system, I have come to the defense of the emotionally namby-pamby.

According to my way of thinking, everything that has happened has occurred because of imperturbable laws, and could not have happened otherwise. Where is the room for criticism? It bursts like a soap bubble. But in spite of an unavoidable fate, one keeps struggling, because the workings of brain, heart, and nerves so demand. . . .

As you know, each of your children has a sum of money deposited with me which, whenever they desire, they can withdraw, and on which I will pay them six percent until such time as the sum is paid out. Pin-money for the girls and a little reserve for the boys!

My older brother, you and I are far down on life's descending slope. The link that binds life and dust to the spirit of the world's totality is a conundrum, and, faced with it, small thoughts and small trouble dissolve into nothingness — a kind of life vacuum. But those who have walked, side by side for a long time, through life do understand each other better, and become closer, as we have, in loyal and brotherly friendship.

Alfred

During the last three years of Alfred's life, he also grew closer to Sweden. He would usually stay at the Grand Hotel during his visits to Stockholm, but later he began to change his habits. While negotiating the purchase of the old ironworks in Bofors, he stayed at the more modest Hotel Carl in Brunkebergs Square, where he occupied a simple suite of two rooms, bedroom and receiving room, "furnished in the dark and heavy style of the 1880s, with heavy curtains at the windows and an overstuffed sofa."

Alfred wrote Robert a letter during one visit to Stockholm, on July 29, 1893, that gives an insight into his mood as he approached his sixties:

Dear Brother Robert,

For what reason do you assume that a distance has grown between us? For my part, I know of none. That our correspondence has stopped I would suppose to be for the same reason on both our parts: the necessity to preserve our eyesight.

Lately my sight has diminished at almost ten times the normal speed, which means that I have to go from one prescription to the next in less than three months, instead of two years, which is the most common condition. The oculist has forbidden me all writing and reading for six months, but how would that be possible?

Yesterday's mail contained 57 letters and 10 telegrams. I have no secretary, and it is difficult to get one for the kind of business I do. But the necessity grows more obvious with each passing day, and the tremble in my hand is making the writing less and less clear. I know that with you, who has an iron constitution compared to me, your vision has weakened, but that luckily you can expose it to less strain and ought therefore to keep it for many years.

I have to look forward, with a certain melancholy, to a rapidly approaching time when everything will be dark in life. I am more philosophical about this than most, but that doesn't help.

The families of Nobel and Ahlsell are actually miserable races, doomed to a short life. In the Nobel brain, an abnormal number of pictures that we call ideas whirl around, and in the case of the Ahlsells, myriads flourish that might hinder the blood circulation and reshape our bodies into instruments of torture. . . .

Do you have any plans to come to Stockholm? Otherwise I will come to Getå. How we are aging, my dear Robert! You are almost 65, and soon I will be 60.

What remains is less than a full life, at least for me, because I have always had too little energy and strength is not refound when one is sliding down on life's sloping plane. But you have always had enough strength, and ought to still have enough for your old age. It is an inheritance from our father's side.

But that with my miserable body I have managed to nearly reach sixty and still remain active is a mystery. But of this and many, many other things we will speak of some beautiful August evening. Since now Ingeborg and Ludvig are going to get married, Hjalmar and Tyra will probably follow soon. Marriage is contagious.

Warmly yours
Alfred

His niece Ingeborg's intention of marrying the young Count Carl von Frischen-Ridderstolpe was the occasion of other letters. Robert was not at all convinced of von Frischen-Ridderstolpe's suitability.

Gmunden
August 24, 1893

Dearest Brother Robert!

In your position I would take things very easy for three
reasons, namely
1) that what has happened can not be undone;
2) that in America 20 million females never discuss matters of marriage with their parents, and that in no
   other country is the woman as happy and as well situated as there;
3) that your little daughter's health is of such nature that
   it cannot be subjected to overly harsh if well-meaning
   criticism.
. . . Your future son-in-law seems dedicated and manly
but not hard, has an easy manner, and is less affected by
the snobbery than any Swedish nobleman I know, except
for Nollan and Pirre.
   Young Riddarsporre ["larkspur" in Swedish — a play on
his name] looks as if he were man enough to handle
things well. He gives the impression of a leader, not of a
passive personality.
   That the place is not that beautiful and the house not
exactly grand does not matter.
   Ingeborg could not be less pretentious. Neither she nor
her husband will want to prance about in a nobleman's
liveries. To sum up, without in any way wanting to give
advice, I would say that the young man's dark spot is his
father, whose senseless waste has done the son much damage, but perhaps also sharpened his nature, so that he will
be much more considerate of his little wife than you
predict. . . .
   Of course I realize, though a bachelor, that it is not easy
to handle daughters, nor to ensure their future happiness.
   But how dimly can even the most sharp-eyed of us read
what is in the book of Fate. It is perhaps better therefore
to let destiny lead rather than to try to lead it: that way, at
least, one cannot be said to be applying the brakes at the
wrong time.
   Without being unrefined, Ridderstolpe has something

ebullient in his nature. Such people are often attracted to a
weak or refined creature.

Their fusion will perhaps result in a better alloy than
you think. A man without his own fortune, who in our
day got married to a girl with two empty hands, is actually an infatuated idiot with every chance of making
her unhappy. . . .

There are two reasons that I am sitting here at one
o'clock in the morning, philosophizing with my pen: one
is that I have to live up to my doctor of philosophy degree, the second that I look like blessed Job: full of impatient wounds. True, they are only mosquito bites but
still . . . they contribute to a philosophical mood. . . .

Paris
September 23, 1893

Dearest Brother Robert,

. . . I almost believe you're already beginning to share my
opinion of Carl Ridderstolpe. In any case he is remarkably
free of the Swedish nobility mania, and that is all the
more delightful in a country where so many so-called
aristocrats prance around with ideas as antiquated as leftover signs from demolished lunatic asylums.

Ridderstolpe on the other hand has a very natural and
dignified manner; it is not his fault that our society has
marked him with a sign of social rank.

My case against the English government has forced me
to come back here. I am totally exhausted from the long
journey and am therefore writing poorly but you are
greeted all the more heartily

from
Alfred

Chapter 60

T hough at one point, Alfred believed that "in your old age you do not acquire any friends," this did not turn out to be the case. A couple of months before he turned sixty in 1893, he met a twenty-three-year-old engineer named Ragnar Sohlman, who would become an extraordinarily loyal associate and his closest friend. Alfred needed someone: his mother and Ludvig had passed away, his partner Paul Barbe had taken his life, and the long relationship with Sofie Hess had mercifully come to an end.

Through Ragnar Sohlman's memoirs, published posthumously in 1950, the circumstances surrounding their first meeting are known. After completing his exams at the Technical Institute in Stockholm, Sohlman went to the United States, where for a time he worked in a dynamite factory owned by the Du Ponts. In 1893, he was offered a job as engineer at an explosive-substance factory in Mexico, but a bout with pleurisy kept him from accepting it, and his family wanted him to return to Sweden.

During the summer of 1893, he worked in the Swedish pavilion at the Chicago World's Fair. There, to his great surprise, he received a telegram offering him a job as Alfred Nobel's personal assistant. Much later — on his own sixtieth birthday — Sohlman would find out who had recommended him for the post: Alfred's chief financial backer in Winter Bay, J.W. Smitt, and Robert's son, Ludvig.

In October 1893, "with a certain trepidation," Ragnar Sohlman presented himself to Alfred, who was visiting Paris. A maître d'hotel escorted him into his famous compatriot's workroom, where Alfred was sitting, writing letters. He was, according to Sohlman, less than average height, had sharply defined features, a high forehead, thick eyebrows, and deep-set eyes "whose glance was penetrating and, like his temperament, animated and frequently changing."

Sohlman spent his first three workdays trying to bring order to the library at Avenue Malakoff. He grouped the technical or scientific works according to their subject and arranged the literary works by language. Alfred was much pleased with the result. During these first days, Sohlman was staying at a small hotel in the neighborhood, but Alfred always invited him to lunch in the Winter Garden.

Alfred quickly realized that Sohlman did not have the necessary

language fluency to be his secretary. On May 24, 1894, Alfred wrote
Alarik Liedbeck from San Remo: "I am not just lazy, but so tired of
writing that I have to think of getting a secretary, male or female
coûte que coûte [at all costs]. Preferably the latter, because they are less
troublesome when you don't have something for them to do. They
just get themselves some persistent beau and you don't have to watch
over them as you do a male secretary. . . ."

In 1895 Alfred employed a Swedish woman named Sophie Ahlström. He told her he would be very demanding. Any secretary of
his had to be able to take shorthand in "excellent English, French,
and German" plus be efficient in "handling the Remington type-
writer. . . . This past year," he wrote Miss Ahlström, "I employed
one Mr. Sohlman as secretary, but one week later it became obvious
that he had more talent for chemistry. Since then, he has been employed at my laboratory in Bofors and become one of my few favorite
people. So you see that even though I am myself a sort of worthless
brooding instrument, I have sense enough to realize and appreciate
others' worth. *Avis à la lectrice* [Take notice, dear reader]."

Sohlman had indeed become a valued addition to Alfred's laboratory in San Remo. For colleagues he had Alphonse Tournaud and
George Hugh Beckett, who had worked with one of the most prominent chemists in England, Sir Alfred Mond. One task Alfred gave
Sohlman was to maintain his extensive patent correspondence.

It seems certain that in Sohlman Alfred saw a mirror image of
himself in his youth. He was increasingly impressed by the young
man's gifts and capacity. For his part, Sohlman showed his employer
and patron great respect. Alfred had asked that he call him by his
first name, but Sohlman continued to address him as "Doctor," even
after he had been urged not to. "Two things I never borrow —
money and projects," wrote Alfred in 1895. "But if somebody as
thoroughly sound as Mr. Sohlman is willing to lend me a little
friendship, I will indeed accept it and be glad for it."

Largely due to Sohlman's presence, Alfred's thoughts more and
more frequently were of Sweden. Another reason was he had begun
thinking, as he wrote in his laboratory journal on October 21,
1893 — his sixtieth birthday — of purchasing the Bofors machine
works. His journal also reveals that he was involved in "patents for
the soundless discharging of a gun" and "elimination of disturbing
sounds in the phonograph" in his San Remo laboratory. The phonograph was the speech-registration machine with rotating cylinder

that Edison had invented in 1877, which in 1910 would be replaced by the gramophone.

Alfred's ambition was to turn the machine works in Bofors into a cannon industry with international scope. "It would be amusing," he wrote, "to see Sweden rival Germany and England when it comes to arms." A bonus was that he would finally acquire a Swedish home in the form of the manorial estate Björkborn. Although the Swedish winters seemed discouragingly long to him, the country's industrial climate was favorable. Any initiative that increased employment opportunities could count on support from the authorities.

He was also looking forward to carrying out his increasingly advanced weapon-technical experiments in a newly equipped laboratory and new surroundings. Moving his laboratory from San Remo to Bofors gave him no feeling of loss.

At the time England was not a viable alternative, since the torturous cordite trial was still dragging on. Moreover, as he wrote Bertha von Suttner: ". . . in England the conservatism flourishes too well for anyone to accept anything at all that does not have some prehistorical tradition." Authorities in France had closed his Sevran laboratory. Alfred felt also that "all French live with the blessed belief that the brain is a French organ." Finally, as for the Germans, he found them "priggishly long-winded and superfluously detailed." He also never seriously considered settling in Germany because of all the unrest after Bismarck's resignation — even though he was the first to admit that the country's chemical and mechanical industries were the best in the world. That was why the idea of acquiring the Bofors works looked so attractive. The conditions for his planned experiments would be the best imaginable in an isolated Swedish milieu.

In the beginning of January 1894, for a cash sum of one million Swedish crowns, Alfred bought the entire stock of the family firm. The weapon smithy was antiquated and the investment needs badly neglected. From his extensive financial experience, Alfred was well aware that he had acquired an enterprise on the brink of bankruptcy, but that didn't stop him from utilizing an option to buy the old works at Bjorneborg, where the blast furnaces, Bessemer converters,[4]

---

[4] Named after Sir Henry Bessemer, 1813–1898, an English engineer who developed a method of making steel by blasting air through molten pig iron in a large container to burn away the carbon and other impurities.

and rolling mills fit his plan of action well. To exploit the hydraulic power of the Svartälven River, he also put in a bid for the nearby stream, Karåsforsen.

When the board of directors for AB Bofors-Gullspång held a special board meeting on February 19, 1894, Alfred was elected as the new chairman. It was also decided that the managing director, Jonas Kjellberg, would stay on, even though the Kjellberg family had sold off its shares.

Alfred presented the new board with a memorandum challenging the management of Bofors with the following assignment: 1) construct a laboratory for the manufacture of smokeless gunpowder and for carrying out chemical experiments; 2) establish a shooting range for small-scale tests of powders and explosive grenades; 3) expand the cannon workshop, for which he wished to receive "a complete project with plans and cost estimations to maximize organization." These guidelines remained the working manual for Bofors after his death.

Alfred's visit to the Bofors machine works the summer after his purchase grew into a lengthy stay, as he took an active part in the construction of his laboratory in the park surrounding the works and the manor. When in August 1894 Ragnar Sohlman assumed his position as superintendent, he had George Hugh Beckett from the San Remo laboratory at his side. The latter began dividing his time between Björkborn and San Remo.

Alfred stopped acting as if his life's work was over. The documents from the early days in Bofors testify to just how hard and enthusiastically he worked. In 1966, eighty-seven-year-old Augustus Åhling provided an account of Alfred's activities to the *Swedish American Tribune*: "Nobel had a whole laboratory sent up on train cars from Stockholm. As little boys we were allowed to help with the transport up to the works where the building was being constructed. He was mostly involved in the projectile manufacture and was himself participating in the test shoots. They were shooting old muzzle guns, trying out different kinds of gunpowder, and I was one of the ones who Nobel had employed to run around and find the cannon balls out in the fields after the shoots."

One problem Alfred wanted to solve was "how explosive loads could be made effective against thick armor plate." In a letter to Sohlman he envisioned "a weapon that shoots a lot of small projectiles that reach an enormous speed and treat the armor plate like butter. They will do the preparatory work for the large projectile and stuff it with food already chewed."

A newspaper notice from October 3, 1894, shows that Alfred was also thinking of peaceful uses for these new products: "Patent is sought by Dr. A. Nobel for ways to produce substitutes for India rubber, gutta-percha, leather, and varnishes as well as the way they are manufactured." He was equally involved in the mechanical manufacture of potassium, artificial silk, sodium, and even synthetic jewelry.

Alfred began spending longer periods in Sweden, and this enabled him to associate with friends such as Liedbeck, Salomon August Andrée, the inventor Wilhelm Unge, and the executive director of the Swedish nitroglycerine company Carl Öberg, as well as the Polar explorers Nordenskiöld and his loyal acolyte Louis Palander. His circle also included the inventor and engineer Robert W. Strehlert. After receiving his degree at the Technical Institute, Strehlert had worked at Alfred's laboratories in Sevran, San Remo, and then in Bofors. A man with remarkable entrepreneurial qualities, he had gone to the United States after finishing his studies and found a way to work for Thomas Edison. He had studied the manufacture of light bulbs thoroughly, and, on his return to Sweden, began working in the Sodertalje Swedish Light Bulb Factory. What most interested Alfred about Strehlert was the method for manufacturing artificial silk from nitrocellulose that he had patented. When the young Swede described his future plans, Alfred saw right away the possibilities for producing artificial silk on a large scale.

A little over a month after Alfred's death, Strehlert wrote to Rudolf Liljequist, who had been elected executor of Alfred's estate: "With his deep concern for progress in the technical field, Alfred mapped out in detail, a month before his death, the plan that should be followed in building the vegetable silk industry. He was even willing to provide financial security to a Swedish business with this purpose, since his own health was shaky. All preliminary agreements to this end were finished when death came and in one swift gesture ended his grand project."

Steel provides yet another example of Alfred's uncanny ability to see new developmental possibilities. In the Björkborn laboratory, he was experimenting to find a new steel alloy that would make production more efficient. To produce better kinds of steel, Alfred was considering various possibilities with both French and German companies, before he turned to the Bethlehem Steel Corporation. His goal was to create what he called an "alliance" with the powerful United States company. Bofors would buy shares in Bethlehem and vice versa. Leading individuals from both companies would serve as members of each other's boards.

The collaborative plans with Bethlehem were at the center of Alfred's interests during the last six months of his life. His death prevented them being brought to fruition.

Chapter 61

Alfred had once read in a medical journal that the eye is capable of maintaining an image on its retina for about one-tenth of a second. The observation was not new, but a few scientists had begun a thorough study of this "inertia of the eye." Alfred's interest was aroused, and he wrote in his notebook: "Double or multiply the light's effect by letting lamp mirrors rotate faster than ten beats a second." He imagined that somehow it should be possible, in one way or another, to take practical advantage of the eye's "inertia." He wanted to experiment with "moving pictures on a spherical horizon" — several years before the Lumière brothers invented the cinematograph at Rue Capucines in Paris.

Alfred never did succeed in solving the problem, but his sketches show that he was on the right track. He believed it would be possible to increase the light flow through a mirror, which would rotate around a flame more than ten times per second. What he had in mind was an "inverted magic drum." He would place a light source with a rotating mirror in the middle of a circular room and project illuminated images on the wall.

Alfred did not succeed in winning his colleagues' enthusiasm for these ideas even if they did dutifully listen to his expositions. The head chemist, Beckett, called his employer's fancies "toy business." Had they taken Alfred's "toy business" seriously, it is not inconceivable that the birthplace of the motion picture would have been Bofors, not Paris.

According to the laws governing joint-stock companies, it is the managing director who, on behalf of the board of directors, leads a company. When Alfred sat down in Bofors's chairman seat, however, he was the one who governed. In memoranda written at the time he is called a "severe taskmaster." When he was not in Björkborn, he would steer the company by remote control; that is, by telegrams and letters from San Remo. He seldom gave direct orders, preferring to write letters, which so often began with: "It has occurred to me . . ." His authority was so undisputed that rarely did anyone voice objections — even though they might have wanted to.

When Alfred took over Bofors, it was a family business on the brink of closing down, and unemployment in the region was widespread. Once Alfred took hold of the reins, things turned around fast. His first decision was to put 2.5 million Swedish crowns (about half a million dollars then) at the company's disposal for reconstruction, and his program was put into immediate operation. The new laboratory was built, the worn-down tool shops were refurbished, and the machine park for the manufacture of the famous Bofors cannons was reconstructed.

Bit by bit, the tension in the small foundry village, and the paralyzing feeling that the business was doomed, disappeared. Writing to the board of directors in March 1894, Alfred's assurance and determination are clear enough: ". . . from a pure business point of view, it is even more important to produce something of so high quality and specialized that it exceeds anything existing. Only if such is the case will we be able to look forward to large sales to other countries. Specialization and profit almost always go hand in hand."

The "specialization" that Alfred was referring to had first and foremost to do with steel. He wanted to make the Swedish steel famous the world over for its superior quality. He had also advanced plans for the manufacture of cannon powder and, "following Krupps's example, prescribe[d] its use for the cannons we produce. That makes the most sense."

Alfred's demands for the highest quality possible were not limited to the raw material and the finished product, but included the workers' contributions. If someone in a position of responsibility did not live up to his expectations, he didn't hesitate to act. As he said at one point, he "practiced honesty but not sentimentality." He never wavered when it came to firing a dishonest person, regardless of the person's rank.

In time, Alfred's concern for his employees' welfare became almost as famous as Ludvig's. As chairman and director, in effect, at Bofors, his philosophy could be summed up in a few words: when people have been assured material security, then and only then can they be expected to contribute satisfactory work. He had put this same view into practice at all his dynamite companies for many years. Consequently, there were waiting lists for positions at his companies. His employees received free medicine as well as medical care. Early on, Alfred would raise the issue of their right to a pension after lifetime employment.

A right-wing publication called *The Worker's Friend* once tried to convince him to distribute the paper among his employees, since "nowadays so much poison is sown among workers by agitators that it ought to be every employer's duty to find an antidote." Alfred's response was memorable: "I would regard it as improper for the workers at Bofors to dictate what I should or should not read. So too should they be able to demand that I refrain from such interference with their freedom."

In the 1966 newspaper interview of August Åhling, the former employee gives a firsthand account of Alfred as the new owner of Bofors: "Nobel had a soul of fire. He worked hard, burned with ideas, and spurred his collaborators on with his contagious energy. At the same time he wanted to appear as an unpretentious man and liked to emphasize that he was not soft, underlining that his needs were no greater than anybody else's, and that he would have been content with a dog house. But when he lived at Björkborn, he did want certain comforts and had water toilets and electric light installed."

Åhling might have added what was already well known, namely that Alfred was so worried about cold and drafts that he slept in a kind of box: he had four secure wooden walls built around his bed. Possibly this also warded off chilling memories from his childhood — the drafty home on Norrlandsgatan and the no-less-drafty apartment in St. Petersburg.

Alfred left the furnishing of Björkborn to his nephew Hjalmar, to whom he wrote in the fall of 1894:

I would like to make a couple of remarks, namely
1) that the gentlemen who come to see me, as long as I can afford it, will receive good tobacco and that therefore a smoking room is not really needed;
2) that an unmarried man cannot allow himself to have one guest room for a lady, but he might be allowed to have several. It might therefore be a good idea to furnish a few rooms to be suitable for either gentlemen or ladies of modest requirements.

Alfred had once told Jonas Kjellberg that his living quarters demands were trifling. "But I do need," he added, "a very good bed since otherwise I am unable to sleep, and a very good kitchen since I am dependent on it. Not being squeamish, but having a troubled stomach, I need to follow a careful diet. My needs are otherwise limited to a cupboard for books and whatever other furniture is available."

It is true that he had a "troubled stomach" that had difficulty digesting homely Swedish fare and, in spite of his assurances that his demands were simple, he sent for a French kitchen staff.

The chilly Swedish autumn forced Alfred to return to Italy earlier than he had planned. He was therefore in San Remo when Ingeborg's wedding took place. He wrote to Robert in Getå:

San Remo
October 31, 1894

. . . How happy I am that all went so well with little Ingeborg's wedding! And that she is said to be healthier and happier than she has been for years.

In Russia poor Emanuel is suffering from business trouble and too heavy a burden for his young shoulders to carry. It is a mystery to me that things are going as well as they are and that our company manages to stay afloat. It seems to me as if Emanuel himself is beginning to realize the necessity of hiring new people in managerial posts, but perhaps he will wait too long or choose poorly.

I feel very tired and have frequent heart trouble. It would therefore be impossible for me to come to Emanuel's aid, as I am increasingly forced to limit my own tasks, which are forced upon me. . . .

P.S. Many thanks for your warm greetings on my birthday. It gives me great joy to hear that you keep rather well and chipper and that the ship seems built for a good deal of sailing into the 20th century. . . .

Eleven days later, Alfred wrote another letter to his brother:

San Remo
November 11, 1894

. . . I cannot deny that the contents of your letter of 11/5, which crossed mine, somewhat astonished me. The simplest thing, of course, would have been to ask me openly why I did not come to the wedding.

As you know, the sad case against the British government was imminent just then, and every managing direc-

tor from every company had a meeting in Berlin, partly
to compose a plan to bring to the House of Lords, partly
to revise their contractual relations with me, as I myself
had asked.

Several times I had asked Ingeborg about the time of
her wedding with the intention of trying to attend, and
what you mean by "feelings" that could have caused my
absence is a puzzle to me.

In this life if I could follow my emotions or my reason,
I would avoid every kind of festivity at which drinking
and feasting occur. I do that so far as I am able, living like
a recluse for the simple reason that an undigestible piece
of food or a couple of glasses of wine aggravates my gas-
tritis and forces me to undergo a torture that may last for
months. In Stockholm I live in a perpetual hell because of
the cooking, which is unsuitable to me, and varying the
mealtimes does not agree with me.

That I am still alive is due only to my extreme caution
when it comes to gatherings. However, used as I am to
putting aside my own well-being, I would gladly have
stayed for the wedding if I had been able to do so without
discrediting myself before a great number of colleagues
awaiting me in Berlin.

It was all the more unpleasant to travel, because I ought
to have gone back to Bofors to attend the annual meeting.
But one cannot be everywhere.

I have aged enormously this last year and feel very
strained and tired. No wonder, since for almost my whole
life I have been a kind of half corpse. . . .

Back in Bofors Alfred took great pleasure in trips by horse and
carriage, as he had in Paris. He had asked Emanuel to buy some
Orloff horses in St. Petersburg. "Nobel was an agreeable fellow but
of course he had his peculiarities," Åhling commented in the Swedish
newspaper interview. "One of them was that when he went somewhere, he liked to get there fast. So he had three Russian stallions
shipped in — two black and one gray — which he harnessed to his
landau and then took off at a terrifying speed."

Åhling also reports that Alfred had electric lights mounted on the
carriage as well as mudguards, so that "it shone and thundered when

the Lord of Dynamite swept by." A local newspaper described one of Alfred's trips when his gorgeous Russian horses experienced some difficulty holding back on the slopes: "He came traveling at a rapid tempo in his powerfully driven closed coupe. Only the flying hooves of the stallions could be heard, since the carriage itself was soundless, equipped as it was with his own invention: rubber belts around the wheels."

Alfred's coachman in Björkborn was named Anders Karlsson. When he turned eighty years old on March 4, 1938, the newspaper *Karlskoga Bergslag* interviewed him. "When Alfred Nobel came to Strömtorp," he said, "there was no train connection to Bofors. He asked the stationmaster if they could order an extra train for him, but the stationmaster answered that it would be an expensive undertaking, and he did not think that the gentleman could afford it. Nobel asked what it would cost, and the answer was fifty crowns. Whereupon the doctor brought out his wallet and flashed a couple of thousand-crown bills. The stationmaster went off immediately and ordered an extra train from Kristinehamn."

During this time, the Swedish two-crown coin carried the profile of the union monarch, Oscar II, and the motto "The sister nations' weal" (The "sister nations" were Sweden and Norway). The king decided to visit Bofors, and his visit was later recalled by Karlsson:

I remember when Oscar II came here to see the doctor [Nobel]. He was the most magnificent person I had ever seen. A big, fine beard he had, too. He was probably right to give Norway its freedom, because otherwise there would never have been an end to the squabbling between us sister nations.

His Majesty arrived in Bofors at eight o'clock in the morning and when he passed through the flag-decorated triumphal arch, a salute was shot using genuine Bofors gunpowder. After the king inspected the workshops and laboratories, accompanied by Alfred and Emanuel, who had made the long journey from St. Petersburg just for the royal visit, there were lofty speeches. Alfred declared that to them the royal visit symbolized an encouragement "that would spur them to further efforts for the benefit of king and country. For my own part, I will do all I can to bring the industry here forward."

KENNE FANT 301

Oscar II answered by proposing a toast to the Nobel family "of which several members have been and remain a credit to Sweden and have made the name of Sweden honored all over the world."

A couple of years following this exchange of praise, King Oscar would summon Emanuel to his castle to try to convince him not to carry out Alfred's last will and testament.

Chapter 62

During his stay at Björkborn in the summer of 1895, Alfred seems to have been in a mood of near harmony. Despite suffering from angina pectoris — for which he took daily doses of nitroglycerine spirits, now being used as a vasodilator — he was very productive.

About this time he had begun to take an interest in the inventors Birger and Fredrik Ljungström, brothers in their mid-twenties. About them Alfred wrote to Alarik Liedbeck that "it is fun to work with persons of such substantial ability and such true unpretentiousness." They were working by day and attending classes at the Technical Institute in the evening.

Alfred was helping the brothers develop several of their inventions, notably the Svea bicycle. The Ljungströms had designed the first bicycle with changeable gears. Birger had been only sixteen years old when he invented the so-called roll catch, a mechanism for power transmission that locks in one direction and permits free motion in the other. With the help of this invention, the rear wheel hub acquired the shape it has kept to this day.

Alfred first decided to begin working with the Ljungströms following a demonstration outside of Stockholm; he was impressed by how the bicycle construction facilitated pedaling. On August 17, 1894, he drew up a formal agreement with the engineering firm Waern and Barth, which, through a newly formed company in England, the New Cycle Company, would market the invention commercially. Alfred invested 40,000 pounds in the firm, and soon a three-wheeled version of the bicycle appeared — with one driving wheel at the rear and two steering wheels in front. This "cab-cycle" used the Asian rickshaw as its model.

Great efforts were made to save the company, but in March 1898, New Cycle was forced into liquidation. The basic idea was sound, however, and Alfred had been an enthusiastic spokesman for "the wheel sport," which, during this decade, came to represent a technological leap forward in the transport field. August Åhling recounted that "Nobel got the notion that he was also going to learn to ride a bicycle during his time at Bofors. He used no regular bicycle, but a high-wheeled machine that was pedaled in a peculiar way. An engineer had to be present the whole time to hold on to Nobel so that he wouldn't tip over."

Wilhelm T. Unge was a former artillery captain who had retired in 1885 in order to devote all his time to inventing. In 1892 he tried to contact Alfred in Stockholm for the purpose of interesting him in his "flying torpedo," a projectile that could carry weapons. Unge's idea was that after it had been propelled and had reached its apex, a rocket would be fired to drive the projectile further. The procedure is well known to television viewers of the space age.

Alfred was impressed by the former military officer, and, to finance the flying torpedo, AB Mars was formed with 40,000 crowns in share capital. The shareholders included King Oscar II and the Swedish nitroglycerine company; when they were 7,000 crowns short, Alfred made it up.

Busy nearly all the time, still Alfred found the time to attend Unge's first test shoots in Stockholm. Further experiments were carried out both in San Remo and on the half-mile shooting range in Bofors, east of Björkborn. Alfred's interest in Unge's idea increased when he realized that the air torpedo might find civilian use, as for instance in the case of catastrophes at sea. He decided to invest another 100,000 crowns.

After Alfred's death, the main part of Unge's businesses was sold to Krupps: the Germans were eager to acquire the patent for the flying torpedo, since they saw it as a potential rival to their own extremely profitable cannon production. Earlier, in a letter to Alfred, Unge boasted that Krupps's "enormous iron monsters will be replaced by the flying torpedo."

The Germans would later find their own Wilhelm Unge in Wernher von Braun. At Raketenflugplatz [rocketflight square] in Berlin, at the beginning of the 1930s, similar experiments were carried out by the Krupps works under von Braun's guidance. Unge's and Alfred's air torpedos were forerunners to the World War II retaliation weapon: the V-2, or buzz bomb.

Another idea that developed during Alfred's collaboration with Unge was air photography. This time the idea was Alfred's. He wrote to Sohlman: "I plan to send up a small balloon equipped with parachute and camera plus a small clockwork or timer. At the appropriate height, the balloon will empty automatically, or the parachute be separated and descend with the camera image." This method, made possible by Unge's rocket, was useful for area measuring and map production, a fact Alfred emphasized in his patent application in 1896.

In the fall of 1896, the Swedish government ordered two 25–centimeter cannons from Bofors for the navy and for coastal artillery. This necessitated new equipment since the old machinery could only accommodate the production of 16–centimeter cannons. The first cannon — weighing thirty tons — was shown to the general public at the industrial exposition in Stockholm in 1897, a year after Alfred's death.

In three years Alfred had managed to reorganize Bofors and make it competitive with the largest foreign companies in the field. The breadth of its productive capacity was impressive: from artillery material, ammunition, and armor plate to innovations in the chemical field that later would make Bofors the world leader in production of X-ray contrast substances, medicines, and color substances. Today, the business possesses a nearly unique specialty in regenerating nitric and sulfuric acids. Bofors's evolution would not have been possible without Alfred's initial contributions as an inventor, financier, and inspiration. Up to the very end, when he was working on the construction of an explosion-proof steam boiler, Alfred believed in exploring new territory.

Given his enthusiam and energy, it is no coincidence that Alfred's library contained plenty of adventure stories. He liked to hear about bold exploits, the more arduous the better, in which heroes beat the odds. His support of the Swedish explorer Sven Hedin and the balloonist Salomon August Andrée therefore makes sense. Alfred gave Hedin money to explore "Tibet's desolate mountains" and gave Andrée money when he was making plans to reach the North Pole in an air balloon.

In his memoirs Sven Hedin writes that he hesitated for quite some time before approaching Alfred. He had assumed Alfred would prefer using his money for the manufacture of "15 mm cannons and projectiles of treated steel for the country's defense." When Hedin did write to Alfred during the summer of 1893, he received the following response:

Paris
July 17, 1893

Much Honored Doctor,

Since electricity and in its wake the dream of traveling

around the world in a quarter of a second, I have developed a supreme contempt for our globe's petty dimensions. For that reason I am less interested in treks of exploring and discovery than before. I have to admit, however, that I harbor the most lively interest for a far, far smaller part of the world, namely the Atom. Its shape, movements, fate, etc., both individually and as a participant in the life of the Cosmos, fascinate me. I am also a miserable businessman, and my purse has lately been heavily beset by my blunders. Drained by mistakes and by various contributions, it is beginning to develop vacuous caverns. However, I do not want to abstain totally and am therefore enclosing a check in the sum of 2,000 crowns.

With the greatest respect,
A. Nobel

Hedin was grateful for what he got. Two thousand crowns might not make much of a difference to Alfred, but to him the sum corresponded to a caravan of "fifteen healthy camels."

Hedin obliquely let it be understood that, through his royal connections, he could procure an honor of some kind for Alfred's participation. Hedin does not include Alfred's response in his memoirs: "It is just possible that among one and a half billion fellow creatures there exists someone as indifferent, but surely not more indifferent, than I when it comes to honors. One cannot refuse them when they are offered without getting the reputation of being eccentric, but most of the time they cause embarrassment and are therefore loathsome to me. I hope that the twilight of my life will not be troubled by them. I have another wish that is actually a condition, namely that no newspaper is informed of my contribution."

Alfred waxed enthusiastic over others' ideas and impulses, however outlandish, such as when he encouraged the brothers Ljungström and their plan for an air machine. The idea was that air travel would be possible by imitating the movement of birds, a so-called ornithopter — a wing-stroke flyer. This was of course twenty years before Orville and Wilbur Wright constructed their first usable airplane, but even then Alfred had clear visions of what was to come: ". . . we should not think that we will solve the problem with bal-

loons. When a bird achieves high speed, it overcomes gravity with
only a minimal movement of the wings. This does not happen by
magic. What a bird can do, so can a human being. We must have
air fleets propelled forward with great speed. A pigeon flies from
Paris to San Remo in three hours."

Alfred's interest in airships led him to support the forty-one-
year-old Andrée's plans to reach the North Pole in a dirigible.[1] The
two had met at the Patent and Registration Office in Stockholm when
Andrée was chief engineer there. His superior was Hugo Hamilton,
who was a friend of Alfred's, even though they had widely different
opinions on patent questions. Hamilton was the first to tell Alfred
of Andrée's project and his method of maneuvering a balloon by
guide rope and steering sail — with up to thirty-degree deviation
from the wind direction.

In the May 22, 1895, edition of *Aftonbladet*, the following notice
appeared: "Grand contribution by Dr. Alfred Nobel to Mr. Andrée's
North Pole expedition! Dr. Nobel has raised his contribution for
chief engineer Andrée's North Pole trip by balloon to 65,000 crowns,
which covers half of the estimated cost, on the condition that the
remaining half be met by someone else within two months." Someone did.

Alfred believed that if Andrée only got halfway to his goal, "the
deed itself would be something to stir human minds." He arranged
a luncheon for Andrée in Bofors after the Arctic explorer's first
scheduled attempt in 1896 had been postponed due to unsuitable
wind conditions. Sohlman, who was present, says that Alfred praised
Andrée's decision. Alfred had also suggested that Andrée think about
using a special French varnish to make the balloon cover, which
consisted of three layers of Chinese silk, denser. Andrée discussed
the possibility with different experts and afterward wrote Alfred that
the varnish wouldn't work. Alfred wrote a hurried reply:

Much honored Chief Engineer!

Do not believe for a moment that I wish to be added to
the list of boring advisers in a matter where others are so
much more competent. I only pointed out *"en passant"*
future possibilities without the slightest presumption of

---

[1] Andrée and his party died of exposure on Vitön Island, east of Spitsbergen, during
their voyage in 1897. A expedition party thirty years later found their remains and
diaries, which were then published.

judging its practical value. That was why I suggested Rieffel's varnish recipe and am sad to see I have caused trouble by doing so. It brings me enormous joy to hear that your tests regarding the density of the balloon have brought such satisfactory results and that our Arctic hero's horizons are ever widening.

Very respectfully
A. Nobel

During the spring of 1896, Alfred discussed the friction co-efficient between the line and the ice with Andrée and how a varying length of the guide rope might diminish the speed of the balloon. In May, the Arctic balloon, with a dimension of 4,500 cubic meters of gas, was close enough to completion that it could be exhibited in the Dome on the Champs de Mars in Paris before being transported to Sweden. By the end of the month, the expedition was on its way. Before they started out, Andrée wrote to Alfred that he hoped that "you will have the satisfaction of seeing the work for which you have put down the cornerstone completed."

One of Alfred's ideas was that Andrée should use carrier pigeons to stay in touch with the rest of the world. He wrote that in the north of Russia "there is a multitude of pigeons who can easily endure the wintry cold if they are well fed. . . . Imagine the shouts of joy they would cause and how useful they could be for the safety of the expedition." Andrée was skeptical. When Alfred paid up what he had promised, he wrote to Andrée that "the interest thereof could cover the costs for the dovecote." As happened most of the time, he would see his wish fulfilled. Andrée relented, and a few of the pigeons would indeed return with messages. In his diary on July 16, 1897, August Strindberg, whose young relative Nils was on board Andrée's balloon, writes: "In the afternoon saw two pigeons fly from north to south. . . . Said Herrlin: There are Andrée's pigeons!" On July 17 he made the following note: "In the morning I was awakened by a scream which came from the air and sounded like the mocking of a dying man — I thought of Andrée's balloon — it was horrible."

Six days earlier, Andrée's balloon had taken off from Spitsbergen with Knut Fraenkel and Nils Strindberg. They disappeared without a trace over the Arctic Ocean. Their remains were finally discovered on August 6, 1930, on White Island (Vitön) by the crew of the Norwegian seal ship *Braatvaag*.

Chapter 63

In 1890 came ominous news from the Ardeer factory: Alfred's old ally and adversary Frederic Abel had been granted a patent that deeply worried the management of Nobel's Explosives. The company had acquired the English patent rights from Alfred for his ballistite. Now it was announced that Abel and the physics professor James Dewar had received a patent for a smokeless gunpowder that was identical in principle to ballistite.

At first Alfred could not believe that these two men — both of whom had over the course of the years become friends, despite their differences — to whom he had paid generous consultation fees for their many years of service to his English company, would be capable of such deceit, and because of his disbelief at first he took no action against their obvious patent violation. He informed the management of Nobel's Explosives that he wished to settle out of court. Normally, Alfred's will was law, but not this time: against his wishes a lawsuit was instigated, which was formally possible since Alfred did not have a majority interest in the company.

The judicial proceedings turned out to be lengthy, strenuous, and expensive. Alfred continued to recommend some kind of settlement with Abel and Dewar, but the company management and its lawyers persevered.

Alfred's smokeless nitroglycerine powder had gotten as much attention in England as in Italy. In 1888, the English government had appointed a committee whose two most prominent members were Frederic Abel and James Dewar. Their task was "to investigate new inventions generally but particularly such that could have an effect on military explosive substances and provide the war department with suggestions regarding such technical improvements that the commission considered suitable for recommendation."

Alfred's two friends on the war ministry's Explosives Commission applied for, and received, information about his ballistite — in the strictest secrecy, naturally. The commission gave its recommendations and objections, some of which Alfred found useful. The fast-evaporating camphor, for instance, was exchanged for acetone, the glycerine's acetic acid–ester. Abel and Dewar, meanwhile, were experimenting on their own in the state laboratory to produce a nearly smokeless powder type consisting of 58 percent nitroglycerine, 37 percent cottonpowder, and 5 percent vaseline, which, at Alfred's suggestion, was gelatinized with acetone — the colorless evanescent solution that even today is used in the manufacture of smokeless powder and celluloid goods. It was given the name "cordite," since the powdery substance was pressed out into strings or cords. During the years after Abel and Dewar had received a patent for their version of smokeless gunpowder, they managed to keep it secret, in order to get more detailed information out of Alfred.

As a consequence, the commission, dominated by Abel and Dewar, recommended their own cordite, and the ministry decided to use the powder in the military. That Alfred might have priority rights to the invention was not considered.

Abel and Dewar's patent first came to light when Nobel's Explosives offered ballistite to the war ministry. The startled company management immediately contacted Alfred in Paris. It was an unpleasant message, and it came at a most inconvenient time. The French police had just invaded Alfred's laboratory, and the campaign the press was waging against him was at its peak. More bad news arrived: Abel and Dewar had surrendered their patent to the English government, but had kept the foreign rights.

In court, Abel and Dewar admitted that they had been informed of Alfred's experiments but insisted that in no way had that privilege influenced the creation of cordite. They pointed out differences between the patent descriptions for cordite and ballistite. To Alfred these dissimilarities were meaningless. His patience was at an end. Now it was not a question of money but honor. Alfred was also morally outraged that a highly placed civil servant such as Abel would privately feather his nest with proceeds from an invention that he had worked on in a state-owned laboratory.

Alfred's already fragile health was subjected to new trials during the drawn-out judicial process. The uncertainty of whether true justice would be administered, or if, in fact, the case had already been decided ahead of time tortured him for three long years. After it had been dealt with by the chancery division, the case went on to the Court of Appeals, and finally to the House of Lords. In his testimony, Alfred recounted how he had worked on and off to produce a smokeless powder, and that the problem was finally solved when he began looking more closely at celluloid.

"I left the problem for a while," he went on to say, "and then returned to it. It is rather often my way of working. But I do always return to a task when I have a feeling that I must finally solve it."

The claims for damage made by Nobel's Explosives for patent encroachment were rejected in 1895, and the company had to pay 28,000 pounds in court costs.

The judgment was based on a vague formulation in Alfred's patent description, where reference is made to "the ingredient nitrocellulose of the well-known soluble kind." According to the court, this eliminated everything that was "insoluble." That the company's attorneys proved that "insoluble" nitrocellulose powder could, under certain conditions, be "soluble" did not help.

Though the verdict was not in Alfred's favor, during the final pleading one of the three judges gave him moral reparation. The judge explained that, for strictly judicial reasons, he felt compelled to join his two co-judges in rejecting the demand for damages, but he added:

"It is totally clear that a dwarf who has been allowed to climb up onto the shoulders of a giant can see somewhat farther than the giant himself. . . . When it comes to this case, I cannot but sympathize with the owner of the original patent. Mr. Nobel has made a significant invention which is theoretically remarkable and truly new — and then two skillful chemists get hold of the patent description, study it carefully, and discover that by using practically the same ingredients and with only a minor modification they could achieve the same result. It must be considered urgent to see to it that, if possible, this does not occur in a way that deprives Mr. Nobel of the value of an exceptionally significant patent."

This remark could not alter the fact that Alfred had been robbed of the fruits of his invention. He viewed the judgment as an affront, and his attitude toward judicial systems and lawyers in particular became even more bitter and fierce than it was before. Lawyers were "blood-suckers who devour fortunes after delivering short-sighted interpretations of meaningless court rulings, whose obscurity darkens even darkness itself."

But the case was over and the injustice a fact. All that remained for Alfred to do was to appeal to history, which, it was to be hoped, would revise the judgment. *Nemesis,* which expresses so much of Alfred's spleen and anger, is still the best expression (Alfred had also begun writing a satire called *The Bacillus Patent,* of which what remains is only a few scattered pages, incomprehensible to anyone not conversant with the twists and turns of the cordite case) of his outrage.

August Strindberg told the French newspaper *Le Temps* on January 14, 1895, that "drama and the belles lettres were just pastimes" to him, and that it was his intention to dedicate himself to science as a chemist. It was nearly at that very moment that Alfred was turning his energies to *Nemesis.* Alfred wrote to Bertha von Suttner in March of 1896:

> Since I have not been able to participate in any more serious work tasks during my time of illness, I have written a tragedy. I have just finished it except for a few remaining minor changes. Like Shelley in *The Cenci,* I have based it on the touching true story about Beatrice, but have shaped it differently. . . . It will be exciting to see if anyone will put on this little drama whose scenic effect, in my opinion, is rather good. It is written in prose; I do not like conversations in verse — it makes such an unnatural impression.

Only a few days later, Bertha received another letter from Alfred. Now he feels that the scenic effect is not just rather good but very good. He informs her that the drama was written in Swedish and in "poetic prose," and that someone else ought to translate it into German, since he hadn't mastered that language well enough and "besides, I have other things to do."

Those who have read *Nemesis* have noted its obvious weaknesses in both character development and wording. The language is stiff and bookish, and not at all, as Nobel believed, poetic. Alfred was himself conscious that at the very least his spelling and usage were weak "as a consequence of my many years of living in other countries." In a letter to a relative — his nephew's mother-in-law, a writer — he says, however, that he "will not accept collaborators within the field of literature. . . . A writer ought not let someone else change a single word. Criticism on the other hand ought to be always welcomed — the sharper the better." She had apparently read the play and offered only mild suggestions.

Historically, the tragic story of Beatrice Cenci ended on September 11, 1599, when "the determined father murderess" was executed in full view of all Rome. To both Shelley and Alfred, her story was about justifiable patricide. The theme indeed fit Alfred's mood, for in it he could vent his fury against the judicial system —

"justice exists only in our imagination" and "the best excuse for prostitutes is that Mrs. Justitia is one of them."

To his nephew Ludvig, Alfred wrote: "I have written a theatrical play, a tragic play, you can be sure, and sad as hell. The scenic effect is good and might perhaps make overly sensitive women suffer fainting fits." The casual tone was an act. Alfred was serious about *Nemesis* and the injustices it expresses are deeply felt. Using Beatrice's voice, he can speak from the heart. When she exclaims, "I am the defiled virgin and the downtrodden avenger of justice," one can sense Alfred's identification with martyrdom.

Nemesis was printed in Paris, and Alfred hoped to have it translated both into Norwegian and German. His ambitions for the play seem curious. How could someone as intelligent and well read as Alfred not perceive the obvious flaws in his play? One answer is that *Nemesis,* for all its imperfections, was his spiritual testament, a *cri de coeur.* One last time he wanted to translate his view of life into language. The drama's narrator tells the audience:

> . . . a glimmer of light emerges out of Europe's terrible darkness. A more humane way of thinking is taking shape everywhere. The thought lends its wonderful aura to a seduced and broken-hearted world. We should be proud that it is our country that raised the flag of civilization. It is our Columbus, our Galileo, our Leonardo, our Bruno, our Campanella, our philosophers, poets, and artists who have been the world's first guides to purposes higher than burning our fellow beings and drying out their brains.

> [Act III, scene iii]

Autobiographical references in *Nemesis* abound: the references to the Mediterranean (location of San Remo), the fear of spies (as in the czarist St. Petersburg), severe migraine attacks, a girl (such as Sofie Hess) who ought to have chosen a mature man over a youth, and — inevitably — the fear of being buried alive. There are references to explosives, rockets, balloons, light bulbs, and cameras alongside talk about the church, death, and eternity.

Through *Nemesis,* Alfred seeks a higher jury and a fairer verdict, yet he knows that may be possible "neither here nor beyond the grave."

Chapter 64

In the fall of 1896, Alfred was told by his physician in Paris that his health was not good. Alfred, however, did not seem to anticipate just how near the end would be. He was buying new horses for San Remo and ordering expensive furnishings for a newly acquired villa next door.

He returned to San Remo on November 21, 1896. The letters he wrote during the last weeks of his life reflect no worry or anxiety. This could be as much from resignation as denial. He became involved in an intense discussion by letter with Andrée regarding the dirigible balloon's gas losses and the subsequent diminishment of its ability to rise. His last letter was to Ragnar Sohlman:

San Remo
December 7, 1896

Mr. R. Sohlman
Bofors

The samples you sent are exceedingly beautiful. The pure
n/c powder seems splendid to me. Unfortunately my
health is again so poor that I write a few lines with effort,
but, as soon as I am able, I will come back to the subjects
that interest us.

Your affectionate friend
A. Nobel

About an hour later Alfred suffered a stroke. His servants carried him upstairs to his bedroom. An Italian physician diagnosed a cerebral hemorrhage that was severely affecting his ability to speak and remember. Suddenly Alfred could only recall the language of his early childhood — Swedish. Later his manservant, Auguste Oswald, would tell Emanuel, Hjalmar, and Ragnar Sohlman that Alfred had tried in vain to make himself understood, but that he grasped only one word: "telegram." He wired Alfred's nephews and Sohlman immediately.

Alfred Nobel died three days later on the morning of December

10th. Neither Sohlman, Hjalmar, nor Emanuel were able to reach San Remo in time. What he most feared had happened: he died alone, surrounded only by paid servants.

The family decided to bring Alfred to Stockholm for burial in the family grave at the North Cemetery, but a small ceremony would take place at Villa Nobel first. The young Swedish minister, Nathan Söderblom, was asked to come from Paris to officiate at this memorial, which was set for December 17.

Upon their arrival at Villa Nobel, Sohlman, Hjalmar, and Emanuel, not daring to trust Auguste Oswald or anyone else, began an immediate and systematic search for valuable documents and money. They found the second last will and testament with Alfred's notation: "Canceled and replaced by a last will of December 27, 1895." This final will was on file at Stockholm's Enskilda Bank. Sohlman sent a telegram to the managing director of AB Bofors asking for a copy as soon as possible.

Sohlman recalled that on the evening of December 15 Emanuel received a telegram from the bank that informed them that the will had been opened. The deceased had selected Sohlman and Rudolf Liljequist to act as executors of his last will and testament. There was also a stipulation that the departed's arteries should be opened and the corpse be cremated.

When Sohlman recovered from his surprise at having been chosen as executor, he contacted the physician who had signed the death certificate. The doctor expressed his amazement at the request and said that the actions that had been taken in connection with the embalming would be as effective as any cutting of the arteries.

On December 17, the coffin was placed in Villa Nobel's dining room, and Nathan Söderblom gave his eulogy:

> By a strange coincidence, the departed, a few weeks before his death, allowed me to become acquainted with a manuscript from his hand. After the message of sorrow had arrived from San Remo, my eyes fastened on the following words on one of the last pages, words that he would hardly have guessed would be applied to himself. To such an application we have, however, complete right at this moment, because the words let us sense his thoughts about life and death.
>
> "Silent you stand before the altar of death! Life here

and life after constitute an eternal conundrum; but its ex-
piring spark awakens us to holy devotion and quiets every
other voice except that of religion. Eternity has the floor."
[*Nemesis,* Act IV, scene ix]

When Alfred Nobel allowed someone to look beyond
his multifarious interests and discussions, and into his inner
soul, one would find new proof of the perpetual truth that,
more remarkable than all daring thoughts and significant inventions, and beyond all the fortunes and excitement, is the
spirit of a human being, who lives, struggles, and suffers,
who loves and hopes and believes. There was without a
doubt a great measure of loneliness and suffering in his life,
and, in the eyes of his fellow human beings, he was considered by too many as a rich and remarkable man, and by
too few as a human being. Let us not perpetuate this error
now that he is dead. For to the land beyond the grave we
can take neither acquisitions nor reputation nor genius. . . .

So at this bier will fall silent every vain panegyric eulogy and the boisterous voices of earthly fame. In death
there is no difference between the multimillionaire and the
shack dweller, between the genius and the fool. When the
curtain falls, we are all equal. In death, as in religion, it is
only a question of being human.

Alfred was indeed conscious of religion. In Act I, scene vi of
Nemesis we find Cenci saying:

People are tortured by conscience and fear of God. That
has never happened to me. That God exists, I do not actually
doubt, because the Creation speaks wordlessly but elo-
quently of His omnipotence. Thus far does my faith take
me. But when people speak of His eternal justice, it's the
silliest of all fables. That institution of penalty they call hell
is an excellent invention, because it allows the priests to
fleece all of humanity. But they can't fool me with such
babbling. In nature's great work, there is no mercy, no
profit for virtue, no punishment for crime. Everything is
corrosive or being corroded, torturing or being tortured,
and God's reward, like that of the State, goes to the
strongest.

After the ceremony at Villa Nobel, Alfred's coffin was taken to the San Remo train station to be sent on to Stockholm. Emanuel sketched the guidelines for the funeral to take place at three o'clock in the afternoon of December 30, 1896.

The funeral procession went through the Swedish capital on a wintry afternoon, replete with torch-carrying outriders and illuminated cabs. The church was decorated according to Emanuel's instructions. When the guests entered through the large portal, they were met by the sight of laurel trees. The center aisle was transformed into a lane of palm trees with laurel garlands, which were joined by a splendid canopy that was, in accordance with Italian custom, held up by a white dove. The coffin was made of olive wood and equipped with silver handles.

At the head of the coffin was a silver plaque with the inscription:

Nobel, Alfred Bernhard
born Oct. 21, 1833
died Dec. 10, 1896

The funeral was one of the most extravagant ever held in Stockholm. In addition to relatives and associates from near and far, guests included his business associate J. W. Smitt, and the explorers Nordenskiold and Andrée. No representative of the royal house was present.

The ceremony was performed by the curate Kiellman-Göransson, after which the opera singer Carl August Söderman sang a selection from Verdi's *Requiem*. Around four-thirty, the coffin was carried outside, where a large mass of people had assembled. The funeral procession included forty carriages, of which four were filled entirely with wreaths. Thousands of people lined the road to the crematorium at the Northern Cemetery. At Norrtull, more torch-bearers on horseback joined the procession. "The light from torches and cressets at the graveyard threw a magical glow over the white snow drifts," read an account in the *Dagens Nyheter* newspaper, which went on: "Outside the crematory at the Northern funeral grounds, the lid was unscrewed and a white inner coffin was carried inside to be entrusted to the oven's fires. The clergyman said a few last words, an organ harmonium hummed, and the mechanism by which the coffin is loaded into the oven rattled while the torches outside blazed."

Chapter 65

If they were to find out about the little project that my fantasy is now caressing, it would be a dearly bought pleasure to me. But whatever happens, nothing will keep me from performing my little caprice. It has been an eternity since anything stimulated my appetite to such a degree. By means fair or not, happen it must.

Nemesis, Act I, scene vi

The day after the San Remo memorial, a copy of Nobel's handwritten will arrived. From a quick first reading, it was established that the heirs would not — as in his earlier will — receive 20 percent of his estate, but instead only personal bequests.

Hjalmar did not hide his disappointment, but Emanuel's reaction was restrained. When Alfred and he had spoken in Paris, they had touched upon the subject of the will, and this disinheritance did not come as a surprise. He and his family were already very well off, which was not the case with Hjalmar and the rest of Robert's children.

Emanuel's concern had more to do with the sentence, "All of my remaining property shall be handled as follows: the capital, which is to be invested by the executors in stable securities, shall constitute a fund, the annual interest on which shall be awarded as prizes to those persons who during the previous year have rendered the greatest services to mankind." Emanuel correctly feared that a drop on the stock exchange — affecting the shares of all Nobel enterprises — would occur when the contents of the will became known in the world's financial centers. Emanuel might have wondered how an experienced financier such as his uncle could have formulated such a capital-destructive stipulation.

Perhaps when Alfred wrote his final will he was convinced that everyone's life was doomed to oblivion, and so putting a capital-destructive stipulation into it was of no moment. His money was only important if it led to some understanding of what he believed. His unique bequest, therefore, was not self-destruction but self-revelation: he wanted to reward men and women who created something in the same "idealistic" spirit as he had.

Moreover, all his life, Alfred found some of his relatives' interest in his money intrusive and repulsive — the antithesis of idealism. It must have given him certain satisfaction to formulate his will the way he did. One of his letters to Sofie Hess suggests that it would. Writing from the Hotel du Lac in Switzerland on September 1, 1889, he raises the issue of inheritance and revenge: "Probably nobody will miss me. Not even a dog like Bella will shed a tear for me. Yet she would probably be the most honest of all, since she would not go poking around for gold left behind. Besides, in that respect, my dear people will be awfully disappointed. I am taking great delight in advance in all the widened eyes and curses the absence of money will cause."

Studying Alfred's last will and testament carefully, one is struck by the somewhat absentminded division of his large fortune. His will was afflicted with so many contradictory stipulations and formal flaws that the executors Sohlman and Liljequist were at first confused about how to begin their job.

As early as 1889, Alfred had decided to formulate his stipulations regarding his estate on his own, a direct consequence of his continued bias against attorneys, whom he called "formality parasites." On March 3rd of that year, he wrote to a friend in Stockholm: "Would you be so kind as to ask a Swedish lawyer to prepare a suitable form for my will? My hair is gray, I am shopworn on the inside, and I must prepare for shuffling off my mortal coil. I ought to have done so long ago, but I have had so many other things to keep me busy."

It turned out that the form he had requested was of no great assistance. The friend who had sent him the document had asked him in an enclosed letter to remember the University of Stockholm. "Thank you for the last will form," was Alfred's reply. "I will indeed remember the University, but it is not yet clear to me if it is better for growing youth to dig like Nebuchodonsor or brood like Newton."

Alfred commented further on his first sketch for a last will — which he later destroyed — in a letter to Sofie on November 11, 1889: ". . . what a sad end I am going toward, with only an old servant who asks himself the whole time if he will inherit anything from me. He cannot know that I am not leaving a last will — I have torn up the one I once wrote. Neither can he know that my fortune is becoming more and more hollowed out."

The second will is interesting because in it Alfred stipulated no definite sums, but put aside 20 percent of his fortune to twenty-two named relatives and co-workers as well as male and female acquaintances. Another 16 percent would go to various institutions, among them the Oesterreichische Gesellschaft der Friedensfreunde [Austrian Society of the Friends of Peace] in Vienna, the sum "to be used to further peace ideas" — a tribute to its founder Bertha von Suttner.

Also among this 16 percent were remembered the Swedish club in Paris, the University of Stockholm, Stockholm's hospital, and the Karolinska Institute (for medical research), the money for which would create a fund "whose amassed interest every third year, according to a decision by the management, will be awarded as a prize for the most important pioneering discovery or invention in the field of physiology and the medical arts."

Of the remaining 64 percent, this second will stipulated:

> The total remainder will go to the Academy of Science in Stockholm to constitute a fund, from which annual interest shall be given by the Academy as a reward for the most important pioneering discoveries or works in the field of knowledge and progress, with the exception of the domain of physiology and medicine. Without thereof making an absolute condition, it is my wish that those who through writing and action have managed to fight the strange prejudices still harbored both by nations and governments against the establishment of an European peace tribunal would especially be considered. It is my express wish that every prize designated in this will be given to the most deserving person, without the slightest consideration if the person is a Swede or a foreigner, a man or a woman.

Alfred's letters of the time suggest that he felt uncertain about who he was; the inventor, the poet, and the businessman all struggled for the upper hand.

The second will contains significant formal advantages over the third and final will. For example, specific recipients are named. Had these directives become the final ones, "Alfred Nobel's Fund," later named "the Nobel Foundation," would not have been deemed a money-distributing, and therefore taxable, institution.

Another difference between the 1893 and 1895 wills is that in the earlier version neither the Norwegian parliament nor the Swedish Academy were appointed to select the award recipients. Alfred's original intention was that the Academy of Science would handle these tasks. Regarding the peace prize, the Academy's duty was not absolutely defined. In the 1893 version, there is no mention of a literary prize. The instructions to the Academy of Science were so vague and elastic, however, that it would have been capable of giving prizes for literary works. Alfred probably realized how delicate and difficult it would be for the Academy of Science to select a literary achievement, a discovery in chemistry, and a contribution to the peace movement. Far better that he transferred the choice of the winners of the prize in literature to the Swedish Academy and the choice of the recipient of the prize in medicine to the Karolinska Institute.

In the 1893 version, the peace prize would go to someone who had worked for a "peace tribunal," while the 1895 version — still in force — stipulates that this prize shall be given by the Norwegian parliament to whoever has "done the most and best work for the brotherhood of nations and the abolishment or reduction of standing armies as well as for the establishment and spread of peace congresses."

Alfred deposited his third and final version in the Enskilda Bank during the summer of 1896. It had been witnessed at the Swedish Club in Paris, and Alfred had kept utterly silent about its contents. Emanuel knew only about the second will, and Alfred had told him that he would inherit Villa Nobel and that Alfred's house in Paris would go to Robert's daughters. That did not happen. The second will also directed that his relatives would receive about 2.7 million crowns (about $500,000 then) in securities and cash, plus buildings with an assessed value of around half a million crowns. In his final version, Alfred changed this to limited personal bequests, amounting to a million crowns.

The personal bequests were divided as follows: nephews Hjalmar and Ludvig each received 200,000 crowns; nephew Emanuel 300,000 crowns; Miss Olga Boettger, the sister of Sofie Hess and a young actress for whom he had a definite weakness, 100,000 crowns; Sofie Hess (Mrs. Sofie Kapy von Kapivar), an annuity of 26,000 florins; Mr. Alarik Liedbeck, 100,000 crowns; Miss Elise Antun, an annuity of 2,500 francs; Mr. Alfred Hammond, a young author and brother of Alfred's former housekeeper, whom Alfred had helped in different ways, such as by introducing him to Victor Hugo (Hammond had emigrated to the United States), 10,000 U.S. dollars; Emmy and Marie Winkelmann (daughters of a German business friend), 150,000 marks each; Mrs. Gausher, Alfred's French house-keeper, 100,000 francs; the manservant Auguste Oswald, an annuity of 1,000 francs; Auguste's wife, Alphonse Oswald, employed at Alfred's laboratory in San Remo, an annuity of 1,000 francs; former gardener Jean Lecoz, an annuity of 300 francs; the postal employer Mrs. Dessolter, an annuity of 300 francs; and Mr. Georges Fehren-bach, a yearly pension up to January 1, 1899, of 5,000 francs.

Alfred had already given Robert's children — Hjalmar, Ludvig, Ingeborg, and Tyra — 20,000 crowns each.

The contents of his will had hardly been published (on January 2, 1897, in the Swedish newspaper *Nya Dagligt Allehanda*) when the voices of protest began to be heard. Some went so far as to suggest they might try to prevent execution of the will. The radical press declared itself "opposed in principle" to donations and private gen-erosity, even when it involved idealism. Hjalmar Branting, the editor-in-chief of the *Social-Demokraten* and from 1896 a member of Stockholm's City Council, published a four-column article under the headline "Nobel's Will — Magnificent Intentions — Magnificent Blunder." He thought the bequest "a major bungle," referring par-ticularly to the fact that the literature prize was to be awarded to "whomever, within literature, has produced the most outstanding work, in an 'ideal direction.' " "It must be said aloud about this whole donation," Branting said, "that it is a major bungle to choose the Swedish Academy as the awarder of the prizes," given what he assumed that conservative institution's interpretation of the words "ideal direction" would be. Gösta Mittag Leffler, a mathematician and friend of Nobel's, argued that Nobel was an anarchist, and that by ideal "he meant anything that takes a polemic or critical standpoint toward Religion, the Monarchy, Marriage, the Establishment as a whole."[1] Professor Knut Ahnlund is more precise: "When he speaks of 'ideal direction,' he was probably giving more play to rebellious and independent tendencies than his contemporary interpreters understood, to the extent that they wanted to understand this."

It will probably never be possible to define exactly what Alfred Nobel intended by the word "ideal." That may have been his inten-tion. Anything is possible. It is even possible that as a Swede who

[1] Kjell Espmark, *Det litterära Nobelpriset*. The English translation is entitled *The Literary Nobel Prize* and was published by G.K. Hall & Company, Boston, in 1991.

322   A L F R E D   N O B E L

lived outside the country for many years, Alfred had lost his sensitivity for certain nuances in the Swedish language and had actually meant "idealistic" but had happened to write "ideal." (In Swedish, the two words are *idealistisk* and *idealisk*.)

Not even the peace prize found favor with Hjalmar Branting. He expressed appreciation at the choice of the Norwegian parliament as the awarder of the prize, but added that "the only road is through a merger of the working masses in all countries. . . . The truly great work for peace is never one human being's accomplishment. . . ." Branting finished with a declaration of principle: "A millionaire might personally be worthy of esteem, but it is better to avoid both the millions and the donations."

Generally, however, the press reactions both within Sweden and outside were positive:

Nya Dagligt Allehanda (Sweden):
This will, whose content without doubt is designed to awaken the attention of the entire civilized world, creates one of the most magnificent dispositions for the good of humanity that any single being has so far been able, and wanted, to make.

Dagens Nyheter (Sweden):
Alfred Nobel's will was opened here on Thursday afternoon, December 31, 1896, which therefore marks a major event in our cultural history.

Svenska Dagbladet (Sweden):
. . . [There] exists only one noteworthy action comparable for promoting spiritual growth in Sweden, namely when Gustaf II Adolf transferred his privately inherited estate fortune to Uppsala University.

Köln-Zeitung (Germany):
The gift is the largest that any single man so far has donated for idealistic purposes. Sweden has earlier had the fortune to claim a number of men who furthered scientific aims. . . . In Nobel it has a patron whose nobility surpasses every Croesus, because the benefits of the means he has put into the service of science and humanity are not limited by any national borders.

Le Figaro (France):
The will, whose most important stipulations we have here
reproduced, will remain a monument to philanthropy and
thereby save Mr. Alfred Nobel's esteemed name from
oblivion.

The New York *Daily News* published a letter from the Swedish
engineer and cannon instructor Axel Welin:

Those of your readers who had not the pleasure of knowing
the late Mr. Alfred Nobel personally might find the para-
graph in his will which stipulates a reward to the most
successful promoter of peace to be in disharmony with his
activities during his lifetime, especially when they discover
that he was almost the sole owner of Sweden's largest cannon factory. However, that Mr. Nobel harbored a deeply
rooted antipathy toward war was a familiar fact to his
friends. When I wrote to him once about improving certain
war material, I received an answer, dated San Remo, January
5, 1896, with the following ending words: "For my part,
I wish that heavy cannons with carriages and all else belonging to it would be dispatched to hell, which is the most
suitable place for their exhibition and use."

But the most unrelenting criticism of Alfred's will came from
Robert's children Hjalmar, Ludvig, and Ingeborg, as well as the
latter's husband, Count Carl Ridderstolpe. They were not as well
off as other members of the family and had inherited their father's
bitterness. Year after year, they had heard from their father that
"everything that was done in Baku since I left the city has been
expensive and of poor quality." His relations with Ludvig and Alfred
had improved over the years, but Robert had never completely freed
himself from his jealousy of his younger and extremely successful
brothers. For the remainder of his life, he had trouble accepting what
he felt was a niggardly retirement compensation, especially since it
came during the years that Branobel was showing great profits.

Alfred was in favor of general prosperity but not of inherited
wealth. Large fortunes, he felt, ought to be put back into the public
arena, and the children of the very rich ought to get only enough to
enable them to acquire a fine education and "the essentials in life."
This train of thought underlay his generous but limited bequests to

his brothers' children. Robert's children did not share their uncle's opinion.

The will's irregularities meant that it could not be executed in its original form. Weighty responsibility therefore rested upon Sohlman and Liljequist. Emanuel would also come to play an important part. He had much in common with his uncle. A bachelor, it was quite natural for him to take over responsibility as the head of the family. His willingness to cooperate with Sohlman and Liljequist was of major importance, since Robert's survivors soon brought suit protesting the will. Furthermore, Robert's son-in-law, Professor Hjalmar Sjögren, was suing his brother-in-law Hjalmar Nobel in Karlskoga district court and his other brother-in-law, Ludvig, at Stockholm's magistrates' court. His reason was that Alfred had given Hjalmar and Ludvig 200,000 crowns each in the "document entitled 'last will,' " whereas his wife received only 20,000.

Earlier, Hjalmar Sjögren had protested to the French authorities against Sohlman's and Liljequist's actions in Paris and demanded that garnishment proceedings be brought against the total existing fortune. He knew very well that French courts had a tendency to be more formal than the Swedish courts, and that certain of Alfred's vague stipulations might result in the will's being declared invalid. According to Sjögren's logic, the whole estate would then be divided between the relatives.

Others weighed in. In February 1898, King Oscar II summoned Emanuel, who was a Russian citizen. Oscar II was of the opinion that a will that did not exclusively reward Swedish citizens was "unpatriotic," and he admonished Emanuel: "It is your duty toward your sisters and brothers, who are your wards, to see to it that their interests are not neglected in favor of the fantastic ideas your uncle had." The king was also hinting that Alfred might have been under the influence of "females" — he was obviously referring to Bertha von Suttner.

Emanuel did not bend to the royal pressure but answered frankly: "Your Majesty! I will not expose my siblings to the risk that in the future they will be accused by highly deserving scientists of having appropriated for themselves what would rightly go toward science."

Ragnar Sohlman wrote to his co-executor Rudolf Liljequist:

I have been brooding a great deal over how the expression "all of my remaining property . . . to be invested by the executors in stable securities" ought to be understood.

If he meant that all his industrial shares must be sold and
transformed into state or other guaranteed obligations,
then these instructions would bring about the greatest
misfortune to all the Nobel enterprises, the dynamite
company, the naphtha company, and especially Bofors.

By "stable securities," Alfred was referring to state bonds that
were tied to the fluctuating value of gold. It was not a preposterous
idea at the end of last century, but became so in 1931, when the gold
standard was abandoned.

Sohlman's concern over Alfred's Bofors shares did not last. The
former owners, the Kjellberg family, managed to gather a number
of shareholders together and form a consortium that reached an
agreement with the estate, which meant that Bofors and its weapons
industry — now so critical to the country's defense — remained
under Swedish ownership. In complete accordance with Alfred's
wishes, the manufacture of ballistite was placed in a new Swedish
company: AB Bofors Nobel Powder, which later also acquired
Alfred's laboratory at Björkborn.

In January 1897 Ragnar Sohlman traveled to Oslo, where the
Norwegian parliament became the first of the prize-awarding bodies
chosen by Alfred to accept their assignment. From there, he went
to Paris, where he consulted with two prominent attorneys, Paul
Corbet and René Waldeck-Rousseau. He learned to his relief that it
was technically possible to insist on the validity of the will in spite
of some of its formal oddities, but that this meant running certain
risks.

If the will was declared valid, all of the estate's assets, including
the significant fortune Alfred had deposited in banks and brokerages,
would be taxed in France. Given that Alfred had not lived in Sweden
since he was nine, it would be difficult to insist that Bofors, where
he had lived for only two years, was his actual residence, or what
in France is called *domicile de fait*.

Sohlman made a fast but wise decision: he resolved to remove
immediately all valuable documents in order to prevent possible seizure. The Swedish consul general, Gustaf Nordling, assisted by is-
suing him a *certificat de coutume*, which specified the rights of an
executor of a will under Swedish law. In a locked room at the consulate, Ragnar Sohlman packed up those shares and securities that
were to be sent to London to be sold. Other securities were addressed
to Enskilda Bank.

French postal rules limited the amount that one could insure each mailing to 20,000 francs, but Sohlman was not stumped by this. He quickly drew up and signed an insurance agreement with the Rothschilds' banking house, by which he could send the documents in packages up to a value of 2.5 million francs. Sweden's consul general and the young executor carried loaded revolvers when, by horse-drawn cab, they transported the major part of Alfred's assets in France from the consulate to the Gare du Nord.

Ragnar Sohlman continued on to St. Petersburg to sort through Alfred's assets with Emanuel. Emanuel's willingness to cooperate meant that Sohlman quickly found the sources for an accounting of the estate's Russian assets.

On October 30, 1897, a legal inventory of all Alfred Nobel's goods and chattels was made at Björkborn. Summons had been sent to the heirs. Hjalmar and Ludvig, as well as the Ridderstolpes, appeared in person. Robert's widow, Mrs. Pauline Nobel, was represented by the assistant district judge, E. Hagelin. Carl Lindhagen, Stockholm's assessor and later mayor, and Jacob Seligman acted as administrators while Sohlman and Liljequist formally presented the estate. It was established that, outside of Sweden, Alfred had left assets in France, England, Germany, Scotland, Italy, Austria, Norway, and last but not least Russia.

At Lindhagen's recommendation, Sohlman and Liljequist had divided the assets into two groups:

1. Assets on which inheritance tax in other countries was not due. The combined inventory value of these were 18,123,043 Swedish crowns.
2. Assets in other countries on which inheritance tax should be paid. The combined inventory value of these were 15,110,749 Swedish crowns.

Combined assets before tax were, in other words, 33,233,792 Swedish crowns [just under $7 million then]. Pauline Nobel, along with Hjalmar and Ludvig as well as Carl and Ingeborg Ridderstolpe, protested the validity of the proceedings.

The legal process that was now beginning in Sweden caused much worry and a huge waste of time. Early on, Sohlman had sensed a glimmer of hope that an understanding could be reached, as the heirs expressed their assurance to the court that, whether or not they won the case, they would endeavor, as far as it lay in their power to do so, to carry out "the principal intentions of Dr. Nobel's will." Finally, two reconciliation agreements were signed — on May 29, 1898, and on June 5 the same year. These granted the heirs certain pecuniary advantages corresponding to the estate's profits over eighteen months. They then approved the will, after which the garnishment of assets in different countries was canceled.

After the personal bequests had been paid and the taxes and costs for inventory and court had been regulated, the newly established Nobel Foundation had at its disposal, as of December 31, 1900, 31,225,000 Swedish crowns.

According to the conciliation agreement, the regulations for prize distributions were to be ratified in joint deliberation between the foundation and a chosen representative of the Robert Nobel family and then approved by His Royal Majesty. It was further stipulated that the Nobel prizes must be awarded at least once during each five-year period; that under no circumstances should a prize sum be less than 60 percent of the disposable portion of the fund's yearly yield; and that a prize must not be divided between more than a maximum of three recipients. The conciliatory agreement was accepted by His Royal Majesty at the beginning of September 1898 and was turned over to the district court in the city of Karlskoga on September 29th.

Emanuel's stalwart support during the sensitive negotiations was of decisive importance to the creation of the Nobel Foundation, as is seen in the notes of a meeting held February 11, 1898: "Mr. Emanuel Nobel stated that it was his wish to respect the intentions and wishes expressed in the will of his deceased uncle. He would therefore not dispute the content of the will. In order to give effect to the lofty aims the testator had intended, alterations and supplementary provisions would undoubtedly be required, and these could not be introduced without the consent of all the heirs."

Emanuel had reminded Ragnar Sohlman at an early stage that the Russian expression for an executor of a last will and testament was *dusje-prikasstjik,* which meant roughly "agent of the soul." Alfred's final wishes should be guiding them, Emanuel felt, and nothing else.

Chapter 66

Whatever a human being manages to accomplish during his or her lifetime, there are so utterly few whose names will remain on the pages of history for any extended amount of time. Rarer still are those whose renown grows after their death. Alfred Nobel belongs among these.

If Alfred kept at a distance from his fellow human beings, this was in part the self-protecting instinct of a hypersensitive man. His keen sense of betrayal rendered him depressed and reticent. As an expression of his nearly uninterrupted melancholy are two lines that he seems to have jotted down hurriedly on a piece of paper, found in a pile of unsorted newspaper clippings in November of 1956:

> Then the reality of life is bared and of the
> dream of happiness only the ghost of memory remains.

From his "dream of happiness" remains more than a "ghost of memory," however: every year on December 10th, when the Nobel prizes are awarded in Stockholm and Oslo, the whole world is witness to Alfred Nobel's dream.

In accordance with his express wishes, the prizes are awarded independent of ideology, race, sex, or nationality. They have become an enduring monument to a brilliant inventor, a visionary empire builder, and an unprejudiced humanist.

TESTAMENT

I, Alfred Bernhard Nobel, hereby declare, after due consideration, that this is my last will with regard to the estate that, at my death, I will leave behind. . . .

All of my remaining property shall be handled as follows:

The capital, which is to be invested by the executors in stable securities, shall constitute a fund, the annual interest on which shall be awarded as prizes to those persons who during the previous year have rendered the greatest services to mankind. The interest shall be divided into five equal parts. One part shall be awarded to the person who has made the most important discovery or invention in the realm of physics; one part to the person who has made the most important chemical discovery or improvement; one part to the person who has made the most important discovery in the realm of physiology or medicine; one part to the person who has produced an outstanding work of literature in an ideal direction; one part to the person who has done the most and best work for the brotherhood of nations and the abolishment or reduction of standing armies as well as for the establishment and spread of peace congresses.

The prizes for physics and chemistry shall be awarded by the Swedish Academy of Sciences; those for achievements in the realm of physiology or medicine by the Karolinska Institute in Stockholm; those for literature by the Stockholm Academy; and those for the promoters of peace by a committee of five persons to be selected by the Norwegian Storthing. It is my express wish that the prizes be distributed without regard to nationality, so that the prizes may be awarded in every case to the worthiest, whether he be Scandinavian or not.

This Last Will and Testament voids any previous instructions of mine in any other Last Will, if such were to be found after my death.

As executors of my will I appoint Ragnar Sohlman, resident at Bofors, Varmland, and Rudolf Liljequist of 31 Malmskillnadsgatan, Stockholm, and Bengtsfors near Uddevalla.

Paris, the 27th of November 1895
Alfred Bernhard Nobel

INDEX